WATERMARKS

Life, Death and Swimming

By Lenka Janiurek

Watermarks
Life, Death and Swimming

a&b

WATERMARKS
Life, Death and Swimming

Lenka Janiurek

Allison & Busby Limited
11 Wardour Mews
London W1F 8AN
allisonandbusby.com

First published in Great Britain by Allison & Busby in 2020.

Copyright © 2020 by Lenka Janiurek

The moral right of the author is hereby asserted in accordance with
the Copyright, Designs and Patents Act 1988.

All rights reserved. No part of this publication may be reproduced,
stored in a retrieval system, or transmitted, in any form or by
any means without the prior written permission of the publisher,
nor be otherwise circulated in any form of binding or cover
other than that in which it is published and without a similar
condition being imposed on the subsequent buyer.

A CIP catalogue record for this book is available from
the British Library.

First Edition

ISBN 978-0-7490-2595-3

Typeset in 12/17 pt Adobe Garamond Pro by
Allison & Busby Ltd.

The paper used for this Allison & Busby publication
has been produced from trees that have been legally sourced
from well-managed and credibly certified forests.

Printed and bound by
CPI Group (UK) Ltd, Croydon, CR0 4YY

*Thanks to my ancestors, my children,
and the Earth*

Some names have been changed

CONTENTS

SUBMERGED

I am in water, submerged and suspended. It feels too tight. There are murmurs, doors bang, there's the thump thump of going up and down the stairs. Clattering, of cutlery on plates, the coal scuttle, a poker. Voices in different registers, and sometimes silence. An owl, right outside in the dark air. On the radiogram, Tchaikovsky. I kick in a desultory way, my heart's not in it. The womb gets fuller and tighter still, I am outgrowing the jar and I can't stop. Even I realise that. And I'm not at all sure what happens next. There's this serpentine connection to my host, cumbersome, lolloping around my limbs, my face, floating round my neck. There's the noise of an organ, muffled. There's a pulse of sustenance, of care, and in the background there's unease and fear. And then the camel scrabble of kneeling, a lot of gabbling and frankincense, and bells ring. My mother is in her own envelope of faith, and hope.

When it happens I'm waterless. The jar empties, and I'm slithery, viscous, amniotic. I'm hurtled, crushed and squeezed beyond bearing. All I can hear is,

'Bear down, bear down. That's it. Just breathe. That's good. Pant. Pant. Now breathe. And . . . push.'

Voices with a hint of panic in them, under a surface of sensibleness and a whiff of the nobility of suffering. There are the noises of pain. God is mentioned. The bed is ready to receive the fifth child. Two girls, two boys already, they wonder which I am. They pray, they are always praying.

'In the name of the Father, and the Son, and the Holy Ghost, Amen.' They pray, 'Hail Mary, full of grace.'

I slip out to my mother bellowing. I taste blood. There is air all of a sudden, a gasping shock like crawling out of the primeval swamp, with fins and gills and webbed feet. Air is too much for me, then it's not. The lightbulb light cuts into me like ice. I have emerged, and it's all shocking and strange. The taps run on full in the bathroom. They cut us apart. I'm slippery. They dry me, I'm a girl. They wrap me up. Too tight, but it loosens. They bathe my mother's face with a flannel. There's a glass of water on the bedside table reflecting the light. There are tears in my mother's eyes. She stares and stares into my face.

'Hello, you. Hello, little one.'

A tall shape, like a shadow, of my father stands by the window. It rains, splattering the windowpanes. It's dark outside.

In the future I will give birth to children myself. In pregnancy I will swim, letting the water bear the increasing weight and form. Proud of my shape as I pull myself up out of the pool, seal slick. Training in breathwork, preparing for the marathon of birth. Up and down the pool I will swim, counting, growing, my child's body adrift in me. In transition, that worrying limbo between the cervix being fully open and being allowed to push, I will want to cross my legs and go home, want them all to go away. I will throw a bloody pad across the room, and the nurse in short white wellies will look shocked. In my mind my baby might turn out to be a fish or a monkey, and then everyone will know I am not human after all.

My first day. Daylight is a cloak of mist. And milk, yellowy, watery, sweet. Mine. My father brings a breakfast tray. I meet my older siblings, they meet me. Each fingernail is so very small, I clutch without understanding. When my navy sister sees the black sticky mess in the nappy she will be disgusted although she must be used to nappies and baby shit. I wet myself happily, it's warm. My mother is trying to balance her Graham Greene novel as she feeds me. People come and look at me. My grandmother, wearing a special shirt with little birds on it, says babies like patterns. And there is talk about baptism. For Catholics the unbaptised child is not good enough for heaven. So I am new and perfect, but not.

Soon enough my mother is weary, clumping down the stairs, are the boys wearing clean shorts, and the girls' dresses ironed? All the shoes are polished in a line by my father in shirtsleeves in the back kitchen. We don't have a car, so we walk to church. It's chilly, echoey, stone-cold. It smells of polish, candle wax, ashes, and earth. I have godparents now. I bleat because the water splashed on my head is stone-cold, and they all pray over me. I am not struck by a thunderbolt of God's love or light, although Mary was possibly in the corner of the bedroom when I was born. There is only a chipped plaster statue of her in a niche in the church. Her hands stuck in that double blessing pose, she wears a tawdry necklace. The heavens open on the way home, it's winter. I am a January Sales baby. My birthday is too close to Christmas and New Year, all everyone longs for is an ordinary normal day with nothing to celebrate. A day that isn't special, with no pressure. My baptism is an anticlimax. The water a dribble. Even the cake is dry.

My eldest son won't be baptised. When he is ten days old we'll go swimming, and standing in the pool I will let him go, release him from my hands into the warm chlorine-sharp water. And he will sink down and then float up, and swim, waddling like a soft creature taking steps on another planet. He'll be the best swimmer, Tom, a high diver.

SEASIDE

Now I have a younger brother, so there's six of us children. Quickly we become 'the Little Ones'. My father manages a bookshop, the owner has a flat in Filey on the Yorkshire coast, and so we get to go to the seaside in August. For two whole weeks, my father comes for one. The four youngest go in a taxi to the station with the navy trunk. You can pull out the top drawer and it has all our swimming costumes in it. The older ones walk to the station, and we meet up and sit on the long bench with green Twiglet iron struts and wait for the train. There's our trunk, there are bags, there are lots of bags, and coats. There are steam trains. The whole platform fills up with steam hissing. There are whistles and stoking and clanking and the engine is beautifully grotesque. We sit in a compartment holding sandwiches in brown paper bags. The countryside hurtles by backwards, I can't quite believe we are the ones moving. We have to change trains at Seamer. The navy trunk is like a butler accompanying us, stoic and loyal. Finally we are in Filey, craning to see if we can see the sea. There's another taxi, craning from the back of that too, I see a glimpse, a strip of it, but 'hurry up now', we're at the flat. It's upstairs and all lino. We tramp around the rooms. I'm squeaking with excitement, my sister says stop squeaking. Oh, I can't wait to get to the sea.

At the bottom of the road are the Crescent Gardens. We can see the sea, and it never ends. The gardens are overlooked by vanilla ice-cream terraces, we skirt round flower beds along the warm path then follow the steps down. Down, round this corner, round the bend, down, and down some more. There are 104 steps, I think. And then we come out across the road from the promenade with the railings, and there's the boating pool. And Filey Bay spread out before us glistening and wet. The sand licked by the tide. There's Flamborough Head at one side, and the Brigg at the other. The beach held in their claws. There's the horizon, and the frills of tiny edge waves on the flat sea. It's calm, it's sunny, it's sandy, salty, fishy, it's all there. And I want to run.

We walk along trailing our bundles, the blankets, the towels, drinks, more sandwiches, buckets and spades, the cricket bat, the wickets, the bails, the balls. I want to drop everything and just run. Down the cobblestones into the tunnel and out onto the beach, we turn right and find our spot and unpack. I changed into my blue swimsuit with the fish on the hip at the flat, slipping on the lino with excitement. So I can peel off my shorts and jumper, throw them down in our new mini home at the beach. Mum has a book and the bags and they are parked along the grey whale curve of the wall so she can lean back and watch and sunbathe and snooze. And I run, the tide's half out and has left those crumpled ridges like mini desert dunes that are hell to walk on, but I'm running. There's a spell in my head, I'm spellbound. The first touch, toes sinking, cool waves, rivulets, and white and clear and that sound of being washed by it all, the air the sun the sand the salt the water. It's holy. My older brothers are wrestling, splashing and shouting at each other, I don't care, their noise sails out on the air. One sister is wading, the other is back at the promenade wall with my mother, arranging her hair. My little brother hums as we stand in it, beside each other, and are embraced. This is the holiday, now. We are in the sea, it's in us.

In Filey we join the library temporarily each year. Books have to be had, my mother has to have books. Of course we go to church and the Filey priest listens to all our confessions. At low tide we walk to the Brigg with Tata, my Polish father. Following the seaweed-strewn undulating concrete path, up and down, across mussel beds, transfixed by the miniature worlds of rock pools and along to the very end, so we can go round the corner of the headland that's like an old sleeping reptile. There is a wooden cabin painted grass-green where someone sits and sells purple-wrapped Cadbury's chocolate. We get this as a reward for all the walking. Sitting on the other side on the rocks Tata shares it out, counting, snapping the squares apart. I wee behind a rock, my brothers point and laugh, I grimace, and they point and laugh some more.

We climb along and there's the Emperor's Pool, a stone shelf askew, of emerald water named for Constantine. I want to bathe there, to bask. To be a creature of the deep, an empress with handmaidens. Tata says it's much too slippery. We troop back to Filey along the clifftop. Climbing the iron ladder, rusty, treacherous, wobbly, vertigo-inducing. The path up the cliff is a long nose, with rabbit holes and gravelly muddy grass, it requires surefooted balance. I don't have it, my feet hurt. They've been hurting a while. The others laugh, imitate my whines, my pleas to be carried or to stop and rest. There's no more chocolate.

This curve of the bay is made of the profiles of stern elders with aquiline features, clay faces that watch forever. We pass the yacht club yachts' halyards tinkering in the breeze. And it's possible to get back to the harbour because I'm high sitting on my father's shoulders now. At Coble Landing there's ice cream, candy floss, and Corrigan's, the amusement arcade with pyramids of pennies, miniature cranes tantalisingly about to snare a prize, but never quite. Metal horse races, flashing lights and bleeps, whirrs and the smell of cigarettes. There's the lifeboat, you can climb a ladder to look at it properly, painted navy and white with a swooping belly. The fishermen wear waders and the tractor rescues the boats as they come in on the tide with great chains, and my father sits with us on the sea wall and stares. While my older brothers whack each other with a tennis ball. They are never tired.

My mother has stayed behind on the beach, just sitting, knitting, reading, snoozing even, she's on holiday, she takes it seriously. My father is watered down by all the space and the air, even when he shouts or chases my sister with a cricket stump. I never mind so much about him in Filey. At the bakery here there are floury baps, my mother makes prawn cocktail sauce and crams fresh prawns inside. This is my quintessential mother, leaning back into the curve of the promenade wall, chewing a bap with a bit of lettuce hanging out the side, tea from the tartan-patterned thermos beside her, a library book, a rug, sandals off, and sandy toes. Staring out occasionally at the sea and the sky, watching her children from a blessed distance. She very rarely goes all the way in, to swim. Mostly she stands in the shallows, water lapping her ankles, towels and jumpers slung around her like ropes. I wish I had known her when she was girlish, less responsible, less tired or likely to be cross. I wish I had known her without being interrupted. I have to go all the way in, I have to try to swim.

Sand in the beds amongst all the sheets and blankets, sand between your toes, sand in your clothes, your hair, sand on the lino. Scratchy, gritty, irritating, sand in your shoes. I keep two small heaps in my shoes on purpose, to take back to York, for after the holiday. Real beach sand. Not the stuff delivered in heaps and wheelbarrowed to the sandpit in the garden. In the future, on a wide Welsh beach I will become a grain of sand in a giant egg timer inside a huge round mandala drawn out with garden rakes. Someone with a drone will film the sand, us people, falling through, marking the time that will be running out.

On the last night in Filey we trail along to the Vinery, a cafe in a greenhouse, and eat Knickerbocker Glories. Real grapes hang from the roof, there is salt in our hair and on our skins. We are dreading going home, licking the tall glasses and our spoons clean.

STORM

Round and round the garden we run and eventually my father picks up the hose and makes a great arch of spray we have to run through. Fleeting rainbow colours, and fear that he might suddenly deftly lower the hosepipe and splatter you full on, controlling the flow with his thumb. We shriek, the grass is getting waterlogged, and slippier and slippier. Then with a great show of huffing and puffing he inflates the paddling pool. Square, canvas bottle-green, slidey inside and repaired in places with the puncture repair kit on the outside. He chases us, he threatens us, he gives us chores in the garden.

Weeding, picking up grass clippings from the edges of the rose beds, picking up sticks. We groan and moan, unsure of our ground, of each other, but mostly of him.

In the garden my father is more crazy. Especially with the lawnmower, which lives in the pigeon house and smells of oil and petrol and rags. He has hurled it around before now when it won't work. He swears, he shouts, he rants, we can't go anywhere near him, we can't do anything right. He seems to swear in several languages. He goes very quiet and contemplative by the bonfire. And standing beside him, he seems unfathomable when he burns stuff in the brick square he calls the 'incinerator'. He is always foreign in England, his name, his accent, his gestures, his tastes, his bark, his smell. His memories are foreign, although I don't realise this, not yet. This is him. And I am me. All I know is he is different from other fathers, but I don't know why.

Sitting at the dining-room table when his mood is palpably filthy, we are all strung on the edge of our nerves. Waiting. This is what it is like to live with fear. He holds it in his body, ready to pounce. We try to humour him, it doesn't always work. All eyes are on him, even when they're not. It's like living with a big bear with very bad moods. When he comes home from work I listen with absolute precision to the way he opens and then closes the front doors. Is he in a bad mood and is he raging, or merely sulking, simmering? Can he be coaxed cleverly or is it better not to try? Should this great dark cloud of mood be ignored, or sympathised with? I suppose I pick up on this tension and these questions without noticing, from my mother. My father left his country and his parents when he was a teenager. Letters in Polish on thin paper like the hard loo paper at school come sometimes, but not often.

There was one trip to Poland with my eldest sister and my eldest brother after Tata's mother died. He couldn't get permission to go before. They wouldn't let him behind the iron curtain. He pronounces 'iron' with the R hard, even though we tell him not to. I can see grey metal, I can't see anyone behind it. I was small, but very jealous about Poland. Because my brother didn't even want to go, and had to be bribed by taking cornflakes and tomato sauce with him. There was a fuss. He wanted frozen peas. This brother hates thunderstorms, and will get an award for helicopter pilot brilliance in the future. He never takes his jumper off on a hot day either.

Only when I go to Kraków fifty years later and hold the faded pieces of orange card with the photographs of us all stuck on, photos of the fringed pram on the promenade, my father's legs lanky, my mother steering her brood wearing a home-made dress, do I feel I've met my Polish grandmother. Those photographs she must have looked at again and again, wondering if she would ever meet any of us, her six grandchildren. She never did. I will look up at the windows of the flat with the view of the convent opposite. I will walk along the river beneath the castle that the Nazis under Hans Frank occupied. I will hear the sound of their highly polished boots, and their drunken sadist jokes echoing on the staircases and through the courtyards. From when they ruled that dragon town.

On the window seat we are surrounded by playing cards. I've lost again, inevitably. It's just me and my poker brother, it is always poker or pontoon with him, played with matches. I think he cheats.

My parents met at Oxford, and moved to York before I was born. It was a promotion for Tata, to manager. Catholics need room for all their children. Although a bookseller is never well paid, my father had a job and ten pounds in the bank. It was enough. So we live in this big house, renting out the top floor to foreign students from the university. A Lady Guisborough lived here before us, apparently then everything in the house was white. It certainly isn't now. There was a vegetable garden beyond the rose garden that was full of cabbages when my parents came to look round the house. We thenceforth called this the Cabbage Garden although it's all grass now. It is surrounded by brick walls and conifers and is a battleground between the washing line, the need to play cricket and football at all hours, the grass and compost heaps, the bonfire and, in the corner, the incinerator.

Defeated at cards, I stand on the window seat and look out at the trees in the Cabbage Garden bending, listening to wind belting down the chimney. The sky turns a magnificent slate grey, backlit with yellow, like the sky's ill. The trees are going berserk out there. I open the window and the air is warm and full of static, bristling. The sky is about to crack open, and I want to be there. I want to see behind the sky. I race to get on my swimsuit with the fish on the hip, to ridicule from my victorious poker brother. I don't care. On the stairs I see my eldest, helicopter, brother looking worried.

He goes to hide in the linen cupboard. This is the brother who never takes his jumper off in summer and needs frozen peas and cornflakes. I wonder if these traits are all related and logical somehow. I can't work it out.

And I'm running down the veranda steps. The steps my little brother fell up one lunchtime running in for fried egg and chips, and his face came up bloody like the tomato sauce. He had to have stitches and I felt bad about eating the chips and egg anyway, when he couldn't in all the ambulance drama. But it seemed such a waste. Anyway, I'm running down the veranda steps thrilled, with a laugh in my throat and the sky's lit up and cracking and violent drums play overhead and I dance round the garden, and jump into the paddling pool. The air is prickling, the sound is deafening, the light magnificent and terrifying, threatening and cataclysmic, and still the rain holds off. I can feel it taking a deep breath. There's another pause, I ignore my poker brother shouting at me out of the window. The sky's about to break and I think I'm ready.

Everything has gone darker, and still darker and the trees are rustling and swooping like crazy. The bigtreeinthecorner that's hollow inside, the copper beech, the chestnut trees, are as excited as I am. Anything could happen. My eldest (navy) sister is upstairs in my parents' room, knocking on the window and looking cross and bossy and then she gives up, tossing her hair at me.

And I'm sitting back leaning on the walls of the paddling pool, bottle-green, blue with my fish, wet from a foot of paddling-pool water, and waiting to be drenched. And it comes on quickly, the rain, the blessed rain. So I'm dappled, then damp and then my hair is plastered to my head and the pool is being hit by spikes, lances of rain and the grass is flooding and I'm wet through. And alone. And it is the most glorious feeling in the whole world. Me in the paddling pool in a thunderstorm and no one can stop me. And the rain takes over completely and the storm slowly travels off a little way and the thunder is not so deafening, more booming than crackling and I sit there and sit there, the trees still dancing all around, leaves and grass floating in the pool, and it's a long time before I realise I'm shivering. A long time before I go in and peel the costume off into a wet creature to slop on the floor. Before I wrap myself in my light blue sister's birthday bathrobe without asking. They all say I'm mad. And for once I don't mind what they call me, what taunts come my way, what looks they exchange amongst themselves, how much they snigger or hum horrible ditties. Because I have tasted bliss, drenched and soaked to the skin. This, in the paddling pool in a thunderstorm, was my true baptism. Christening my soul and my elemental spirit.

THIRST

We didn't wash the body. My grandmother looked through Mum's dresses and chose her best one, cerise with gold borders. I privately preferred the blue one. Granny looked out pink lipstick to match. I never played with my mother's jewellery box again. Never touched the pearl teardrop pendant. We, the Little Ones, my little brother and I, used to pretend her wardrobe was a bus. We'd wear her shoes and lose them, fall off the bus. Putting on funny voices, taking names like Gladys and Ethel. We didn't play that game again. Like we didn't pretend to be window cleaners in the bath.

It was to do with corpuscles, white and red. It was 1968. My mother was doing some marriage guidance training, my mother went to Hull. She caught a nasty cold and was in bed for a week. And that horrible January went on and on.

By the end of February there was a plastic beaker on her bedside table, with a toddler's spout. She couldn't drink otherwise. She was waiting for the Spring, she'd make it to Spring. I could pick snowdrops and put them in the blue-and-white stripy egg cup. Surely she would smell the lilac, and then the roses, surely I could make her a daisy chain? A scientist would come up with a cure miraculously, we could pray more, we could pray harder and faster and longer and do more penance and say more rosaries and surely Our Lady would intervene in blue and cut a swathe through all this red and white corpuscle nonsense, and sort them out. My mother's face was going yellow and a bit green. She was always thirsty but she couldn't drink. And there was a tide mark around her lips. One good thing about being married to a bookseller was all the new books, piled around her bedroom, strewn across the eiderdown. Voracious, she was reading Charles Lamb and Iris Murdoch. Except now there were no books on the bed, no newspaper, no concentrating, no more chatting, no knitting, no listening to the radio. Only looking at the curtains, and out at the sky. And I didn't want to climb in with her, because of it, the Leukaemia. I had to keep going to school, we all did. I perched on the bed and told her I was going to be a toad in a well, under a spell, but only I could help the third son find the Bird of Paradise. I would lie behind stage blocks and leap out crying 'Caramba'. I could stuff tennis balls up the back of

30

a green jumper to be toad-like. My mother closed her eyes to imagine it. And I closed mine realising that I would have to ask Tata to come, and he'd be the only dad in the whole audience.

I changed her water, I filled up the cup in the bathroom, then held it up to her lips hoping she wouldn't dribble. And I told her Spring would come. And I told her it just wasn't fair.

'Life isn't fair.' And 'Love never dies,' she said.

These were the talismans she gave me as she came closer to her bed being her deathbed.

She died in the night on the Spring Equinox. We all trooped in, the others kissed her cheek. I couldn't, I just touched her hand, and it was cold. And the miracle hadn't happened. The undertakers came and they seemed particularly tall and anonymous like they weren't people at all. My mother had said her many goodbyes, all the priests all the mothers all the family, all the friends and neighbours. She took her death seriously. Only with her little sister did she express fear, asking her to come with her on the raft. Otherwise it was all Jesus, and Heaven and so on. Praying.

There was a Requiem Mass, there was purple everywhere in church, then it was Easter, but no one thought to give us extra eggs, although we privately thought they might. Spring going into hot Summer days seems to betray us. Can I enjoy lying on a blanket on the grass in the rose garden in the daisies licking a vanilla ice-cream wafer with cheese and onion crisps afterwards? Death is not mentioned at school.

My mother wearing a black mantilla singing the hymns heartily, loudly, while surreptitiously doling out chocolate biscuits to us along the pew. My mother in the kitchen, peeling apples, peeling potatoes, in the back kitchen wrestling with the mangle, in the garden, her Scholl sandals clip clipping along, with the washing to hang up in the Cabbage Garden, telling the boys to keep the football away, my mother with pins in her mouth cutting round a pattern with pinking shears, my mother standing in the roses in a flowery home-made dress, my mother drinking sherry with her Cabbage Club intellectual friends, discussing George Eliot, not wanting their brains to dry up with motherhood. My mother clutching, clawing at the sheet, in bed and yellow and dying, and I couldn't accept it for a long time. Will I ever really accept it? My mother being buried, all daffodils flimsy and fragile in the rainy cemetery, limp jokes about God crying, no Resurrection. Wondering if I shouldn't have worn my red kilt. Stuffing the black corduroy trousers she'd made me and I'd ripped to the back of a drawer, I didn't want anyone else to touch them, let alone mend them.

Going with my father to the tap near the grave to fill the aluminium watering can with water for the peonies and lupins from the garden she'd never see. I didn't realise how her death would change absolutely everything and everyone for good. How the temple of our home, of our family, was torn asunder the day she died. I couldn't have known quite how her absence would always be there in the background like a cumulonimbus cloud, how the space she left behind could be so lonely, the landscape so bleak. Even when I forgot her face.

THE BECK

It's the same year, 1968. My mum died four months ago. We've driven to Hutton-le-Hole in the car (a Triumph Herald, light blue, 7761DN, my father passed his driving test last year). We're on the edge of the Yorkshire moors, there's a rug, grass, sheep and their shiny black pellets, a picnic, my father is flat out snoring on the rug. My feet are in the beck, as streams are called in the North. My brothers are involved in an army game which involves stalking through the bracken, lying down, shouting, and pointing sticks at each other. They are on manoeuvres. My sisters are giggling and fiddling with the glove compartment. I wonder if there is chocolate in there. I don't care, but they beckon me over.

I'm always a sucker for being included by my sisters. I think of them as the navy one and the light blue one, the very oldest and the second oldest, it is hard for me being the fifth child. Singly I worship them. My navy sister has peacock feathers and velvet curtains in her bedroom which also has a bath in it. Her hair is blue-black and bushy, her eyes are shoe-polish dark brown. She sometimes lets me ride on her back on the bedclothes when she doesn't want to get up in the morning, sometimes she tells me to 'piss off'. She has her own record player and listens to Bob Dylan and The Incredible String Band, and lets me read John Lennon *In His Own Write*, with 'Good Dog Nigel', which I pronounce 'niggle'. She has an Aubrey Beardsley poster of Salome that I covet. My light blue sister lets me talk to her when she's in the bath, her skin is milky. She is like a bigger version of me but not, we are curly-haired and blue-eyed, but she is womanly. I get her clothes handed down. She prefers Paul to John in The Beatles. She is terrified of dogs, more than I am, she screams. We sat on top of the piano when we briefly got a dachshund we called Bilbo Baggins. He never stopped barking, and they smell when you're frightened. So he had to go to another family.

Unfortunately when my sisters are together they are horrible to me, they work as a double act. I am jealous of them being born in Oxford, they had Polish School outfits with hats and sequinned waistcoats made by Mum. I will discover that when it was just the two of them, before the boys and before we, the little ones, were born, my parents used to give my navy sister presents on my light blue sister's birthday, or she'd be unbearable.

'Did you know Tata has a girlfriend?' my navy sister now says unbelievably.

She is always straight out with things.

'What? Of course he hasn't,' I say.

What can I say, are they teasing me?

'That's what you think, but he has.'

'And we've got proof.'

My light blue sister likes saying 'we', meaning not me. They giggle and there is a lot of eyebrow raising. They do this a lot these days.

'But . . . well. No one would want to be his girlfriend. And what about Mummy?'

'Well, he has. Do you want to see her? Do you know what she's called?'

'Don't tease me. What do you mean, see her?'

It is too much for me to think she might have an actual name.

'Why on earth do you think we've made this up?'

'He told us. He always tells us everything first.'

'What?'

'He told us all about her. Honestly.'

'I don't believe you.'

'Look at this book, then.'

'What's that got to do with it? Tata can't have a girlfriend.'

'He can. And he has. Look.'

A black-and-white book jacket. Photographs of a straight-haired woman with a lot of teeth. I wish my feet were still in the stream.

'That's her. S.'

'No. It can't be true.'

The woman is twenty-three, it says on the cover. My father is forty-eight, my father has six children and a dead wife. My father still has black hair, he is lean, tall. I would not say my father is handsome, but other people might.

'He's going to tell you all about her. He wants us to meet her.'

'Don't be silly. You've made this up. All of it.'

'You'll see. He hasn't told the boys yet, but we thought you'd like to know.'

My father is grunting in his sleep next to the bracken. It can't be possible that he has a girlfriend. In the same way he told us about the Leukaemia in stages, oldest, the girls, first, then the boys then us, the Little Ones, last. I have leapfrogged into knowledge I don't believe or want or understand. Fathers can't have girlfriends. There is some chocolate in the glove compartment, at the back. My navy sister opens it boldly, snaps it, breaking all the rules. There is a silence. There are sheep, the sounds of warfare in the bracken, a car goes past, a family floats by looking bored out of the windows. I envy them. I envy their boredom, and the fact that they all fit in the car without anyone having to sit in the boot. The fact that there are two parents looking bored. I look at the pictures of S. I don't want to, but now I have to. Then I go back to the stream, back to building my own private dam. Selecting a stone to take home. Wait for my father to clear his throat and tell us little ones finally about S. Using the same hesitant and embarrassed tone he had when he decided he should sleep in our room after Mummy died, with me and my little brother. And he scared us with his coffin-shaped sleeping bag on the green camp bed, and the earth he'd stowed on top of our wardrobe from Poland. It shouldn't have been so frightening, but it was. We were glad when he went back to his own room having agreed privately that although he'd said we needed him to sleep in our room, we'd thought he couldn't face sleeping in his room without her.

My feet are waterlogged and freezing. Tata wakes up and shouts at the boys. We visit a church on the way home, for the first time he doesn't loudly whisper, 'Pray for your mother.'

He doesn't even mention praying. He tells us before bed that a woman, a good woman called S, is coming to stay and meet us next weekend. From London. We might like to go and collect her at the station. We might have steak and ice cream for supper. There is no mention of girlfriends. I pretend not to listen or really care what he says.

My little brother speaks out of the dark, after Tata has turned off the light and we have listened to his footsteps going downstairs, he says, 'We might be allowed cider.'

'We never have steak,' I say.

'I think it can be a bit rubbery, chewy.' He sighs. 'Well, it's obviously ridiculous. It won't last.'

My little brother still sucks his thumb, there is a knobble on his knuckle from it. He is seven. My navy sister is sixteen.

Pool

Somehow I still haven't learnt to swim. We've been going to the swimming baths for years, and I'm embarrassed by the calluses on the soles of my feet, and by my father trying to make me, force me to swim. I can't breathe with water wings, arm bands haven't been invented yet, I panic. There are too many people and I don't like the echo. My father clenches his teeth, like when he clutches my feet too hard and slices, it's all tense, all nerves, always near to shouting. My mother used to calm him down.

S had a custard-yellow going-away suit, the boys were altar boys, we girls the bridesmaids. S's father is the same age as mine. Really. In the photographs his teeth are braced in a smiling fury. Tata and S went to Formentera on their honeymoon, where her parents have a villa. They ate watermelon, she said on the postcard. Granny looked after us, but I haven't seen her since. People have stopped talking to my father. We are not allowed to mention my mother, we've got S now. She is hard to explain.

I've been to London now, the furthest I went before was Oxford. Before the wedding we were taken on a whirlwind of sights, the Tower, the planetarium, the waxworks, the boys hated the National Gallery. We went to see *The Mousetrap*. S's parents live in St John's Wood with her old nanny, who makes apple pies with cloves and walks an Afghan hound in Regent's Park. S's book made her famous, and her parents aren't sure about this. We were all photographed ranged on the climbing frame at home, and it was in the *Daily Mail*. 'That rag,' my sisters said, and refused to smile for the camera. They refuse to talk to S. S's father reads the *Financial Times*, his father owned mines in South Africa, her mother plays bridge and tennis and is always a Caramac-brown colour, all year round.

The wedding was in Hampstead, and my poker brother got so drunk on the champagne he had to be carried outside and laid flat out on the grass. My navy sister made us kaftan dresses, with flared sleeves – her flared sleeves you could hide things in, mine were tiny, hardly flared at all. I thought the white socks I wore with the black shoes didn't go with the teal corduroy, but I didn't say anything. Really, in the last while there has been a lot of posing for photographs. As if life is happening so quickly and we keep trying to hang on to it, but we can't. I have a new brother now, a half-brother technically, but a person isn't a half, even if they are a baby.

Anyway, now we've come to stay in a manor house in the country, it's amazing, there's a boat and a swimming pool and a croquet lawn and chairs on wheels to sit on in the courtyard. We brought our dog, Fuzz, but he's eaten some ducklings and so we locked him in the dungeon that's a table-tennis room, but he ate through the door, and so S had to go into Oxford to get some hardboard and paint to repair it and hope no one would notice. It's an extremely old door with metal studs on it.

The pool is surrounded by a yew hedge. Apparently from above it is shaped like a grand piano. The straight line of the keys hold the shallow and the deep end, the curvy bit is all deep end. But you can't really tell on the ground about the piano, you'd have to be told. There's a massive slide with water that trickles down it to stop your bum sticking. I sit up there with my legs hanging down onto the slide bit and S is down in the pool treading water, and encouraging me to slide down saying she'll catch me, 'It's fun.' Her teeth flashing at me. I sit up there for half an hour until she's gone away. Then I retrieve my legs, turn round and creep back down the ladder like a spider. S's method with children is half humiliation. It would be better if she left me alone.

I decide to teach myself to swim in my own way. In the shallow end, slowly, in between people coming in and out. I am the safest person I know. S is noisy, she drinks gin, she smokes, she wears jeans, she swears a lot, she laughs, the au pair looks after my new brother. My father is working.

I suppose S is solving the problem of holidays for all us children like this, by asking her rich friends to help.

I develop my own swimming style, the one that's best for me, without anyone shouting or encouraging me. I do it quietly and gradually with just the birds for company. When people come into the pool I cling to the sides, or sit on the edge. I do breaststroke arms and crawl legs, it's easier. And I build up to actual swimming. Even though S was Olympically trained, like her mother practises at the Wimbledon club and gets the used balls from the Championships (they only use them for seven and then nine games, that's why they're always saying 'new balls'), I don't follow S's advice. I swim my own way. My sisters have left home. The navy sister has gone to university, my light blue sister has gone to stay with another family. So I'm the only girl. S isn't really like women I have known before.

I've done it at last, I've taught myself to swim. And I beat my poker brother at croquet. He hasn't worked out how to cheat at that, yet. I swim four or five times a day now. You can here. My feet and hands get waterlogged like a crocodile but I don't mind. And there's a big log fire in the house with a kind of chainmail curtain as a fireguard. They have a butler here, there's a bell on the dining-room table. When my father comes for Easter, he says, 'I just don't like ringing it. It's silly.'

His finger hovers over the bell like it's a slimy sea anemone. S laughs loudly from the other end of the table. My helicopter brother reaches over and rings the bell instead. The butler appears, he has striped trousers.

We eat a whole salmon on Easter Sunday. It has been flown down from Scotland for us. M, the rich man whose house this is (he has a few), caught it on an island there and had it sent here, by plane! My father says we should help with the washing-up, but anyone can see that the butler and the housekeeper don't want us in the kitchen. It is clearly their kitchen. But we do as we are told, the boys clear the table. There are loads of different sets of plates and platters and cups and saucers on loads of shelves in the kitchen. I don't like the green set. There's an Aga, and a whole room full of wine. I fill up one of the sinks to wash the glasses. Of course I break a wine glass, it just slips, then there's blood in the hot water. So I run out of the kitchen, down the passage past all the storerooms, across the gravel and round to the back of the barn, and then along the path to the boathouse. I am frightened of being told off. There's a rowing boat just sitting in the boathouse. We are allowed to use that too. I can hear them calling me, well, S calling me. No one finds me. I only go back after spending a long time in the boathouse, where there are all these reflections so it's almost all in black and white because of the shade. There are ducks, I don't know if they are the parents of the ducklings that got eaten by the dog. I am shivering when I go back, and bracing myself. But everyone has gone off to the tennis court.

I like the river here, it's the Thames. There are bulrushes and you can just sit on the bank in the grass away from everybody and everything, and listen to the trees. In the future I will have sex here. No one at my new school would understand about S, let alone this fairyland place, so I'll say nothing about this holiday. However much my brothers mock me, I can swim. I can float on my back like a starfish and look at the sky in the deep end. All the deep dark green water holds me, like I'm weightless. I've discovered it's easier to swim in the deep end because you can't touch the bottom. I was all wrong about swimming. And because my feet are painful with too much walking, it's a new piece of freedom. Swimming doesn't hurt. I know I used to have a panicky comical birdlike hop along the bottom in pools, now I just breathe in and glide.

BATH

I'm washing my hair in the bath. I don't have baths with my little brother any more. I kind of miss it, we used to play being at sea, or scrubbing the sides and talking in funny voices. I was in charge at the front and rowed the hot water to the back. My little brother would call me bossy. I liked it when we were the 'Little Ones', that's what Mum used to call us. I liked playing pirates with the settee cushions. I liked the little-people-who-lived-in-the-flower-bed stories she told us out of thin air, we and she never knew what was going to happen next. I have my own bedroom now, up in the attic opposite the au pair's room. I painted it orange and antique gold. Tata did the window in gloss. I have my own washbasin. There is ice on the inside of the window in winter, but I can see the stars better from the attic.

I go to an all girls' school now, uniform, navy blue. I don't go to the convent where everyone else from primary school went, so I am the only Catholic. We have been doing the Battle of Thermopylae in ancient history. In needlework I've made an apron and a shirt with a collar from scratch, buttonholes by hand and everything. I know Mum would be proud. S doesn't sew and she hates cooking. I just wear my self-made shirt anyway, unfortunately no one in my family is that impressed.

It seems like most of the girls, in fact everyone else, have got their periods. It seems like I'm the last one, still waiting. Sometimes I wonder if I'm not really a full girl, because it hasn't come. I'm nearly fourteen. And I don't understand why the biology teacher Miss Smedley got so angry with me. We have this subject called 'Hygiene' once a week. We cut out pictures of food and stick them in our books and labelled them. We drew diagrams of rabbits' reproductive systems. And then the human reproductive system. The week before half term she asked us if we had any questions, and told us to write them down and put them in a question box. It looked like she'd wrapped a Kleenex box up in brown paper to me. Of course we were all hoping she'd start talking about sex, we hoped she'd be embarrassed and then forget to give us homework. But she only asked us for questions, anonymously. To be put in the box by next lesson.

And of course I forgot, so just hastily scribbled something in the notebook I got in my pillowcase at Christmas, then tore it out, folded it up and put it in the box. No doubt some of the swots had thought up complex enquiries. Miss Smedley gave me a particularly fierce stare, she looks like a walrus, although that could be unkind to walruses since I have never actually seen a walrus close up, or at all. My hair was probably coming loose again, she is very big on tying your hair up, and doing up your science overall properly.

Miss Smedley is not overkeen on me, she makes me feel improper. Possibly because I felt-tipped my initials on my science overall rather than having elaborate embroidered ones, and possibly because one of the overall ties fell off and I lost it and made another one out of pink velvet. I don't think she appreciates me.

The next Hygiene lesson arrived in due course, and Miss Smedley made a great show of drawing out slips of paper and answering some of the questions from the box. All dull. And then she paused dramatically and said, 'Now, I'm very sorry to say one of you has taken it upon themselves to use this opportunity to write something shameful. And not only that, they have tried to make an exhibition of themselves by writing on yellow paper. Their question was quite beyond what is proper.'

She always purses her lips into puckers. People were looking round and rustling with interest. Dear me, I realised she was talking about me. The yellow paper.

'They will know who they are, and I will not stoop to

giving them any satisfaction to ridicule this exercise . . . by being so very . . . unhygienic.'

I spluttered, and most likely went bright red in the face. I just can't stop blushing happening.

Anyway, I'm lying in the bath wondering if I'll ever have a period. And I never got an answer to what to me was a perfectly innocent question.

'Can you still wash your hair in the bath when you have a period?'

Anyway, I've got a good spring crop of pubic hair, I smell more when I sweat. I can't say I really have breasts yet but there's time, maybe at some point I will have a bra and periods, and then I'll grow up. My sister (light blue) told me all about periods ages ago. After Mummy died and before she went away to live in the caravan. We were eating fish fingers, mashed potato and peas with tomato sauce on the veranda.

'It's agony. You won't be able to bear it. And all the blood.'

'What? How much blood is there?'

'There's so much blood, it pours out of you.'

'But where from?'

'It's your eggs bursting, stupid. Do you want to know about sex now, what they do?'

'Who?'

'Grown-ups. Tata and S. How do you think babies come? How do you think they get in there?'

I was thankful when the front door slammed and it was the others coming back from a football match. S was in London. My light blue sister left soon after, with two cardboard boxes of clothes. She took her bike too. She was the only one of us with her own bike, a brand-new Moulton, she'd saved up for it for ages with the money her godmother sent every year. My godmother went to live in Tasmania, and my godfather is a missionary in Lesotho. I only have a small fur purse to show for this, with a few shells with pink spines inside it, from a beach on the other side of the world. And presumably there are prayers coming over from Africa when he remembers me, but nothing I could ride.

COFFEE

I get the bus into town and walk over Lendal Bridge, past the
Bar Walls and the peacocks in the Museum Gardens. There
are two rivers in York, the Ouse and the Foss, the Romans
were here in style and called it Eboracum. The city is built
on bones and broken pots and mud. The bridges are like
relatives, I know them so well, Lendal and Skeldergate are
metal with shields, Ouse Bridge is stone. If you walk along
the Bar Walls you can see why York floods, the city's like an
upside-down hat. The nearest proper hill is Garrowby Hill,
fifteen miles away.

I'm working in the shop. Not the new university bookshop in the library building with the cafeteria and phones with helmets like space men, with the lake with the plastic bottom. I'm working in the shop in town, in Stonegate, the street leading up to the Minster. The building is new books downstairs, secondhand and 'antiquarian' up. There are loads of staircases and creaky rooms, the one with no windows was used for cock-fighting ages ago. The art books, secondhand, are in the front room on the first floor with the bay window overhanging the street so you can examine all the tourists and they don't even know you're there. People used to shake hands across the street through the upstairs windows. Well, I must say, they must have had long hands. Maybe that is in Whip-Ma-Whop-Ma-Gate, or the Shambles near the market, markets are a bit of a shambles, so it's a good name. That's where Margaret Clitherow was crushed to death for being a Catholic. My father is the manager so he is in charge, and he makes sure everyone knows it. They freeze when they hear him on the stairs. There's the children's shop next door, I want to be in charge of the window and arrange my favourite books in there. My father has unilaterally banned Enid Blyton, you have to say 'go to Smiths' to her fans, and then they look crestfallen and puzzled and back out of the shop. In the rear of the children's shop is the coffee room where all the staff come on breaks and try not to complain about my father. They call him Mr Jan. They call Mrs Shimiratska, Mrs Shimi. The others all have English first names. Mrs Shimi is the only other Polish person I know, except the man who brought the plum trees for the garden and he lives miles away. Mrs Shimi does the accounts with a little machine and takes out her false teeth. Later her office will move up the road and round the corner to Coffee Yard.

I sit in a back room with a lot of dust mote columns and falling-apart cardboard boxes full of duplicates of invoices that need filing in alphabetical order. They're not very important, but quite important, and I'm getting paid. You file them under the publisher's name. They are flimsy, almost see-through, and either an insipid lime or lemon colour.

On a good day Tata buys eclairs for everyone from Betty's and the staff all behave as though he's done something extraordinary. On a bad day he makes a huge racket, running up and down all the different stairs swearing under his breath, berating and belittling people, including customers. He's particularly rude to Germans on purpose. He pretends not to understand German, and then breaks out into it, then they look astonished and horrified, God knows what he is saying. He is not fond of Americans either, particularly if they are wearing tartan trousers. He throws up his hands in the air in exasperation, he's a big gesticulator.

In the future, I will learn from a friend who attended The Mount, the Quaker boarding school, whose swimming pool my school borrows on Thursdays, that a favourite pastime on Saturday afternoons when they were allowed 'out', was to go into town, visit the bookshop and provoke 'Mr Jan' into exploding. Like a sport. After his death I will google his name idly, although he will die long before the Internet, and I will discover the immortal phrase: 'Mr Jan was well known for his volcanic temper.'

Right now, he is not impressed that I have filed the flimsy invoice copies correctly.

'There is plenty of dusting to do. Glory be, and where is Charles? Is no one efficient at all? Reliable? They drive me up the wall.'

He really drives himself up the wall, I think privately, as he bangs the door and runs down to the post room. He has metal segs on the soles of his shoes, so everyone knows where he is at all times. In the future, my brother (poker not helicopter) will try working for my father and fall out badly with the man who runs the post room. The man who runs the post room where all the parcels are dealt with wears a brown overall and is plodding and territorial. My poker brother will hatch a plot to undermine him, and come up with the elaborate scheme of buying laxative chocolate from Boots, melting it onto plain digestive biscuits carefully, forking in a convincing pattern before it sets, and offering them in the post room. A diarrhoea emergency and loss of dignity will ensue. My brother will decamp to the bookies, then the Star Inn to drink Guinness. He will not last long as an employee, but the laxative vendetta will not be uncovered by my father.

Now, as directed, I'm dusting shelves and the tops of books, arranging, alphabetical ordering. I'm upstairs in secondhand, art. Trying to just lose myself in the job as people are meant to.

The thing is, the thing I'm trying not to think about too much, is that S and Tata are always fighting. I have two little half-brothers now. It is either shouting and banging doors, or a static electricity of sulking. My father can get through a whole meal with everyone sitting round the dining-room table without speaking a word. It's hard to know what's going on. The au pair looks after the boys. S goes to London for days and days and Tata just goes on going on, standing over the porridge while it goes gloop gloop, waiting for the coffee to rise up and percolate, reading the paper and going to work every morning, going to church a couple of times a week, watching football, mowing the lawn angrily, making us do chores, and that's it.

My father says to me every schoolday morning, 'No porridge?'

'No time,' I say.

'No toast?'

I glug black coffee standing up.

'Bye,' I say over my shoulder.

Sometimes I feel faint in assembly, we have to stand up and my ankles go all itchy. I'm used to having no breakfast, from fasting on Sundays before Mass for years and years. At church I mostly found myself retching in the flower bed outside by the time the Offertory came round. I suppose the congregation got used to me going yellow and stumbling out every week. I can't even have coffee on Sundays.

We go to a different church now, because of the article in the colour supplement. Where S said our church was too busy raising money for tarmacking the car park, when there were hungry families in the parish over Christmas. And that they should sell off the Vatican treasures to feed the poor. This didn't go down well with the priest. S doesn't go to church any more, but we still do. And when it got to the middle of the sermon on that particular Colour Supplement Sunday, my father suddenly stopped blowing his nose into his handkerchief, stood up in actual pin-drop silence, and said out loud, 'Father, I'm taking the children home. You should preach charity.'

And we had to follow him solemnly out of church, past everyone we know and have always known staring at us. My older brothers were the altar boys as usual, and they stayed blank-faced and angelic-looking. I suppose flinging off their surplices and striding out behind us down the aisle would have been too melodramatic. It is hard to know what God would think really.

Island

Apparently we're going to Formentera. The smallest Balearic Island, it's south of Ibiza. But I don't know, even if Tata has ordered a whole crate of books to take with us, on the plane then a boat, whether it will be entirely safe to be alone in a villa with only one other villa in sight, and just the sea and sand and lizards and so on, with my so-called family. There's a well in the kitchen. I have never been abroad, or on a plane, and am worried. Worried it will be too hot, so I am imagining the hottest setting of the oven, and hopefully it will be cooler than that, it must be. I practise a little psychology on myself now and then to make life more bearable. I hope this works, about the temperature, because I do want to enjoy it. The island, I mean.

As my little brother says, it's sad and a waste of a good holiday when people go away as a patching-things-up exercise. I think of Mummy's knitting bag with the darning mushroom for a moment and wonder where it is. Well, we'll all have to put up with them. Arguing, I mean. And we could do with a break. I have been saving up my working-in-the-shop money. I'm a good saver, 'a good miser' my brother says. I've put it in a wooden box, and called it, half in jest, 'my running away money'. I have a brown suitcase ready in my room, S points this out to visitors and laughs as if I am a character in a book, not a person at all.

Well, the plane landed. The boat had chickens and a goat on a rope on it, but luckily no coffins. It's not as hot here as I feared. Not quite. There are salt lakes inland, so it's like there isn't an inland on this island, it's all water and salt. We eat melon and watermelon every day, very dribbly, watermelon is a bit gory really. The well does have a bucket, but it's just under a wooden cover in the corner of the kitchen, not like a nursery rhyme well. You need to drink a lot of water in the heat. They drink wine, it comes in flagons. S says, 'I like it, it's rough. You can drink as much as you like.'

'I wish you wouldn't,' Tata says.

'I'm on holiday,' says S.

My father just clears his throat then and goes and spits in the bushes. He is a big spitter. He sometimes tells the old story of his teacher falling into the spittoon in his classroom, as if this was really hilarious. To me it is just pretty vile.

We have big straw baskets and go to market in the villa car and load up with bread and cheese and Spanish salami and fruit and more wine. It's too hot to cook. I swim five or six times a day. You can. You just walk over the little stone wall via a little foot bath to get the sand off on the way back, then walk down through the cactusy plants growing in the sand, you're already on the beach. The villa is a hundred yards from the sea. That's it. There's not much tide in the Mediterranean, and there's nothing else, just beach, some rocks, scrubland and a rock to swim out to. There is one other villa in sight, and that's it. The sea. I'm in it all the time. It's milky in the morning, clear turquoise shimmering later. Deep blue when it's overcast. We had sheep lightening, or is it sheet lightning? Just the whole sky charged with flashing clouds and the sea nearly black.

I went snorkelling with my (helicopter) brother, and the whole sea bottom opened right up beneath us into a space bigger than a cathedral. There were shoals of little fish everywhere, flashing in the light, refractions, reflections, movement, colours incandescent and electric, I had no idea underwater was so miraculous, so very otherworldly. My brother practised using a harpoon on an octopus.

In the future I will follow a giant cloth octopus round Parliament Square to St James's Park by the Treasury, and up to Trafalgar Square. The octopus will be accompanied by a mean samba band, dangling skeletons, cut-out fish, enormous puppet birds and lines of police. It will be part of the Extinction Rebellion.

Rays flipped up the sand and hazed up the water. My poker brother stepped on a sea urchin and got a spine stuck in his heel, he was in agony, the neighbour from the other villa had to suck it out. It's the only way. We all watched.

We walk round the headland to a beach with a light sprinkling of Germans with salami-coloured tans. There is one restaurant. It has no walls. I have a fish stew, and the bits of octopus in this stew are like thick rubber bands, I don't see the point of eating them. Thankfully the children in Biafra aren't mentioned when I leave the octopus in the bowl. I can't think of a better place to be: on the island, on the beach, in the sea, with no time limits, no one saying we need to pack up now. We are here for a whole month. I read books from the crate, I eat, but mostly I swim and lounge and laze in the shallows. I dance my own swim dance in the sea, turning over like a water snake. I take my clothes off and swim naked in the dark, it's warm and there's the moon, flooding light in a path on the water.

They argue. A plate is smashed, there is drunkenness. (S, inevitably.) There are angry words and shouts and sulks, and it's less final and claustrophobic than at home because there is so much air here on the island. I know it is probably just the same amount of air as at home, but it doesn't feel like it. Everyone goes around barefoot except me in my flip-flops. The villa is mostly open downstairs, lizards hang about on the ceilings, dropping down when you least expect it – I have got used to them, my brother finds them scary. Outside is always ready and waiting, the cicadas are there like a backing track. Even the whole palaver of dealing with mosquitoes, bites and burning coils, is somehow watered down because we're not at home. My little brothers are easily pleased, easily carried, they easily sleep at night. It is easy to walk away from all of them. To make a den of my own in the sand dunes, to be beyond shouting distance. On the shoreline I run, I jump, I sing, I spin, and no one laughs at me. There is enough room for me to be me.

THE KNAVESMIRE

It is strange now my sisters have both gone away. The navy one has written to me from university, but I can hardly read her writing. My light blue sister is living in a caravan in another family's garden twenty-two miles away. There are goats there. My sisters hate S. They were always whispering, smoking as well, and laughing behind their hands. They refused to even speak to S. And all the time the boys have been spurred on by her, bribed, my sisters said. My sisters said they expected me to be loyal, but to whom? They hardly spoke to Tata either. I'm in the middle of the boys, and it's a hard place to be. Gone are the days of trying to stand around the loo and piss with them, of asking my helicopter brother to make me a cardboard willy from a cornflakes packet, like the kind of thing you see them do on *Blue Peter*, but probably with no sticky-backed plastic and we never had many empty washing-up-liquid bottles or tubes of glue either. And my request became a joke. I was too young to realise that. Or think about the cardboard going soggy, it not being reusable. Or comfortable.

I never actually wanted to be a boy, they smelt, but I wanted to be able to join in. They put me in goal. My poker brother commentates while they play football, his face heated, beetroot-coloured. He is always coming up on the wing with a glorious stride, timing, pace, grace, and he's always a winner, the crowd go crazy as he does his victory dance, which is obviously not a dance because he's a boy. And the intrinsic difference is always being rubbed in, about girls being feeble and weak and silly and pathetic. And I'm not. But them thinking I am is lonely. If I make a great save, even one that's not a fluke, there is no commentary for me. And as we all get older, I think they are amazed I even agree to be in goal. It becomes target practice, a toss-up between a superb bend into the back of the non-existent net off his left foot, or making me shriek and flinch with genuine fear. And if it goes over the wall it's a toss-up between the boys scaling the walls like Colditz, dodging the Nazis, or sending me over and laughing if I cut myself on the broken glass embedded into the top of it.

Anyway, basically I am now the only girl left in a family of five brothers and Fuzz the dog, who is also male. The new au pair thankfully is a seventeen-year-old girl from Norway, Ida.

Ida has posters of Edvard Munch paintings and listens to jazz. The arguments are worse now. Nasty, scary arguments. Cruel. And that's when S is actually here. She goes to London in the week. And the au pair incredibly runs the household. We can't bear it: the boys, the rows, the sulking. The amount of washing, cooking, cleaning, child-minding, is endless. I'm glad I have to go to school. I realise I have become one of those sad people who actually prefer school to home. At least it is more predictable.

At the bottom of the road is the Knavesmire. There are no visible knaves, stalking and causing mischief. Although there is the place of Dick Turpin the highwayman's gibbet. There's the racecourse, there's the smell of chocolate from Terry's factory, and there's a lot of mire, and cow shit. The cows sit down when it's going to rain. My mother used to ask me to look at what the cows were doing if she wasn't sure about hanging the washing outside. Sometimes we used to go to the start of the racecourse if it was a full two-mile race and hang about trying to be captured by the TV cameras. The others would be at home seeing if we were on. The sight of racehorses in full pelt is scary, you see all the blood vessels swollen, the sweat, the straining, the mouth foaming. It all feels too near, too real, and brutal.

The only way to survive home at the moment is to go out on the racecourse, right in the middle, well away from all the dog walkers, away from the cows, and scream. So that's what we do. The au pair and me. Sometimes after supper when the boys have to do the washing and drying-up with my father, we lift eyebrows at one another and just go.

In the middle of the Knavesmire, it's like the sea. On a beach you can go a bit mad and no one seems to mind. We scream and let out steam to our hearts' content. Like pressure cookers, like whales, like volcanoes. We scream and scream, and it's best in the rain, then we come back with our clothes completely plastered to our bodies. We come back partly hysterical, still giggly, and purged and puffed and feeling both naughty and happier. And then we listen to Ella Fitzgerald in the attic with cocoa if there's enough milk. And we talk about how crazy they are, and how sane we are. And how easy life could be.

FLOW

At last, my period has finally come! I can hardly believe it, I have been waiting so long. Checking my pants and stuff. But I don't know what all the fuss was about from those big moaning lumbering girls in the cloakroom at school. I like it, the blood, the woman-ness of me. Even though my brothers make jokes about jam rags within earshot, on purpose. I just look away, think of my modesty, and feel smug, they don't have periods, and they never will. How do they know anyway? How do I know they know? But I reckon they do. I refuse to rise to it when they joke about tossing-up or any of the other grubby phrases they use amongst themselves. I don't get what they think is so funny. I really hate their sneering and snickering, but I hate on the inside, because there would be no point saying anything, it would only make them far worse.

The other thing I find hard is the feeling of the ridiculous belt, the towels and the loops and the safety pins and the bulges that surely everyone can see, lumpy under my clothes. It all feels cumbersome and stupid. And I'm hyper-aware of it under my pants and skirt. Surely any- and everyone can see the lumps it makes, and surely everyone can tell that the spot in the furrow between my nose and cheek is clearly a period spot. I'm on my period. Like I'm riding it, where does that come from?

The whole pad paraphernalia was handed to me wordlessly by S. I mentioned to her that you can get stick-on towels these days, we are in the second half of the twentieth century after all. Hinting doesn't work with S, she just behaves like she can't hear. I can't for the life of me imagine having a conversation about tampons with her. I bought a small box in Boots with my working-in-the-shop money. Tampax, beginners' level, but I haven't got much beyond the standing with one foot on the loo seat bit yet. The diagram of inside vaginas is a bit deceptive, and there's always someone at the door. At home and school. It will have to wait.

I'm bleeding now, I am. I am the last in my class, but it's happened. Lying in bed it feels pretty special and almost sensual and I keep reaching down to feel and remind myself that it's real. I'm a woman. Finally. It feels clean and dirty at the same time, in a pleasing way.

It's my time of the month, I've got the curse. But I don't feel cursed, it feels exciting, no one mentioned that either. There is too much shame and furtiveness around. Sandra from school's mum was putting bloody newspaper packages on the fire and went mad when she asked her what they were, meat or something? Her mother swore at her, and she doesn't swear, and she stomped into the kitchen and started banging things around. And Sandra became a detective in her own house. Finding the shoebox on top of the wardrobe filled with a stockpile of nestled pads. I don't feel ashamed, why should I? I'm just annoyed with my brothers, and boys in general. My father patted me on the head.

'You are growing up very nicely,' he said.

S just seems bored and impatient with me, like I'm a chore she's not that interested in. And she has au pairs for the chores anyway.

None of this matches up to the fact that I'm bleeding, I'm a real woman. In the dark I feel soft and strong. My menstrual blood is really red. I would like a full fanfare of trumpets, a procession, everyone wearing red velvet cloaks. I'd like to be showered with peony petals, and drink a special draught, a potion of womanhood.

And all I get are nasty sniggers from schoolboy/altar boys who ought to know better. All I get is their sense that being a girl is a joke, an embarrassment, a game they can't play, so they try and make the rules. I could have a child now, me! And I feel their incomprehension, ridicule and a hatred like a sulphurous mist, of my body. It's mine, and they can't do anything about it. My body is me. And as I bleed at night in my own bed in my own pleasure, I can feel their derision through the walls, the nasty old cheese sock smell, their grey underpants with what they call skid marks, the sweat smell that's too strong, the frantic way they talk about football, the wrestling matches we have that aren't about being tickled or beaten entirely. But are always about being teased. I hate the way they sniff and sneeze loudly on purpose, I hate the way they push me around, and cheat at cards and laugh at me. I hate the way they stare at my legs when I wear tights. The way they weigh me up, size me up, gang up on me and then take me to one side alone and ask me to carry a note to a girl in our sixth form. Or ask me to go round town, when we've never ever gone round town before. My helicopter elder brother has never wanted to be seen dead with me before. He's been a ringleader, conducting humiliations ever since I can remember. And suddenly he's admiring my new jumper, a Mondrian-esque job that I wear with my black loons with huge flares I sent away for. Suddenly he's telling me what to wear and wanting to walk round town with me. And like an idiot I can't resist going.

On my own I feel powerful, even, I feel sexy, and amazed. And all the time as these sexual stirrings float around the house, S's underwear goes missing, my brothers smell stranger than ever and the arguments go on. The visits to the Knavesmire in the rain multiply. S, when she is even here, is drunk on gin and smokes incessantly. And before I know it I am involved in gender warfare. S's sons are too small to be involved, toddlers are gender-neutral. And I feel like I want to drown. I want it all to stop, and I don't know what *it* is. And there's no one to talk to, no one to say 'enough', no sun to come out after the storms that threaten behind every cloud.

S begins to charm me, it feels like being tempted in the Bible. She's going to go to London. She has to get away from this hell house, surely I won't want to stay here without her, and Ida will be going back to Bergen very soon, for good. She ramps it up.

'Do you really want to be left here in this house of arguments and the memory of arguments, in this house of death, in this house of secrets, with your father and the boys? Think what you will become, a drudge, a lackey, your schoolwork will suffer. And think, you're fourteen now, think of the delights of the big city. Think of London. And look at the way your father behaves, he's frightening, he could be violent, he's always at work anyway, and he's not to be trusted. This is no kind of place for a young and intelligent girl to grow up. You know that.'

There is always more gin, she lets me have her lemon with tonic and ice in a glass. And I look at my thighs in my jeans and I think of London. I go to my school in my dyed uniform and I think this is all too small and strange. I think, *This can't be my life.*

THE RED BOWL

In the sink in the kitchen we have, we have always had, a red bowl. Somewhat the worse for wear, a round red plastic washing-up bowl. There it is, reliable, ever trustworthy at the heart of the home. I block my ears to the rows and icy silences. I wriggle in secret delight at my own bleeding, because it isn't all that bad. As I insulate myself with my imagination from the antics of my brothers, as I tire of changing nappies, tilting bottles and holding the tiny hands of my little brother, tire of squishing up bananas with a fork and being a slow shoveller-in of pap. As I realise that despite the scream of Edvard Munch, the passion-spent glory of his black-and-white lovers, despite the sass of Ella scatting, my one true friend, Ida the au pair, is going back to Norway. I muse on the solidity of the red bowl in the kitchen.

It's there in the steam of the straining of pasta and potatoes, frizzing up my mum's hair in memory as she moves about with spoons and whisks and bowls and pans, stacks up plates, swabs the surfaces, travels to and from the pantry and the fridge and the scullery and the back door and the phone and the front door and the kettle's boiled and the plates are dirty again, and again, and the pudding hasn't set properly and the cake is burning, and the washing needs bringing in, 'Now, immediately, there's a downpour.' Her face is harried, harassed, the cupboard doors slam, cutlery falls to the floor, and there's still the shopping . . . and she needs to darn and knit and cut out that pattern for the birthday dress, finish her teacher training, and those curtains could do with re-hemming and . . .

Actually she's not here at all, and all that homemaking, mothering, listening, pegging out the washing, running baths, combing our hair, is gone. Dead as a doornail. She's really dead and gone so far away, she'll never see me like this with breasts and blood, or even talk to me about spots. And the whole of my house, my family, is riven, cracked, there's a slow earthquake going on and everyone is pretending, we just go on going on, shoe polishing, taking tests at school, getting caught in the rain. I brought my school report home and opened it on the way back and rain dripped from the silver birch at the bottom of the road onto the ink, creating a genuinely Japanese arrangement of watermarks, and yet my father said nothing. Only nodded at the splodgy writing he could read. And I was so terrified of his anger, I was quaking, shaking. And S was away and she doesn't care about school anyway, she was expelled by nuns.

So sadly, this small domestic moment of swishing the mugs around in the red bowl, for my brother to dry (this is our designated chore), makes me see that it is the red bowl that is in the middle. Like a mother, except it's a bowl. When you're ill, it's 'Get the red bowl, pass me the red bowl, I feel sick'. And after the retching, the stringy bile or the full lumpy vomiting, 'Empty it and slosh it out with Dettol.' 'I'm cleaning out the fridge, get the red bowl.' 'We'll need to bathe that knee, it looks like a nasty cut with a bit of grit in it, let's get the red bowl with some warm water.' And it's always there, the bowl, the phrase, making life continue, making it all right again, allowing rinsing and cleaning and washing and dabbing and disinfecting and, 'It'll all be all right, get the red bowl.' *How can this be?* I think as I drearily shuffle the cups around in warm soapy water. How pathetic that I no longer have anything like a mother, that this house is no longer a home. That in the future visiting anyone's house I'll offer to wash up and take extra care to clean their washing-up bowl, red yellow blue green or otherwise, wiping the bottom carefully. Clearing scum away. That I'll clean round their taps, rinse under their drying racks, that I'll even clean their soap dishes and the rimed saucers under their plants. All in the same sad spirit of making everything all right, cleaning up, washing it out, giving it a rinse. And it's the red bowl still in my heart in my head in my sub-, un- and superconsciousness, at the centre. Like the mother I no longer have. And how offensive is that? To even think of equating my dead-of-leukaemia mother with a washing-up bowl. But it has come to that.

We still go to the cemetery sometimes with Tata. He takes a trowel and weeds around the rose bush. The headstone is already sunk and slightly askew. My father makes a great performance of going to the tap, using one of the watering cans there. My (poker) brother stands beside the tap pretending he's pissing as the water spurts out. He is always looking for comedy even when it isn't there. The sound of the water in the watering can is forlorn, it's like the water itself is dying. The graveyard is flat, there's no church. There are soldiers buried here in anonymous rows, with plastic red poppies. We water the earth between the headstone and the grass covering my mother in her coffin. My father says nothing, apart from mumbling, 'Pray for your mother.'

I try to talk to Mummy silently, because I find I can't pray for my mother. I can't help thinking she doesn't really need my prayers for her, now she's in heaven. I need her prayers for me now, and for all of us, down here. I think that she is the only person who would understand this thought and not be shocked by it.

My father stands by the grave after the quasi-gardening, in silence, then he looks at his watch, he's always in a hurry. My father cannot live in the moment. I realise that the tools I've picked up since childhood, like the three-pronged fork with a flat triangular blade on the other side

72

that's so good for wresting up buttercups, my father never had. The emotionally intelligent, personal growth toolkit implements, he would never even hear of, and most likely would have had nothing to do with anyway. He had the loss of his country, Hitler's war, being a foreigner and officially an 'alien' here. He only had the Catholic church, my mother, who was dead forever, and now he was losing S. She had come to hate him.

My best memory of Mummy: outside, we're paddling in the river at Nunnington. There's grass, there's a picnic, we children are not quarrelling, there are no tears. My mother dozes, flicks through a book, listens, thinks, makes a sparky remark that shows she knows exactly how I feel, whatever I say. This belief that someone understands me has faded. I cannot begin to explain to anyone at school what is going on at home, really, everything about my family is beyond explanation. Home is not home any more. Did I dream it? Now no one is allowed to talk about my mother, about the time before S, ever. The perceived school-friendly version is that we live in a big house and that my brothers, especially the eldest, are handsome. My father's a foreigner, my mum died and he remarried, and that's it. These are the years before stepmothers were commonplace except in fairy tales. I am living in a time and a place where divorce is scandalous, it is just not done.

I wash up the mugs in the red bowl each afternoon for my little brother to dry, and the earthquake continues. Willy-nilly, the crack becomes a shaft, a chasm, an abyss, and we will be torn asunder. And I know this sounds melodramatic and biblical and not applicable. But I'm not exaggerating, I wasn't to know fully at that time, but the family, that word that can sound so ominous, or just cornflake-advert dull, will be blown apart by death and the shenanigans of the S years, the love story that wasn't.

At the eleventh hour, I receive a letter from S's old nanny, who usually provides home-made apple pies, sad echoes of my mother's. The letter is not a pie, but a plea. She believes only I can save the family, only I can make S see sense and remind her of the sanctity of marriage. I am only fourteen, I feel forty.

Washing Machine

Well, marriage guidance counsellor, peace envoy, I am not. A career at the United Nations will not beckon. The worst thing is I left my little brother behind. We were the Little Ones, we shared everything. Sometimes I couldn't tell if we were holding hands or not. I remember once in that twilight darkness with the curtains drawn and the lights out, half whispering, 'Hey, could you go to the loo for me?'

And believing that in a way he could.

In fact he was the one who wet the bed and was punished, blasted and shamed by S, and made to rinse his sheets out by hand in the back kitchen with cold water, sniffing. We had a washing machine, but she said he would have to learn. S is only seven years older than my navy sister, but she is old-school, boarding-school, material. We were unlucky to be born just before more liberal times. When the extra Easter eggs would have come after Mummy died, the grief counselling, the children's books with a light touch about losing a parent with spindly illustrations were yet to be written. And my father, well, he might have had therapy for the grief of my mother's death, triggering the griefs of losing his mother and his mother country etc. etc., he might not have been catapulted into marrying S at all. I can hear him snort at the thought.

'Stuff and nonsense. Quackery. Self-indulgence.'

He survived concentration camps.

Anyway, we've left. Me and S and her two little sons, we've left my father. We left the North and York crammed into S's red Mini and drove South with a set of Norwegian bowls. Then we had a weird summer in the country at the manor house again. And I realised I'm not a child any more, not invisible in that way, in my stripy bikini. I feel like a grandstander, an audience for S when she's telling stories about herself and her exploits. She doesn't send me to bed so often. I raise my eyebrows and meet other people's glances. People pour me wine. I've become 'the stepdaughter', like S and her sons are real and I'm provisional, a bit iffy. I don't have a blueprint for this role. I don't know what I'm doing half the time. Everything this summer was up in the air, except I swam and swam in the green piano pool and even in the river naked in the moonlight, just because I felt like it.

Now we're in a pebble-dashed house in North London, in a street named after an Ethiopian prince, a new au pair is due, because as S always says, she doesn't like small children. She's talked her way into getting the house bought for her to live in by the millionaire. As she always says, 'Why ask the poor for money?'

The river is miles away from here. There must be underground rivers and streams lurking. I feel lost. I go to the nearest school, round the corner. It all seems very random to me, this new life, we've got lodgers. Maybe life is always a bit random and un-thought out, I get the feeling this situation is particularly unusual, though. I suppose I thought London and living here would be more exciting. I do a lot of babysitting, for other people as well as S. I bathe their children and read them stories and tuck them in. I make them laugh and blow their noses when they cry. My very youngest little brother, the eighth of my father's children, has a recurring dream and appears on the landing rustling in his sleepsuit with built-in feet.

'Blood coming downstairs, blood coming . . . blood's coming to get me,' he says quite clearly, factually.

He doesn't rave or wail. He is in a state that is neither waking nor sleeping but another form of consciousness. As I comfort and reassure him, I wonder. He talks about crocodiles. I wonder about past lives, and if this shady, airy but gloomy house has a morbid history that he's picked up on. One we wouldn't know about because we've just landed here as if from another world, the only thing the same is us. *Except we're not even the same*, I think, *so nothing is*. The only stuff in the house when we moved in was a stained rug and a large television. The Nigerian lodgers are confused too, yesterday asking me, 'Where's the river? Er . . . or the stream?'

'What?' I said.

I had a feeling they, Benjamin and Joseph, had somehow read my mind as I was feeling that yearning for water I always have.

'Well, you see, we need to do our . . . how do you say this? Wash our clothes? Where is the stream?'

They both mimed scrubbing and rinsing, smiling at me encouragingly. Joseph does the talking, Benjamin echoes him. They wanted to do their washing. They weren't joking about streams and rivers, that's what they're used to. Well, probably women doing it actually, convivially by a river, they're not used to washing machines and the silence apart from the washing machine. I try to imagine their small town, and the thing I see is people gabbling, laughing, and gesticulating. I've noticed you don't hear people talking in this road, even though it's named after an African prince.

PIER

We go to the pier in Brighton, Mary and I. We are both trying to navigate the rubble created by divorces. We are fifteen and have coincidentally both moved from the North to the South and are trying to settle down and fit in and fulfil our potentials, and have fun. I have some weak grass and Mary has half a bottle of whisky. These are secreted at the back of the cupboard in her bedroom. Mary is now the one person I know outside my family who knows all the characters in my life, she knows S, she knows my father, she knew my mother, so I don't have to explain anything or anyone. Mary used to come to my mother's nursery school in the front room, and we fought over a tricycle. Once I refused to come downstairs because Mary was in the house. My mother once forced me to change into a dress out of my beloved shorts to go to tea at Mary's house. After much screaming and cross hair-brushing and being dragged there, who was wide-eyed and wearing shorts herself, but Mary? She had an enormous doll's house with working lights. There was a horse called Paintbox in a field at the bottom of her garden. She was the eldest child, and she was not a Catholic.

S stopped me from going to the convent in York. I can only remember being patted on the head by nuns for years and years and years, and their black boot-like shoes. I remember feeling a bit breathless and uncomfortable around the word 'vocation', and the way they looked me up and down as if my levels of piety and purity were visible. My sisters had been to the convent, but I went to the girls' grammar, my Catholic primary school classmates were deeply shocked when they found out and stopped playing with me for that last term.

I was ambivalent towards finding Mary in my secular class. Even a bit bitchy. I was trying to make myself new and anonymous. This was the first time there had been no sibling before me. Uncharacteristically, at first I got up early each morning to plait my hair neatly. My friendship with Mary has been through a few hedges backwards. Now we have settled at being friends at a distance, between me in London, and her on the South coast.

So we're on the pier, laughing, trying to be clever, seeing ourselves as merely ironically putting money in Dr Renner

B's Astrological Machine. It looks like a weighing machine, but with green-tinted swirling illustrations of the star signs. Mary is older than me and I feel she will never let me forget this. She is Sagittarius and I am Capricorn. We wait for our tickets to burp out, the wind in our hair, salt and vinegar fresh on our lips from a shared bag of chips. We are definitely, intelligently, not taking this Dr Renner B seriously, it's highly ridiculous, it's a slot machine. And yet in a shoe-shifting focused way we wait, strangely suspended above the sea frilling on the pebbles far below, held up by a latticework of rusting metal. Mary has an archive of her life, carefully glued into scrapbooks. In the future we will notice that she has kept my ticket. And lost hers.

We giggle, talking non-stop, too loudly, changing the world in every way we can possibly think of, interrupting each other, swearing, smoking the damp loosely rolled spliff out of her attic window and drinking neat whisky out of bright picnic beakers. We know nothing, it's all ahead of us, we know everything, and we wear the wreckage. We hate men, and we adore them, we can't stop ourselves. We both love and hate our new comprehensive schools, we are readers, thinkers, budding intellectuals. It is 1975 and we are inside the wave, the tube of the surf, of change, of growth, of feminism.

The following day Mary's mum drives us to Seaford. It's a pebbly beach, a stormy sky. We have driven past Newhaven and the port entrails, the warehouses and railways lines. We were going to go swimming at the beach, but it becomes overcast and then crack, and the sky is going black. Still, we have our swimming costumes on under our clothes so I go on my own, I insist. I suppose I am desperate, coming from beach-less, sea-less London. Mary and her mum stay in the car, her mum looks puzzled. As I hobble-run over the ridges of pebbles towards the waves, I shout out because no one can hear me, throw off my outer clothes and plunge right in and under. The sea. It's warmer than the air and the rain makes me feel drunk, buffeted, I'm jumping, yelling, flailing around, and the sky cracks again and rumbles nearer, darker, stronger, and I'm part of the music of no music, of harmony and disharmony, of sun and storm, the sky reflects how I feel perfectly.

In the car we have hot coffee from a flask, and I steam up the windows. I feel that somehow I'm not a virgin any more. The storm, my wild engagement with it, makes me think clearly and for some reason say, 'My childhood is over.'

TEARS

S is always melodramatic, without fail. She would be better on a stage, she doesn't know how not to perform. I think she has never got over having a favoured elder brother, and has been compensating ever since. There are bottles filling up the high shelf that goes all the way round the square hall. Gin and wine mostly, with the odd brandy bottle. She has instituted bottle signing, so there are smudged signatures on all the empties if you look closely. Her variety of fame has connected her with a motley crew of people who turn up here to sit around the table, which is a door balanced on a smaller table. The handles are still on. Everything seems to be 'donated' or 'found', even the people, because some seem lost.

Francis, someone of S's, has just been to the marble mines in Carrera and has agreed, drunkenly it has to be said, to paint a boot on the wall. He has very curly hair, but wishes it was straighter, and talks a lot about the copper dome of the mosque he is part of building in Regent's Park. He might be coming on holiday with us, to Formentera again. I like some of the people she gathers around her, others I can't stand. Francis is all right, I would class him as only semi-captivated, but I don't know who he is or really why he comes here. S doesn't have lovers, but acolytes. She is still a Catholic in her own way. In the future, Mass will be said daily by a runaway abbot in the sitting room. I have left religion now, everyone is Jewish at school, or so it seems on the Jewish holidays – there's no one there.

M, the manor house man who bought us this pebble-dashed house, has sent his eldest son to help with the decorating. I think that's a standard thing, for any young man whose future is uncertain, of any class, to make themselves useful. It isn't a gap year because W is not up for going to university. And we are about two and a half miles from his house, so it isn't adventurous as such.

But as he says, 'It's different. Not what I'm used to anyway,' I don't mind that W is not in Borneo with a tribe that would rather not be found. Does 'different' mean I am exotic in some way? I wonder, and keep this thought to myself. It is pitiful how much I want to be liked for myself. Pitiful how easily I fall in love. I feel like I have had the rash of it ever since kiss-catching in the playground with Dermot Monaghan, and I was six then. I do wonder sometimes what it could be like not to fancy people and if I just have a love of love, which is not loving, as Bowie sings. Also my blueprint, if you can call it that, has not been great. God knows how to have a relationship, a boyfriend! It seems so uncool these days as well, this need. I hate the feeling that I am pre-programmed. W and I talk a lot, we are like mates, we are. We seem to have the same sense of humour. Sometimes he goes off for a while and I don't know how long it will be before I see him again, and I cannot bear how excruciatingly desperate this makes me feel. I hate myself. I try to imagine what he's doing, and realise I have a very sketchy understanding of him and his life. His real life.

Inevitably we bond over paintbrushes, over dust sheets and newspapers, over water and turpentine, over the sink, over colours, over the midnight movie on Fridays, over a spliff. We watch *Creature from the Black Lagoon*, and stay up until dawn. We dance in the rain in the garden in the hazy night light. We find barrels of home-made wine at the back of the garage and drink it. W carries round a copy of Sartre's *Nausea*, I tease him that he's always halfway through it. I know, we both know, it's a prop. He smokes languidly, he speaks slowly. He says, 'I like to have a really hot cup of tea in a piping hot bath. Then when I sip it, it feels like my skin is paper thin. The heat of the bath heats my blood, then there's the tea, and everything levels out to the same sensation, beyond the temperature. It feels like I'm not there.'

And I nod, trying not to behave like a pet, trying to conceal the fact that I always hang on his every word, that I'll analyse every word, every look, deep into the night, that I'll remember everything. His wrists captivate me, I try not to stare. He meets my eyes, there's such light in his. No one else holds my gaze for so long like this, I think he can see into me.

My life is a mixture of stolid sensible behaviour, the girl with sharpened pencils in her pencil case, the girl who'd let you borrow her ruler, the reliable babysitter, the washer-up and gravy maker, the one who cuts roses and puts them in a vase on the wobbling table. S regarded these with a nonplussed look that said plainly, 'Why?' The other girl smokes dope in the dinner hour, drinks barley wine and wants to have sex, wants to go to parties and forget the whole weekend, or the week. Wants to be loved. Sloppy. If W's hand even touches my arm I am on fire. I am. Oh God, this has been going on for weeks, for months.

I stay in bed until the afternoon. I cry into my pillow until it's sopping wet. I'm in love, it's excruciating. I'm aroused by wrists, fingernails, ankle bones, bare feet. He's gone, the decorating's done. I don't know when or whether I'll see him and the house is full of sycophants. I scheme and dream, S and her demands and opinions and hangers-on disappear behind a thick fog. So I can ignore her, lose her in it. She suddenly storms right into my bedroom and is shouting something or other, I can't even tell what or why. And she lunges at the bedcovers and then at me and she grabs me by the hair and unbelievably tries to drag me out of bed by my hair. Everything goes into slow motion because I can't believe this is happening. Stepmothers are not mothers, and she is now an ex-stepmother, or trying very hard to be. In fact, the divorce will take seven years to complete.

So, these days, the default setting between us is binary, screaming or silence. She goads me in public, I'm meant to find this funny. Or she wants me to babysit and uses charm. This isn't fair, I love my little brothers, but she uses everyone as her pawns. There's a constant turf-war-zone feeling now, fizzing in the background, all the time. When will it erupt? After how many gins, how many bottles? The hall shelf is full fit to bursting and she's talking about sifting them, weeding some out, curating the empty signatured bottles like a madwoman in charge of an exhibition. She has no inhibitions. I just can't understand why she still has hangers-on and meek lodgers, pussyfooting around her, and people interviewing her on the radio and rich men like M making it go on happening.

At times I do ask myself, *Is this all me? Trapped in the straitjacket of being a teenager, with hormones rampaging, weeping, drama-queening it? Or is the world, the so-called grown-up world, just plain ridiculous and crazy?*

And like a true sixteen-year-old, I plot. And imagine a way, any way, out.

Thunder and Lightning

The sash window is wide open. The bedroom is at the back, away from the cars on the high street intermittently lighting up the ceiling of the room at the front. Like searchlights. The sky's cracking open. I feel electricity in my spine, in harmony with the bass line of the thunder. Lightning is in my eyes, and the rain is on the edge of breaking over the windowsill to make the bed wet and I don't care. The sky is purple and monstrous and magnificent. And I'm riding Jamie, shining with sweat, my blood's on the sheet. I'm laughing with relief and exhilaration. I've just lost my virginity. And it has gone a lot better than expected. The thunderstorm is suitably melodramatic, the sound of the rain thrums, fading in and out, and the changing light effects are in perfect counterpoint to my mood. And W's friend Jamie has never slept with a virgin before, so it's a first for him too. It's finally happened.

I never quite knew what people at school meant by 'getting off with'. Beyond snogging and heavy petting – going all the way, was it? Or was it? I suppose most people were lying, boasting, bragging. Jamie isn't a boyfriend, how feeble would that be? He's a friend of W's and one of a group of guys who do stuff together, mostly smoking dope and listening to music. Dylan and Miles and Pink Floyd and Beefheart and The Doors and so on and so on. They know all the references. The LP covers are artworks and neat tables to roll spliffs on. And when I first went for a walk alone with Jamie, he said he didn't want to just, well, fuck me. But now we're here in his flat he does, and he takes me out to eat afterwards, after we've shared a bath. And the petit pois with butter and garlic are like ambrosia.

I don't know if I've been happy and free and loose and relaxed like this ever. Jamie meets my eyes over the wine and I put to the back of my mind and lock it up that I'm not in love with him. He's being kind and focusing on me tonight. He's one of the crowd and so am I. I'm living in the spare room on the top floor with W's family. Because it couldn't go on with S. She's livid. It isn't how I thought it might be, they don't eat together. I get quite lonely sometimes and miss my little brothers. It's a family, but it's as if they don't do family somehow, or if they do it's when I'm not around or in my room on my own. I have a record player and my books and my stuff for A levels to do and school is now up the longest hill ever. They lent me a bike with the smallest wheels ever. People walk past on the steep hill and say, 'Why don't you get off and milk it?'

I don't understand but pretend I do, and smile and nod or think of something smart to reply when I'm puffing like hell. No one really notices what I do here, coming or going-wise.

Jamie is elusive, he seems ashamed, embarrassed to be associated with me. We still screw, as he calls it, but it's furtive. I have never been on a date or anything, it's not like that. In my heart of hearts I do think because we're having all this sex and baths together and stuff that there's more to it. I can't believe there isn't. That we can be skin to skin and orgasmic and yet this chilliness. This unease. This almost denial.

WATERING

The house looks like a gingerbread house in a fairy tale. The hills ripple into Wales on the horizon. We have just planted out a herb garden. It's round with twelve brick segments, like a clock. Anna has kindly turned around the root I planted the wrong way up. Anna and Matt are going off to Badminton, so I'll do the watering. I've been feeding their daughter with mushed-up vegetables, while Anna makes chutney. And clearing brambles to plant proper cultivar blackberries. I painted the metal fireplace in shades of green and white, and Anna just bit her lip when I pulled off the masking tape when the paint was still wet. Anna is a cousin of W's, and M's niece. I'm in their web. I'm a kind of house guest, but not, I potter around and do jobs, borrowing an overall. It's the school holidays. I'm to water the herb garden, the vegetables outside and in the polytunnel, and feed and water the dogs. They don't have cats.

In the evenings especially at weekends they often have friends over, for long boozy and quite druggy meals. Matt rolls spliffs from grass grown discreetly in a corner of a barley field, he took me to see it. He asked me if I'd like to take a sack of the stuff back on the train to sell at school. I couldn't tell if he was joking. But I said no, I couldn't really see how it would work at Paddington. And at school boys are dealers. Matt and Anna trawl country auctions, filling the house with curiosities. I'd say their style is hangover aristo country house, with funky and Gothic thrown in and thrown together. Matt has an enormous record collection and enormous speakers. He opens the window and blasts out stuff into Wales over the sheep and the South American horses Anna had to have sent over. A farm manager runs it all.

I quite like it when they're here. And when we go off on jaunts to castles or to The Sun at Clun. And I'm flattered they are trusting me to house-sit, animal-sit, water everything and stuff. Although in the back of my mind there is a worm of a worry about being alone right out here, a mile from the nearest other house, three from the village. I can't drive. When Matt collected me from the station and proceeded to drive the Beetle so very very fast along the toboggan-run single-track grass-growing-in-the-middle roads, high hedge tunnels all the way, my hands clenched to white bone on the seat, my breath tense as he manoeuvred, spinning the steering wheel, zooming, braking, accelerating through the dark of the night, he laughed at me. I was exhilarated, terrified and thrilled to be way out here, way out of my comfort zone.

The third night here I woke up. And in the half-light, from under the embroidered peonies on the coverlet, I could hear breathing. It wasn't mine. I saw a silhouette of a man sitting. So I just stopped breathing. I didn't know what else to do. He was sitting on the yellow chair with Chinese birds on it, underneath that print of some ruins in Syria. And I was aware through my half-closed eyes to just keep on being absolutely, utterly still. Quiet as the thick night outside. I was afraid but I wasn't in danger. Danger would come if we both admitted we were there and aware. He went on just sitting there. Looking over towards me, with only his breathing there in the room, hardly his thoughts, only his silhouette. In the dawn light the chair was empty.

With clattering, and a little angry bantering, Matt and Anna and their daughter went off in the Land Rover. The quiet bounces off the flagstones, the dogs are fractious and confused by me. They're greyhounds and look at me haughtily as I take them into the field next to the herb circle in the chilly sunlight.

I eat a sandwich outside and read a book, something

I've never got round to doing here before, in the daytime, when they're around. I walk around the whole house slowly just looking. Places without people in them, without the noise, the confusion, the action, speak differently. I can feel the people who lived here before this influx of Londoners.

In the early evening I water everywhere with the hose and the watering can, I give everything a good thorough soaking, watching the soil go dark and wet, seeping. It's the night I dread. The dark, the total aloneness. The first night I'm alert, jumping at the slightest creak, paranoid probably. I wake up more times than I can count. But thank God, at last it's light, at last, and although the house feels enormous and somehow I've shrunk, I go through the motions, in thankful daylight. The dogs irritate me, in a clan of their own, I am incidental. I feed them and take them out to the field as enthusiastically as I can, fill up their water bowl, talking doesn't register with them. They hang around in the yard. I potter, I have a bath, I fall asleep in the sun. I heat up soup, drink tea and coffee and tea again, I smoke my filthy roll-ups. I water the plants like a good house-sitter. I wait, I look at the clock. I dread the night. The house creaks, it moves. And in the gloaming twilight I can't find the dogs. Did I hear distant barking in my dreamscape, or through the steam of the hot bath? They'll come back. And when it's dark they do, scratching at the door makes me start from my dozing – the record I put on ages ago has hit a scratch. How long has that been going on for? Befuddled, I let them in.

I can't understand what's happening to me, to my breath, to my body. In the night I am completely petrified. I hear footsteps, I'm sure I hear footsteps, bootsteps, in the yard. I daren't turn on the light. I lie like a stone effigy in a cold crypt. I'm not there, I hold my breath, my heart hurts, like a drill bit is boring into it, I can't breathe, and yet I am breathing and thinking about my funeral. Lilies, speeches, but who would be there, who would even make a speech? I daren't open the door of my imagination to think what might happen to me. Now in the dark, miles from anyone, in the middle of nowhere, I realise I shouldn't be here. I shouldn't be. I can't be. I am completely alone. Even the thought of the stars in the sky seems frightening, because I realise I don't know anything. I nod off. When it's lighter I wake and sip water, blessed water. As it goes down my throat I feel the tiniest bit more alive. Still too scared to go to the loo, I resist drinking more. I lie there and lie there and feel like a puppet. I wait. I don't get up until past eleven – the dogs! The dogs whining and scratching downstairs. I try to ignore them, but eventually they win and I get dressed and creep down. I feel deeply ashamed that I'm such a wimp, that fear has got the better of me so thoroughly, so easily. As I walk downstairs I blush.

When Matt and Anna come back noisily, the dogs are overjoyed. I nod and lie, 'Yes, oh everything's been fine, no problem, absolutely fine. Yes, the dogs have been good. Did you have a good time? At Badminton?' I witter on. 'Is it anything at all to do with the game, you know with shuttlecocks? Or just horses?'

They don't know. And we all look at each other and laugh.

Later it transpires the dogs have killed two sheep while I was 'in charge'. And they have to be put down, or sent away somewhere where there are no sheep. The herb garden survives, although some of the brambles strangle the cultivar blackberries. The mantelpiece will be repainted, but not by me.

SERPENTINE

I have decided to swim in the Serpentine in Hyde Park. I feel like a goose. The water's dingy. It's the sky that makes the idea of a swim so tempting. The great reflected blue and white, clouds and water dappling and now I'm in it, and we're non different. So, after the numbshock of the cold, to my bones, I swim. And drift and drift, and reach a place of freedom, for about ten minutes anyway. And even goosepimples and over-balancing putting my jeans back onto my damp body don't take away the strength, the power coursing through me. Even the nasty wanker eyeing me up from behind a tree doesn't make me feel dirty.

I put my parcel of swimming stuff in a string bag on the handlebars of my bike and cycle along Rotten Row, the water drips in a higgledy-piggledy line from my wet things, marking my path. My hair's wet, but I don't care. I can't afford hairdressers or new clothes or shoes, I'm on a borrowed bike living in a millionaire's house and I can't even afford to go to a cafe, but I don't care. My hair splays out behind me as it dries into ringlets and there are snooty ladies on horseback here and ridiculous Bentleys and Rolls-Royces on Park Lane, but I've won a playwriting competition. I've been going to the Activists drama group in the Garage, behind the Royal Court, damp, dark and very grotty. The raw material is youth, us. We improvise. I took a large square piece of paper and plotted a play out, like a mind map, but before they get invented. My play is going to be put on in the theatre in Sloane Square. At the age of four I knew I was a writer, no one seemed to care then, but now I've actually written something and this has happened. I have been invited to the auditions and rehearsals. The thought of casually mentioning this to Jamie is very satisfying.

Inside my heart drops like a stone, plummets like a bird of prey. Jamie is very disparaging about my age and competitions in general, and talent blooming and dying and so on, but I can tell he's impressed, and nearly jealous. Since leaving Cambridge he's written a musical, he wants to get 'into the theatre'. He sings me snatches from the songs – he's the lyricist. They're awful, trite, and the music is pap pop. I can't understand why he's so pleased with himself, no one is 'interested'. And here am I, a teenage playwright suddenly, bumping into Samuel Beckett on the stairs at the Royal Court. I will even be impressed by the cheque I receive, for £13.52, for some reason.

And I've got a babysitting job for two little girls next door. They need someone on Friday nights mostly, while they're recording at Abbey Road Studios. They come back in the early hours. I don't mind when they come back, their house is bright and a bit chaotic in a good way. And there's great food in the fridge.

'Just help yourself to anything you fancy,' they say, looking happy.

I realise I don't know many happy people. From my bedroom window I hear them calling out 'Love you!' to whoever's left at home when they leave their house. And I wonder it this is allowed, if this could even be normal. They have a grand piano piled with records, huge fluffy cushiony dogs. There's a green electric gate, fans wait outside their house in a semi-religious way. This is a family who are beyond famous. They often don't have cash on them so they get someone to stick it through the letter box for me next door sometime over the weekend. I bathe the girls, read them stories, put them to bed and then try and do my homework.

I find being interviewed makes me feel both nervous with dread, and excited at the same time. I like the auditions where I get to meet different actors and read in parts I've written. Putting words in other people's mouths. I have to admit I like being sent off in a taxi to be on the radio, I don't like having my photo taken. All of it feels deeply thrilling, but also completely unreal, and it is, all make-believe. I feel fraudulent. But the publicity department is happy with me. I get great reviews. I get commissioned by the theatre to write another play. I have an agent. And all the time my A levels sputter along in the background like a motorbike that won't quite start.

Ornamental Pond

This part feels unscripted, unscriptable, but I must do my best. After 'success', and a thimbleful of attention, things with Jamie got bad. So here I am in an en-suite room with bay windows overlooking a faux Japanese garden with gravel and a curved bridge over an ornamental pond. Funny, because I'm in a mental hospital. Except it's not called that. It's private, there are menus and napkins and an Arab guy on cold turkey confined to his room, probably restrained in his room. I've never met him. Only heard muffled cries, and shouting and running. I have my own television and a double bed and I see the benign bearded psychiatrist who runs this place. It's a Tudor house with a minstrels' gallery, there are only eight patients.

I look out of the window a lot at that pond. It's hard to tell how deep it is. I don't want to go and actually sit by it, because that would mean being observed. So I hang out the window and stare at the sky through the water, and try to overlook the twee arrangement of the garden, presumably to soothe the troubled patients' minds, try to reach some serenity of my own. The pond seems at times to me to be the only source of any real light.

We sit at dinner in a sad parody of family life, in lines at the table, enduring a formal dining experience with three courses and stilted conversation. Prompted by cheerful asides from the staff who wait on us. The Sloane-y girl with bandages on her wrists, the alcoholic man with health insurance who used to work in a car factory, the catatonic ex-teacher, the bald ex-army officer, etc. They're all drugged up. The doctor hasn't given me any medication. I'm allowed out too, for walks. We talk, he and I, in his oak-panelled consulting room, and he's reached the conclusion that I shouldn't really be here, that it's circumstantial. Like evidence in a court.

In some ways I reacted perfectly normally to Jamie not wanting to see me again. Normal for my age. I couldn't believe he wouldn't answer the phone or the door to me. I couldn't take him seriously when he pronounced that he'd be better off with 'a model, an actress, or a singer'. That it was all 'a mistake'. I was stunned (in both ways) when he pushed me down the stairs from his flat. And I was broken. Jamie told M and then M sat down with me and a cup of coffee in his study and said, 'Don't worry, it's normal to have feelings. It's absolutely fine.' And then, 'If you need us, just wake us up in the middle of the night, you don't need to suffer alone, we're here for you. Don't worry about anything. We're like family. We just want you to be well.'

But with The Note that changed. M and his family closed ranks too, in an exquisite act of bad timing. So next thing I knew I got a note left under a stone on the stairs, saying, *Could you arrange to be away for the summer?*

And a suggestion I could put a mattress in a barn, perhaps with their daughter who'd married a farmer. And even when a holiday to anywhere was mooted, I just couldn't face it on my own. I couldn't. Not the South of France, not South America. I didn't want to be alone. So here I am in the psychiatric hospital, spooning my consommé obediently and politely. Occasionally sharing a clandestine spliff with a couple of the nurses. Chatting to the doctor's teenage daughter. The director of my play came to visit me and said, 'Well, why don't you just enjoy the space and the place, and just write another play? This is a fascinating place.'

I think he needs the work. Being freelance is precarious. So I did, I wrote a play. And after the summer was over M arranged a psychotherapist. I see her twice a week. I sometimes see W on the stairs there, he's seeing the husband of my therapist, who is upstairs. We don't speak. He just nods at me, and I nod back, and I probably blush, and his cheeks flush in that way I am painfully familiar with. It still hurts. Jamie behaved like a bounder in old-fashioned language, or in new, an arsehole.

I set the play in the psychiatric hospital. Some of the staff and doctor's family come to see it, they sit in the front row and laugh in interesting places. They thank me, and we hug and shake hands. My photo is on the front of the programme, although this was not my choice. I have bought a moped. And discovered it is very easy to get completely drenched, I mean to the skin, on a moped. I will also discover that being a playwright means people want to meet you. Not to know you or like you necessarily, but to collect you.

In Deep

Doing lengths is helping me prepare my body for labour, I'm fitter than I've ever been. I swim daily up and down the Chelsea baths, up and down. Enjoying the sun when it shines down through the glass roof and breaks up in the pool. I swim crawl, my arms sleek and splash-less, aware of my hands as paddles, and the ball splash my kicking makes. With breaststroke, I make each frog shift last as long as I can, and each breath, bubbling out underwater gently. I don't panic, it's all smooth. I swim deliberately, inhabiting the rhythm. I hold my breath as long as I can and glide, and then flip twist onto my back and float for a while before I kick up my feet again and reach and reach with my arms behind my head. And each day, each week, each month, I feel the little person inside me growing beautifully. I want to be ready. My tummy is a round hump, and I pat and stroke it so often no one could count the number of times. There's a miracle going on in my body each day, and I'm in training for giving birth.

Pregnancy is a whole new arena of female consciousness and hyper-awareness of the body. Hope and worry mixed up. It's thrilling, there are days I feel high on it, and others that are pure drudgery. There's a locked-in, no-getting-out-of-this feeling, with an inevitable clock ticking like a metronome that won't stop. I feel afraid and heavy and amorphous and not myself. I'm twenty, and I don't know anyone else who's pregnant. And there's no one in my life to ask. We go to an antenatal class full of random strangers, only pregnancy joins us. The women are all more than ten years older than me, they seem organised and distant. I feel as though I might wake up one day and all of this will prove to be a chimera. Except then I touch my swelling belly and I know it's real.

My husband was a member of the audience, I met him and his girlfriend in the pub next door after the show. Yes, they came to the play I wrote about the hospital. They invited me back to their flat for supper. I had a lump of dope and the corridor of the mansion flat had a wooden floor that sloped so much it made you think you were drunk. I live there now. It is the strangest thing to reflect that if the stage-door man hadn't given in to my husband's pestering for my phone number after that supper I wouldn't be here now at all.

Small decisions, flukes really, change the whole sky. In my diary after that supper, after a late-night zip on my moped back to North London, I wrote: *Good show tonight, lots of laughs. Met 2 Chelsea flatters, went to eat at theirs.*

And I remember thinking flatters, flatterers, as I wrote the entry, a bit de-stoned by the cold night air and the emptiness of the streets. He works in television and pursued me relentlessly, despite having a girlfriend. No one has written a dos and don'ts rule book about men. I wish someone would. I envy people who have mothers. I ask them, 'How are your parents?' or 'How's your mother?' And they look back quizzically at the question, as though I have asked something a bit rude. Or they complain and moan about their mothers, and I don't understand. I'd love to have my mother around. But I do wonder if she would have liked my husband, I think she had other, more Catholic, plans for me. And for her Oxford was the peak, the absolute pinnacle. She might have been mystified by my life, by the decisions I've made, at my age. They don't feel like decisions, but they are. And here I am now, married in the registry office next door by a woman in a fake pearl necklace beneath a Woolworths clock, it gave me the giggles it all seemed so counterfeit. Here I am now, married and expecting a baby, with this underlying sense of unreality.

After a shower to get the reek of chlorine off, after picking up my thrown-on-the-floor costume and rinsing it out, noticing it's corroding with the chlorine, after combing my hair, pulling on my clothes and rolling the towel up tight, the baby's small foot kicks. I can see it. I caress the heel through my belly. I'm excited, and I'm scared.

MILK

The baby, my new son, is small, is perfect, is in an incubator beside my bed, because he's an ounce under a specific weight and they have rules. I am ecstatic. And shattered from the inside out, and I can't stop staring and staring and staring at him. I can't sleep, I'm too amazed. My husband got a bit cross, he had to go home. The baby snuffles delightfully. The swimming training paid off mostly: I pushed. Only a few stitches down there and the odd gloop and the emptying out the very depths feeling, when the placenta slithered out, but all is well. I want to fly, I want to sing from the top of mountains, and I feel I can. Everything is possible.

At nine in the morning I have barely slept. I'd like to actually hold my child. I can only poke my hands through the portholes of the incubator. It feels all wrong, I'm used to the weight of him. And now there he is lit up next to the bed under plastic. I'd like to know what's happening, I want to talk to somebody. And my mesmeric staring, my son clutching my finger through the little porthole, is interrupted by the scraping of chairs. The renowned consultant in a spotted bow tie has appeared and there are eight students too, all crowding around my bed, pulling up chairs. And I want to hold my baby and I want to be alone with him, I want just a bit of gentle support, not this, being the centrepiece of a demonstration. So I'm tearful as the spotted bow tie cross-examines me, and doesn't even deign to look me in the eye. I'm a lesson for the students: my attempts to be assertive, my distress, my tears, are all part of the lesson, they duly take notes. When it's over, they scrape their chairs back from my bed and move along to the next one.

My lovely son is put in my arms, the incubator was just a precaution. I want to feed my baby, I want to relax and get to know him. And I don't know where my husband is.

Another mother comes and whispers to me, 'If you've got Rotersept for sore nipples, don't let the doctor see it. Put it away when he's on the ward. He's dead against it. But he doesn't even have boobs, what does he know?'

She shuffles off. She walks like she's been kicked in the stomach, slowly, warily.

I feel winded, like I don't understand any of the words any more, it's all in code. When my husband comes we decide to discharge ourselves, and have to sign a document, and they try to instil us with fear.

And then I'm in the company of a drunk, wide Irish midwife who took hours to come. I'm in the bathroom in the mansion flat with the sloping corridor, my son is wailing, and she's making off-colour jokes while slapping my far too tight watermelon-sized breasts with alternate freezing and boiling flannels. This was never mentioned in the books I got out of the library nor at the antenatal classes. The agony of engorged breasts. It is excruciating, my milk has come in, and how. My breasts have taken over and my son doesn't stand a chance at latching onto these rock-hard footballs. The hot and cold flannelling continues, there is spurting. There is the sound of the taps on full again, the boiler sputtering. There is cackling and the whiff of whisky off the midwife. I feel like I am locked in a torturous bathroom cartoon, when I imagined being home would include soft music of my choosing, my favourite nightie, books, flowers, grapes and my sweet son snuffling contentedly, my husband bringing soft-boiled eggs and toast on a tray.

Thanks to the National Childbirth Trust, we hire a mini milking machine, yes really. And it makes an efficient hissing pumping sound, like in a cows' milking parlour. My son drinks this precious buttercup-yellow nectar, the first milk, from tiny bottles. My husband is able to feed him and this allays his jealousy a little bit. He is forthright about it, outright he says, 'I feel jealous of you breastfeeding. The bonding. I feel left out.'

There is no right answer to this. The last thing I want is to be sterilising bottles and boiling kettles morning noon and night, and then there's all this milk, my son Tom's milk. I know it's best for him, I know it's best for me. I have been home a day, and already I'm feeling triangulated, if that is the right use of the word. Words do not flow in this situation, I cannot find them. I cannot express my astonishment at how my husband is behaving. I kind of know he is psychologically self-obsessed and can talk a lot and at great length about his feelings. But this is not the time and place for his feelings taking centre stage, surely? With this new prince, this wonderful small being who stares out at me knowingly, whose little hands are mesmerising. Yes, there will be no more long-distance back-of-the-motorbike rides through the Alps, no more frantic couplings with the sea crashing over the rocks, and I don't care at all. I'm a mess, I don't know where my hairbrush even is, but I'm totally captivated. Everything is changed now, I'm a mother. There are no illusions. I can't understand why my husband isn't high on amazement and wonder too, at being a father.

The books and classes also never mentioned the utter strangeness of suddenly being at home with a small baby with your hormones in charge, your husband moody, and being beyond exhaustion. This is not a manageable, clearly defined territory with borders. Beyond exhaustion is off maps, far from wastelands and treacherous mountains or forests, it is flat, almost hallucinogenic and bitterly lonely. I now inhabit a hinterland of middle-of-the-night light, nappy buckets and leaking nipples, of cot versus 'the bed', of strangers examining your vagina with matter-of-fact boredom, massive sanitary towels, waddling and general emotional overflow. The glow, the bloom of pregnancy, of youth, has been replaced by a crumpled person, who longs and longs to drink a hot cup of tea all the way through on their own. The idea of actually being alone already feels far-fetched.

The health visitor is completely unsurprised that we're in the middle of moving, from the top floor flat to a maisonette with a little garden and a cellar.

'You'd be surprised how many people move house when their baby's due.'

My husband buys a washing machine that's also a dryer, he's immensely pleased with it. I like hanging the washing outside, I find nappies drying on a line in the wind one of the most beautiful sights. He doesn't agree.

NIGHT-FISHING

We've driven to the toe of the boot of Italy. I'm writing a play here by the sea. My husband has agreed to do the childcare in the mornings. I'm still breastfeeding our second son, Frank, who can stand up but not walk yet, wearing the rabbit jumper. The three of them go up into town to the market, round to the port beach and to the playground while I work. Before I start, I walk through the garden onto the beach, barefoot, and run along in the sinking soft sand. There are only my footprints. The waves are often wild, spumy and torrential. I wear cut-off shorts and my favourite big jumper and have the beach all to myself, because it's winter. For us it's like Cornwall in July.

Up the yellow cliff behind us is the town. Men lean over the wall, talking, smoking and staring out to sea, and at us I suppose. You can see their silhouettes. You can see Stromboli the volcano from up there, but we're down here right on the beach, with only the fisherman's family opposite on this lane that finishes in sand. They live in several rooms without interconnecting doors, so they are bobbing in and out a lot. They have seven children, all ages covered. I think Salvatore, a swaggerer, is the eldest daughter's fiancé. The women are loud, and pinch my sons' cheeks whenever possible. Tom grimaces when this happens, Frank looks blankly out at their smiling faces. If he cracks a smile they break into applause. There's a fireplace in the cottage and we want to buy wood. There's a place up in the mountains, they say, making spiral movements with their arms and laughing. Salvatore, who is always up to something with nets and motors and fish and clobber, draws a map on a scrap of paper. The mountains are Ms, the road is a long snake.

The sea is blue green grey turquoise navy, is clear, is always beside us like a great monster mother. We're so close, maybe we're too close. But it feels right when our bodies and the earth's surface are mostly water, to be up close like this, to absorb it in all these moods. Waves stalk our dreams, lull our slumbers, when the wind's up in the night we hear them slap. My hearing is heightened to the sounds, water frilling, still as milk, or crashing out there raging, banging against the garden wall like drumbeats, then slopping and sitting in the dark, innocent at dawn. The beautifully tailored, unusually tall for an Italian, landlord, did mention in his creamy voice, 'It can flood, you understand. The garden. Sometimes in winter, it is full of water. In summer it is perfect, this house. In winter, you cannot say what will happen.'

His hair is steel grey, his hands long and manicured. He smells of citrus cologne and wears a cravat and cufflinks with insignia. The landlord is suave and a bit creepy. Beside him I always feel scruffy, not properly female, despite my children and my nearly leaking breasts.

'We want to be by the sea. For us the house is perfect.' I grinned an obsequious grin.

'Only . . . it is winter. Ah. Did you say you are a writer?'

'Not for us. It doesn't feel like winter,' my husband explained.

The landlord looked over at my husband balancing Tom on one hip, as if he was not fully male. He looked at us all, wondering if we were stupid. I could see that the landlord was trying to understand us, but not too much. He looked at me again, mimed writing on his palm, so I nodded encouragingly. The term 'writer' can explain and excuse just about anything, can encompass the craziness of our scheme, just turning up here randomly because we weren't drawn to stop anywhere sooner, and being in denial of winter. Further South and we'd have had to cross to Sicily.

'How do you like Calabria?'

Of course we were effusive, we couldn't afford to stay in the hotel much longer.

'We love Calabria. It is wonderful. We want to stay here in Tropea, because, well, it feels right,' I said.

I am more of a gesticulator than my husband, his blood is entirely English. I can do both: obsequious and a bit dim, as well as expansive and expressive, I am more emotional and more foreign. The landlord wasn't dealing with my husband, he was looking me in the eyes, and I could see he was thinking that we were unforgivably naive, that we didn't know where we really were, and would never understand anyway. And then he shifted in his immaculate loafers, and I could see that his curiosity was satisfied quite enough, and that he'd be delighted to take our money for the little house on the beach. For the winter.

Calabria is extremely beautiful at every turn. Even the graffiti, which includes swastikas in black and hammers and sickles in red, has a starkness that is exhilarating. I feel a fizz of fear, disbelief and relief that these polarities are all out in the open here. We are having a winter sabbatical from Mrs Thatcher. There is something about the landlord that scares me, an undertow. Like currents that slip away from you before you can adjust to them. He lives up in the old town in an immaculate apartment with stone battlement walls. The house is right down on the beach. So territorial issues couldn't be too much of a problem. We handed him wads of cash for the rent in advance, to be paid monthly.

Salvatore is marrying Lucia, the fisherman's eldest daughter. She has a beauty spot on her cheek and glossy curly hair, she's five foot. He is tall, dark and chubby-cheeked with darting eyes, like he isn't sure where to focus, and a brilliant incandescent smile.

In the middle of the night there's a noise, a motor noise, coming nearer, going away, coming back, and lights flicker behind the shutters on the sea side of the house. It's not moonlight. I've fed the baby and am wide awake, so I go out into the garden in my nightdress carrying him, and look over the wall at the sea. They are standing up in four wooden boats, two men in each, with trailing nets and large round lights behind, like turquoise moons, big round eyes in the water. I stop being annoyed by the phut-phutting noise of the motors and am mesmerised by the spectacle of the night-fishing lights over the water, by the stars, by the cliff looming behind me in the dark, by the majesty of the fishermen standing in their boats in the bay, by the tiny chapel on the rocks outlined in the night, by the lilting turquoises in the dark water, and the thought of the volcano somewhere out there in the bay.

We have deciphered Salvatore's map and made it up and round many stomach-lurching hairpin bends to the wood people in the mountains. Here all the graffiti is red. The wood people are very friendly and help us stack the wood in the back of the car. Then we have water and coffee. They are communists, their son says baldly, 'The mountains are communist, it is Mafia in town, because of the tourism. Greedy people like to control, you understand.'

He makes his fists as if they are bound together. Sometimes a limited knowledge of language means you get things straight out. The grandmother is unable to stand upright, she is dressed all in black and has few teeth and a filthy laugh. She is translated as saying she'd like to keep one of our boys – which one? We all laugh. Her granddaughter, who milked the goat for our coffee, lengthens the tether again. The well water is sweet, it never goes dry.

In town, we visit the stationer for fresh reams of paper, pens and crayons for the boys.

'Ah, you write. We had been thinking you were a dancer,' he says.

'A dancer?'

'Every morning we see you dance on the beach.'

I suppose I do. I may think I am running, but from the top of the cliff it probably does look like dancing. The soft sand frees me from any pain.

Calling at the tiny pizzeria, which is just a booth with standing room only, I lean with Frank on the counter as we wait and watch. Everyone loves children in Italy, and here they love to see them eat. Frank has seven teeth now and uses these to attack the strings of cheese. We down shots of grappa.

We are sitting in the garden for lunch. My husband has got over his yearning for roast meat and vegetables and gravy. We tried, but it doesn't taste right here in this climate. Our diet is now mostly capellini, the thin 'hair' spaghetti, or capelli d'angelo, which is even thinner, with passata, garlic and salad. We eat this every day. We drink the rough local red wine we buy in flagons in tumblers. The men are always up there, watching the sea and watching us from the top of the cliff. I have got used to them now, being up there above us in a seemingly never-ending conversation.

I'm dandling Frank on my knee and shoving a forkful of pasta into my mouth when my glass pops, it shatters out of nowhere. I look up at the cliff. Is it a shot, from a gun? A joke? An accident? Is it true? I am terrified. My husband and I crouch over our children. The garden in the shadow of the cliff seems dark, like the black fascist graffiti. The cacti that once looked charming are sinister. Could it be the air pressure, who can say? We finish eating indoors.

For the wedding of Salvatore and Lucia it has been arranged that we will be driven from the church by a local boxer, Toni, who once lived in Glasgow, to the reception at one of the tourist restaurants in the hills overlooking the sea. We might get lost on our own otherwise. The church service is baroque, punctuated with many pauses and replays of the action for photographs. By the end of it I'm ravenous as we pile into Toni's car, with a complement of spare nappies. After a lurching, nausea-inducing journey, we pitch up finally and disgorge from the boxer's tiny dusty Fiat. The airy dining room is festooned with nets and there are fishing lights rigged up. I fear the proceedings will be protracted. The menu is all fish and crustaceans and curlicues. I am halfway through a large bowl of unctuous soup, the boys have chewed their way through a handful of grissini, when I nudge my husband and whisper, 'God, it's not them. Look, can you see? The bride . . . that's not Lucia, it's not. Or Salvatore . . . This is really weird.'

The atmosphere is hugely convivial, even boisterous, even though things are just warming up. Even when we sheepishly leave with Toni, who is a little surprised, but utterly unabashed by his error.

'The wrong couple. The wrong wedding. No. Och, let me see. *Sì, sì.* Yes. You're right. They are the wrong people. Well, we could stay. Or go. You decide.'

After some confabulating he packs us back in the Fiat once more. Toni explains how his nose was broken several times in Glasgow, and how this look helps now he is back in Calabria.

'Nobody gives me trouble. You are safe with me. Safe.'

He bangs one hand on the steering wheel hard and laughs loudly with a snarl. My husband looks around the tiny crumpled-looking car and says nothing. Toni turns on the radio and sings along. We lurch along and round and up and down to another net-festooned dining room and the real wedding party of Salvatore and Lucia.

BEACHED

The boys got used to the beach. Ever since I was first pregnant, I've had a primal longing to be closer to nature. Since coming back from Italy I have been wondering what's happened to me. These days the inside of a theatre doesn't mean half as much as sitting amongst these chalk pebbles on the south coast, tapping, carving, shaping, building and breaking stones with two curly-topped small children. I look over at my husband on this one day out and am able to feel completely happy, making clacketing sounds over a background rhythm section from the sea. Playing at the

Stone Age with the two boys, the chalk age. Words don't matter, we are creatures of instinct.

The London flat has become a cage. We even have a canary mournfully hanging up in a three-tiered bamboo birdcage by the window. I can't remember who thought this was a good idea. It might have been me. Everything is becoming a metaphor that's shouting at me. My husband works and works and works, all hours. I drive the children to the river, to parks with ponds, lakes, streams, I commune with flamingos and peacocks, their calls reflecting my dissatisfaction. He has promised me a holiday, a break, time to get lost in, time to play. So I can see life stripped down, fresh and new, and be the person who can interpret this strange world the boys have joined us in. I am not convinced by it or myself. The best place, the safest, the place with fewest people, is by the river, a walled garden, flower beds, fruit trees, a lost and forgotten feeling, where my children can take their clothes off and crawl and run and wee into the grass.

But hey, yes, finally, after days and nights of being alone and him coming back at midnight at 2, at 4 a.m., we cram the car with a tent and nappies and balls, a potty and rugs and duvets and food and spoons etc. We go West and South and there's traffic and tears and breastfeeding, and it's hot but not Italian hot. The journey takes so much out of all of us. Tom, pale and peering, peering out of the window, trying to understand where we are, and when we'll be there, and what exactly 'there' will be. Frank guzzling, clutching at my T-shirt, dozing, nuzzling, farting or worse, clutching again, snoring, starting when the car brakes, nuzzling, suckling, burping, sucking, dribbling. My husband, increasingly bad-tempered, impatient, with a short haircut, curt, his mouth's a line. Me, wondering about speed and time, watching the blur of the world, wondering who or what we are, and why, and what for? And why I feel excited, but with a lacing of dread, like a bad liquorice taste I can't get rid of at the back of my throat. And in the back of my mind is the list of things we forgot, a torch, a washing-up bowl, hats. I feel I ought to break the mood and say something, anything.

'Did we bring the camera?'

'Of course I've got the camera,' my husband snaps back.

As if I'm a fool, and I haven't packed what feels like a thousand household items into a small car for a long weekend, as if we're not doing this together. I have to turn the map upside down to navigate, and he sneers. Frank's nappy is reeking, and maybe leaking.

'Can we stop? I think I need to—'

But he jumps in: 'Just wait until we get there. Just bloody wait.'

The nappy's warm and begins to seep.

'Is the beach there?' Tom asks.

'It's a campsite, not a beach.'

'But I want beach,' Tom says, tracing a finger on the glass where his breath keeps him company.

My husband's driving feels angrier and more dangerous. We are off the motorway and we are speeding.

'Shall I drive?'

'No. I'm fucking driving. AND WE'RE NEARLY THERE.'

After the shouting the car is quiet with a hush of ice, none of us dare say a word. There is no humming or singing or chatting or laughing or sharing of snacks. It doesn't feel like a holiday, and we're not even there yet. Half an hour later, after wresting the map off me from the front to the back of the car, and tearing it, he turns in to a track, drives too fast under a tunnel and out into a field next to some corrugated tin farm buildings. There is a tap. There is a pebble-dashed toilet building. There are bulls in the field next door. There is the thrum of farm machinery and the smell of manure and pigs. There is no one around. Not a soul.

'Are we *there* now?' Tom pipes up.

It is 'too late' when we've put the tent up to drive off to the sea, three miles away. We have made camping food, argued while we put the tent up, I've changed and fed the boys and arranged bedding and read stories and fetched water, all the time providing a steady running commentary of reassurance and promise.

'Tomorrow we'll spend all day by the sea. We will. And we'll get chips, and maybe even go on a boat. We'll get up early, and make sandcastles and . . .'

Suffice it to say that my husband has a bad temper. He has the temper of a toddler, unfortunately a toddler in a grown man's body. And so when in the morning we see that in the night we've been joined by another, better, more high-end and smaller tent than our family-sized one that leaked from the drizzle in the night, and that the owner of this high-end tent has a very high-end shiny motorcycle too, and when I have looked at this motorcyclist and exchanged morning pleasantries with him, while emptying a potty it has to be said, my husband stalks up and declares, 'The shower's a fucking dribble, an insult.' And continues, 'That's it, pack up. Pack up everything.'

He starts tearing the tent pegs out of the ground, he angrily stuffs bedding into the car willy-nilly. The boys eating breakfast from stripy bowls, wearing their pyjamas with geometric patterns of Chinese people all over them, gawp. Tom stops eating, his spoon frozen midway between bowl and mouth. There is no reasoning with my husband. He drives recklessly and angrily all the way back to London. We don't even get to see the sea.

Radiator

I weep soundlessly in the back of the car on the way back to London. Remembering what I suppose was a courtship of sorts. My husband's face open and laughing in the Alps, the snowy peaks celestially lit in a yellow pink and purple sunset, while we tucked into the best omelettes ever, served in a gingham room by twins with long grey plaits. After Cocteau's breathtaking chapel we snogged and made love on the rocks in the sea spray on Cap Ferrat. I even found it funny when he pointed out the douche bags on the back of the door in the crumbly and crummy hotel in an alley in Villefranche. I remember Calais, where we had a fight with soggy baguettes after five hundred miles on the motorbike, observed soberly by a passing train of early morning French, we broke into glorious guffaws of exhilaration and exhaustion.

Salty tears streak my cheeks as I cling on to dignity and grace, refusing to shudder and sob. I refuse to argue, I've tried slanging matches and no one wins. I have shifted out of the sight line of the rear-view mirror so my husband doesn't have the satisfaction of seeing me cry. I talk to the boys gently as if he's not there. I long for peace, for a cup of tea, and to feel loved.

In the longing is a memory of my mother. Of being sick or having tonsillitis or chicken pox or measles or flu, and her choosing that moment past the clearing and cleaning-up stage, past the deep sleep and sour mouth and nightmares. Of her coming in and saying, 'Hop out of bed now. I've run a hot bath for you, I'll change your sheets and make you a boiled egg.' Or: 'I got you some Lucozade. Let me brush your hair for you, and here's a cold flannel for your forehead with some lavender on it. Then I'll read some more of *The Hobbit*, where were we up to?'

And on the bedside table would be one of the old big bottles of Lucozade with the yellow cellophane, that we'd peel off and look through so all the world was yellow and ill and yet sunny too. She'd open the window so I could hear the birds better, and the windinthetrees. I wonder if she'd been alive whether my mother would have liked my husband at all.

Back in the London flat I feel increasingly like a fraud as day follows day, meal after meal, wash after wash, bath after bath, story after story. I trim the boys' hair and nails. I take them swimming, I shop, and mostly I take them out, to every park I can find. Frank flops in his car seat, still clutching the loaf that he's picked hollow while we're stuck in a traffic jam. He is warm and full and asleep.

In Oxfam there is more news of floods and I buy a nightdress without going into the changing room. We no longer go clothes shopping together, my husband and I. There are mirrors that face the bed in our room, and a clematis that needs watering on the balcony. I put on the nightdress, it's pink and voluminous, like a nightie for a baby. It is a nightdress as far removed from the idea of sex as it is possible to get. It is a bag, a sack. It doesn't suit me, it would make anyone look like a blob. My husband frowns at me when he comes in, late again, he ate out. He once bought me a dressing gown decorated in lips, something I would never have bought for myself. He grunts, we don't talk in bed any more. Those intimate post-coital chats, soul to soul, punctuated by spontaneous snacks on trays, are over. We used to read the same books – did that really happen? I lie as far away from him as I can, edging towards the radiator. It must look like I'm hugging the bloody radiator in my unflattering pink sack.

I remember our honeymoon in Ireland with fuchsias dangling in the hedgerows, rainbows and rain. How the plane went back to Heathrow when we were already halfway there, because of engine problems. How my husband had decided to be spontaneous about where we stayed, so our wedding night was spent in a hotel like a doctors' surgery by the airport, because of the delay, still half-drunk/half-hungover. How I woke up at 5 a.m. and he was putting on his shoes saying, 'I'm going for a walk. I think I want a divorce.'

I'd tried to forgive his obsessions and infidelities. How much of myself I've given away, it felt like my own flesh, trying to understand and reassure him. How we'd decided to fulfil a dream of mine and go on a honeymoon ride along a beach, and splash into the sea. But the horses were clumsy and spooked by heavy machinery moving endless boulders. The ride was bumpy and horrible, with an atonal note of ill omen.

How little there is left of me now. And that's when I decide, well, I don't decide yet. But I know. Earlier on, before he came home, I caught sight of the mirror and I couldn't see myself. There was someone else there, but it wasn't me. And now here I am lying in a voluminous sack almost hugging a radiator, staring at it, in a haze, and knowing deep down I have to get out. I've sold myself somehow, without meaning to. I'm in danger of completely disappearing. And yes, I too have a bad temper and am capable of airing my inner toddler, yes, I get hysterical, nasty, tearful, uncontrollable. But I don't deserve the mental and physical violence my husband is capable of. I don't deserve to scream for help and have nobody hear me. I don't deserve to be caged like a strange creature in the name of marriage and motherhood. I was not born to be controlled, or frightened or humiliated, and scorned. And there is not enough light, and too much, far too much shade. And I am thirsty, parched dry of nourishment for my spirit. I cannot continue this catalogue relationship that I've kept on keeping on, putting a good face on it, almost believing we're in a good story. I realise my husband is a stranger. I made him up.

I feel wrapped in pink shame that all my hopes have come to this. The marriage is a sham, our hearts are not joined. My husband, the man I thought I married, is a figment of my imagination. And the metal of the radiator taunts me as the timer makes the system click and clank and there's a warmth coming very slowly as the water churns inside the radiator. And I can't turn over, I can't face him. I don't feel any desire and I'm sick of his.

WHIRLPOOL

Tomorrow we're going to the Strait of Corryvreckan. Young offenders from Glasgow are the leads in the film my husband will be working on, we're here visiting the shoot. It's all in Gaelic, a legend of Finn MacCool, who ate the salmon of knowledge. Corryvreckan is the biggest whirlpool in the UK, the third biggest in the world. It's a legend. George Orwell nearly drowned here in 1947 before he'd finished *1984*. The Scottish winter goddess washes her enormous plaid here to make the seasons turn from Autumn to Winter. I like the thought of a whirlpool as a giant washtub. The boys like the castle we're staying in. It has turrets like medieval ladies' hats, and slit windows. It looks like a proper castle in a proper story. It's disappointing inside, there is no roaring hearth, no tapestries or minstrels, but huge soft rugs and boat-size sofas on the flagstones, there's a modern open kitchen. It's all surprisingly soulless. Our bedroom is like a bedroom in a shop window, but with two slit windows.

'Where are the arrows?' Tom asks.

'There are no arrows,' says my husband impatiently.

'And no bows?'

'No bows. No arrows.'

'In the film there'll be bows and arrows, won't there?' I ask.

I am trying hard, to retrieve a mood that is somewhere far, far behind us. Did I lose it in Italy?

'As far as I'm aware, in the film there is mainly a crossbow.' My husband sounds both pompous, and menacing.

'But tomorrow we're going on a boat. To the whirlpool,' I say firmly.

I feel like no one listens to me any more, except the boys. And they're unsure if it is stories I'm telling them. The castle is stone-cold, the wind is battlement wind, the bed is hard. I don't know what I'm doing here, what I'm defending, what there is to fight for, or against. We fall asleep in a heap, the boys and me, I don't make it downstairs to hang out with the crew and the cast and drink whisky on the sofas.

The director wears a linen cream suit with brown brogues and is always smoking or rolling a spliff. One of the Glasgow lads loads crates of beer and champagne onto the boat that's been hired for today's shoot.

'One should always drink champagne for breakfast,' the director says grandly.

I have noticed that male directors have little self-awareness, they are too busy projecting onto actors. The director doesn't see himself as a caricature, like he doesn't see himself as a dictator, he won't be looking through a lens at himself. Perhaps we are all caricatures, and would-be dictators. I am feeling old and jaded, with old eyes, but I am twenty-two. The idea and the whole process of film-making seems peculiar and unnatural, unreasonable, warped somehow. The crew are painstaking and self-important, they have to believe in it.

The director's second wife climbed out of a boarding-school window to run away with him when she was sixteen, they have two small children now. She is slight, and still looks sixteen. He must have thought our young families might keep each other company on location. They live in a cottage here, and he flirts with Glasgow and inevitably London. He has the public-school-and-Oxbridge drawl. The lads in the film are his pet project, with their raw complexions and swearing. He reminds me of S, with her acolytes and appetites, her need to be seen as a saviour, her remoteness. I try talking, but the director's wife is stony-faced and stoned, and in thrall to the director. Her eyes track his every move.

As we chug out of the harbour I realise I'm not in thrall to my husband, and wonder if I ever was. This trip should be fascinating and exciting, and fun for the boys, but looking around the boat at the people sitting about slugging beer, or the director who's just been snorting coke in the galley, it feels tawdry, made up, self-indulgent, a stupid idea. Clutching

Frank, attempting to keep us warm in the chill, I stare at the wake trailing after the boat and reflect how very odd making a film is. Making people act out other people, or re-enact history, filtering this acting through a director suspended in his ego like a gherkin in a jar. The process is so laborious and frivolous at the same time. The costumes, the fake leopard skin the main actor wears over his underpants, the props, the hierarchy of roles, I'm sick of it already. I look over at my husband's profile, and realise I have absolutely no idea what he is thinking in his film-making head. I reflect that my mood is sour. I should feel lucky.

Tom is seasick, it's messy, and I feel queasy myself. And we're actually going to a large and dangerous whirlpool. People have drowned there. The plan is to try and get as close as possible to film it, whirling in a vortex presumably. And also to lower the main actor into the sea in the dinghy for some sea shots. There may be thirty seconds of film from this whole escapade, and God knows how much the boat cost and the castle and the people and clearly I'm having an off day. I should just smoke a spliff, down some champagne and tell myself to bloody well shut up.

On the ferry on the way to Calabria I remember my husband and I clinking brandy glasses and grinning. 'Purely medicinal.'

And we kissed, didn't we? Juggling the boys between us, we snogged, slightly tipsy on the ferry. We were romantic. Now we can barely look at each other, the gazing is gone.

The weather's not right when we get close to the whirlpool. So it's not quite whirlpool enough. It might not come up on film too well. I can't sense any trace of legend, no sea giants, goddesses, or washtubs, in this white chartered fibreglass boat, in choppy, but not choppy enough, waters. The water looks troubled. The main actor doesn't last long in the dinghy, away from the whirlpool for the sea shots, and the shots of the islands. The dinghy looks like it has a puncture, he has goosepimples and chattering teeth, and you can see his off-white Y-fronts under the leopard skin. And come to think of it the leopard skin is completely inauthentic anyway. Tom is bringing up slimy bright yellow bile. The islands lour and drizzle takes over.

Back on dry land again, it's scampi and chips in the pub. Everyone is knocking back Guinness, cracking jokes and laughing. They look like they've had a great day, even though it seemed dire to me. And I wonder if it's just a question of language, do I speak the wrong one? Think in the wrong one?

ICE

My sons love puddles and sticks, and breaking the ice on puddles. They are happiest outside, their cheeks are flushed and their curly hair is like wood shavings. They wear duffel coats and wellies. They stamp and poke, making shards of ice and slush, and chasing ducks. They chew the old bread we brought for the ducks. York floods, it's an upside-down hat. The flooding freezes. I feel like I've escaped into exile.

'Nonsense. Melodrama,' my father would say.

He is the exile, the refugee, the alien, the foreigner, but he would never ever use any of these labels about himself.

He keeps his Polish accent, he likes real bread (as opposed to what he calls 'air bread'), garlic sausage, chicken soup made from the carcass, and the Church. Otherwise he conforms, he assimilates, he doesn't like to 'ruffle any feathers'. He has had a long apprenticeship with Britishness.

How come I have never noticed before how my father has favourites? That is just how it always was. My father favoured my navy blue sister and my helicopter brother, because they were the eldest girl and boy. It seemed normal. Now with the next generation I see how unjust his favouritism is. He accepts Frank, he smiles at Frank. And he persistently ridicules Tom. It's blatant now I can see it. Tom absorbs the slights and criticisms and disapproval, it's giving him little frown marks in the middle of his smooth forehead. He is genuinely puzzled by my father. Frank has his head patted, his efforts applauded. If I say anything about being fair, Tata sighs loudly and says, 'I don't know what you are talking about. I am an only child, I know nothing about family life.'

He has eight children.

After almost ten years in London, I'm back in the North. I jumped ship, I ran away, I ran back. I had nowhere else to go, I am in my father's house. There is a strange symmetry I notice but no one else remarks on. I left here almost ten years ago with my stepmother and two small boys, my half-brothers. And now I am back in the house that I can't call home, with two small boys, my sons. Suffice it to say, I left him. My husband is there and I am here. I am a single parent. Although my father is sure I will go back, I can't.

I feel more out of place than ever before. We were never allowed to speak in a Yorkshire accent, I stick out like a sore thumb here if I open my mouth. My London life is so remote and different from here that it's best not to mention it. I keep quiet if I see an actor I know on the telly. I am familiar with every single noise in this house, I think I know it like I know my own body. But of course time has passed. I have a new stepmother. Before she moved in my helicopter brother painted the drawing-room ceiling in navy blue gloss. It reminds me of a night sea with no moon. My stepmother remarks bitterly, 'It looks like a nightclub.' She is a chintz person.

I can see she is itching to redecorate and put her mark on the place. She's not impressed by the jute carpeting. A hangover from the years of my mother, it was 'bought to last', and it has. My stepmother clearly wishes it wouldn't. We used to have bold curtains in shades of red and window seats in turquoises and green natural fabrics. We had pottery made by people we knew. The floorboards were sanded and stained. Culture was taken seriously, the Sunday papers and new novels were read closely, ideas were discussed. The radiogram blared out The Beatles and classical music. In the S years, although she had no interest in furnishings whatsoever, we had a half-hearted revamp via her mother. She brought second-hand curtains with silver and gold stripes. She brought a bath rack and handed it to me as if it was a mark of true civilisation. I had never felt the lack of a bath rack before.

My second stepmother doesn't approve of me. I guess she thinks I should go back to my husband. She doesn't want me and my boys here and makes this very clear. She shows no interest in them at all, which I think must take a considerable effort.

We come in muddy, but we always take our boots off. The boys like being in the kitchen, helping, their small hands swishing in the red bowl full of warm sudsy water. They like chopping mushrooms. Helping to stir things with wooden spoons, even banging wooden spoons on saucepan lids. Tata has broken it to me that as far as 'they' are concerned, the boys should not even be in the kitchen. That I should cook for them separately, earlier, and eat in the dining room later when they've gone to bed. I can't quite believe my father when he says, 'Simple. The small boys should be banned from the kitchen. End of story.'

My mother would be appalled, and he knows that's what I'm thinking and not even bothering to say. My sisters appear for the weekend. They are aunts who don't like being aunts to my children. Despite them both living around Brixton and hanging out with radicals, they treat me in a very Catholic way. As if I should suffer, for my sins. For my failings. 'Pride comes before a fall', they say. I picture them quaffing champagne at my wedding, and taking a case of it home afterwards. I picture my navy sister flirting with my husband and kissing him on the lips. I cry as she lectures me. I cry wishing I wasn't crying. They always used to call me a crybaby when I was little. I shake and my teeth judder. There will be no hugging, no sympathy, no empathy. I feel the floor beneath me give way, as if I have had no idea of where the ground is, and there's an endless dark space going down and down. I am more alone than when I am alone.

The wallpaper beneath the navy gloss ceiling is beige with flowers. There are begonias and parsley growing in the rose beds. We used to have one rose bed each. My stepmother is talking about grassing four of them over. My father has sold off a triangle of the garden to pay for new tiles on the roof. The symmetry has gone, there is a shiplap fence instead. The roses in my bed were pink, my navy sister's dark red, my poker brother's yellow splashed with red. My stepmother seems to have begun to hide food, tins of tomatoes and pasta, the boys' favourite food. I find tins of tomatoes stashed in a drawer, when the shelves in the pantry are half empty. It is cold round the dining-room table. I don't know what has happened here since I left, I don't know what is happening here now. The work ethic has taken everyone completely over. Work, pensions, holidays.

'You make your own bed and you lie in it,' my father is fond of saying, clapping his hands together.

I look after the boys. I play with them, read to them, do the washing, hang it out, put it away, shop, cook, go for walks, investigate playgroups. It is a half-life. My husband appears out of nowhere, the bell rings one morning and suddenly there he is standing on the front doorstep in his too-big grey gabardine, here to try and talk me round. I don't let him in. I am afraid of him, I know what he is capable of. He rings and rings and rings. I can never go back to him, why does no one see that? Can't he work out why I left?

My divorce lawyer, Mark, asks me out. Or did I ask him? My father is delighted by the idea of this respectable professional Englishman. When he comes to pick me up for the evening, Tata simpers about, shaking his hand heartily, he's agreed to listen out for the boys while I go out. He tells us to have a good time, he even says, 'You deserve it.' Mark could be debarred for getting involved with me. We both know it's wrong, but we do it anyway, my heart's not in it. It just makes the break final in my mind.

When the boys are seeing their father in London, I get drunk, I eat out, I sleep over. In Mark's world there is rugby and drinking, I find the rowing club rowdy and deeply dull. In bed he suddenly says he has a surprise for me, giggling uncontrollably. I wonder what the hell it is – jewellery, a fine wine, a threesome? He presents me coyly with a condom he has filled with water and put in the freezer. He thinks it is hilarious, he is nervous and excited. I am underwhelmed. It melts. He looks humiliated, maybe he wants to be humiliated. We listen to Marvin Gaye's 'Sexual Healing', but I'm not in love. Mark seems to me incomplete as a person, however much he tries, he is implausible, insubstantial. When I am with him I feel like an exotic dish, a strange creature. I long to relax, and not to feel I am performing.

THE LEAK

I go back to London once. To retrieve my belongings, books, clothes, the boys' toys and clothes, letters, photographs. I can't take the piano I bought. Or my moped, I have to give it away. My soon-to-be-ex-husband won't look at me. I am relieved I don't live here any more, glad I ran away. I don't like being here, it makes me jumpy.

I had to trick my husband the night I ran away. I persuaded a friend to buy him a drink and keep him talking in the pub. While I swiftly shoved nappies and a duvet and my toothbrush and a small bag of clothes and the boys in the car and drove away terrified. He would never have let us go. I remember tears falling onto the steering wheel on the M1, my heart still racing with fear. When the boys were finally asleep, I heard a peculiar noise like a throttled animal sobbing, and then realised it was me.

I haven't missed my husband, my marriage, or the flat at all. Particularly the cellar, which was crammed full of books, a spare bed and the washing/drying machine in the corner, like a household god. We would never have known about the suicide, except for the guy who rang our doorbell one foul November night, and begged for the chest of drawers which had been sitting in the cellar when we first moved in. He was ranting in the communal hallway. I was organising the nappy bucket in the bathroom, and then my husband started shouting and the doors were banging and there was the sound of a scuffle. At first I thought it was my poker brother turned up with an empty bottle of brandy in his pocket, mucking about. But no. No one came out of their flats to investigate, but this was a building where people never spoke to their neighbours. They barely nodded.

There was a flat roof above our bedroom covered in pot plants, and a crack in the ceiling above our heads. The crack kept getting bigger, and I kept going to the agent on the Broadway and complaining nicely and less nicely, cajoling, even begging them, to get the plants moved and the roof looked at. Nothing ever happened. We stared at the crack every night, thinking about the roots delving deeper, the pots enmeshing into the roofing felt. We discussed it, we ignored it, we argued about it. I scuttled regularly along to the agent's office.

'It has started to leak, don't you understand?'

'You will need evidence. In writing. We can forward it to the owner.'

'But it could fall down on our heads at any time. I've got two small children here, look. It's dangerous! The whole ceiling could come down on our heads! Don't you understand?'

Evidence in writing had been provided, but nothing changed, except the crack. I would try not to rant or rave, while feeling like ranting and raving. I would leave the office with tears in my eyes, feeling angry and humiliated. And nothing happened. Like the times I'd screamed, choking, for help. And the sound just evaporated into a fog of anonymity. Or when I rang a friend in distress and my husband crushed my fingers and pulled the phone socket out of the wall.

The wind was squalling, all the doors were banging on that foul November night. My husband stomped back into the flat, swearing. I put the lid back on the nappy bucket and washed my hands slowly.

'That guy had a bloody nerve, turning up here off his fucking head. Asking for that chest of drawers. Does he think I was born yesterday?'

'What chest of drawers?'

'Bloody cheeky bastard. The one in the cellar. It's ours, legally ours, it was here when we got here. We've been here more than a year. Said it belonged to his mother, and then listen to this, saying she'd fucking killed herself. In the cellar. Nutter. The nerve. Thought he could just come in here . . .'

I held my breath, I froze. My guts churned, because I'd felt something wasn't right. There was a weird vibe. There was that mark on the wall. It looked like a rune, it had always made me feel uneasy. I'd tried to make it disappear, painting over and over it, and still it grinned through. I hung a picture over it, but I still knew it was there, on our wall. I could see there was no point trying to reason with my husband, trying to point out the guy's distress, his right to have the bloody chest of drawers back if he wanted it. In memory of his mother. But I tried. After he'd grabbed my wrist to stop me running out into the street in my slippers, in the dark in the wind and the rain, to find the guy who'd lost his mother.

'You are so gullible, you'd believe anything of anyone.'

'But we don't even need that chest of drawers. You even said you didn't like it.'

'I said the bottom drawer sticks. Anyway it's the principle of the thing.'

I could think of a few things to say about principles, but my husband was fizzing in his self-righteousness. I was speechless. I just looked at him and saw a person I didn't like.

Now in our ex-bedroom I notice the ceiling has been replastered where the crack used to be. My ex-husband follows my glance up at it.

'Yeah. It fell in eventually. I was in bed, but it missed me, it didn't hurt me at all,' he says.

I can't wait to get out of the building. I have to leave some of my stuff behind, but I get out.

That night I am staying on the ground floor of a house with friends my husband doesn't know, it is three miles away from the flat. But I wake up at six in the morning and through the gap in the curtains there he is, standing in the front garden, staring at me through the window. He must have driven round scores of streets to find the car, looked through scores of windows, to find me.

PADDLING

Everyone secretly dreads Christmas, even people who say they love it. We're conditioned to dread being alone at Christmas, it's presented as the worst possible fate, redolent of failure and loneliness, a kind of destitution. It's a wet, non-white Christmas, and I am alone.

Not so many months since I sat in my father's garden with students I'd known from London and we conceived a plan to share a farmhouse in a village. Hopes and dreams, a vegetable patch dug over, flower beds begun, vegetarian communal meals enjoyed, the sharing of childcare, all came to an abrupt end when the landlord discovered I was not a wealthy divorcee living in a four-bedroomed house alone with my sons. I had been economical with the truth, even to myself. Shame clings like a mist in the face of judgement. The students fled to friends' sofas, and I faced the landlord out. Or rather I tried to, but when he said he'd put his arm in the fire and to watch him, he wouldn't feel the pain, when he pulled the phone out of the wall, I agreed to leave. What is it with men and phones and walls? Is this dramatic controlling gesture an irresistible imperative driven by testosterone, accompanied by some sadistic satisfaction in instilling fear in a woman? I didn't want to be there alone with only a herd of cows, in for the winter, in the barn across the yard. The landlord gave me a week, I hadn't the patience or reserves to fight him.

The council found me a room in a house with shared facilities and fleas. My mail got stolen, the boys enjoyed playing on the pile of rubble by the front gate. Now I'm living in a two-up two-down, bathroom-out-the-back, privy-in-the-yard terrace, in a grid of terraces. At the end of the road is the river, it's the floodplain. There are sandbags.

The 'Campaign' has been in full throes. This is the time of the year when the sugar beet is ready and great lorries deliver it day and night to the factory that looks like it's held together with rubber bands, and pulsates and billows smoke across the floodplain to process all the beet into white sugar. You can see it from the end of the road, you can hear it, you can smell it, like burnt bitter sawdust. The Campaign goes on for three months every year, the jobs are sought-after. It is the other side of York that smells of chocolate.

The boys are with their father. Last night I went to Vigilia, Polish Christmas Eve, at my father's. The axe was under the table, the straw and our purses under the tablecloth, the candles lit, the wafer from church shared, kisses were proffered. The washing-up was done, presents offered. My sisters, high on weed and probably coke, got drunk on cherry brandy. No one said anything that mattered. My father looked through me, as though I am a sinner. And all those words and phrases about women I've ingested from the Bible, since before I could walk, ran through my brain. I didn't stay to go to midnight Mass.

So today, for the first time ever, I am completely alone for Christmas Day. I have one parcel, from Mary who's in America, to open. It's quiet, I get up when I feel like it. I eat leftovers happily with my fingers. I drink a mug of milky coffee, then another one. I sit and stare at the sky, at the bricks and walls around me. I go for a long walk in my Oxfam alpaca coat and wellies. The water from the river comes to the end of the road, the fields are all flooded. The sky has pillow clouds and blotches of blue, and there is sun. There is space and peace and absolutely no one about. There is no traffic up on the flyover. There is this great expanse of water everywhere I look, with green fronds of grass beneath it. There is the sound of my boots paddling through the water, there is grass, grassy water, watery grass. The sky is reflected in the water on the fields, the rays of the sun fall out of the sky from a hidden hand, like in a Blake watercolour, without judgement or damnation. I do not feel like a fallen woman or a scarlet woman, an adulteress or a sinner. I cannot tell exactly where the river is because there is water everywhere I look. I feel blessed by the water in the sky and the sky in the water, in a way I haven't for years.

I trudge, I splash, I kick at the water, I wade. And my only companions are seagulls, hundreds of them, squawking, flying around and landing, flapping about like bad angels, and a few ducks, refugees from the river, making the most of the day. I walk, taking breaks to stand and stare vacantly, for a long time. I sit on a stile and breathe it all in. The city, the sugar factory, the railway lines, the bridges, the river, the grid of terraces, my lungs, my breath, myself. Tears come from behind my eyes without warning, and they are tears of grief certainly, but also tears of relief. Even tears of joy, at reaching some kind of plateau. From feeling bitter about my ex-marriage, from missing the boys, from dreading Christmas, from feeling ashamed of being alone, from feeling misunderstood and blamed for being a single woman, a single parent, I have somehow, because of this bright wet unexpected Christmas Day, wrested a holy moment, just for me, just with me. And I shout for the love of the moment. For the hell of it. A hallelujah, a halle-bloody-lujah.

I go back to the house when I'm ready, when it suits me. I make a sandwich and put a Coltrane tape on. I sit on the futon by the gas fire, and open the parcel from

Mary in America. It's a book that hasn't been published in the UK yet. I devour it into the afternoon, into dusk and evening, I finish it at night. I realise I am completely happy by the gas fire with Alice Walker, reading *The Color Purple* and listening to John Coltrane. My heart thrills, my mind blows, my tears roll. I am alone, but I am not alone.

ADRIFT

It's the day we leave the terrace with the river at the end of the road. The day we leave York the little old lady from opposite hobbles over to our side. I have never seen her outside before. Wisps of hair are scraped into a bun, she has few teeth. She regards the van and our stuff half in half out of it, the rolled-up futons, the plants looking leggy on the pavement, with suspicion.

'Well now, and where do you think you're going? You've only just arrived. It's been five minutes.'

'Bradford. Well, I've been here a year.'

'A year. Like I said, five minutes. No time to even get to know you.'

'It's a pity.'

'Mmm. Takes ten years before you begin to get to know a person. You're not flitting?'

'No. I don't think so.'

'I saw you, you know, with them lasses a while back. When the police came looking.'

'Oh?'

'I don't blame you. Some busybody must have rung 'em.'

The miners' wives and I had been breathless with laughter, puffed from running, then we'd slammed the front door shut, run into the kitchen and emptied our buckets and tins on the table, to count out all the coins we'd collected door to door. They needed the money for food, the strike had been going on for months. I had barely spoken to a soul here in this street all year. Now I learn I haven't been here long enough.

'Big boy's gone, eh?'

'Yes. With his dad.'

She seemed to know everything about me. Maybe more than I knew myself. She would have watched the car coming and going, my husband wrangling on the doorstep of the damp street. The cardboard boxes loaded up with Tom's few possessions. The new box of Lego and the golden arches wrappers in the car. My clenched face, Frank's bewilderment. We will never recover from this loss. However much separated parents listen to what children want, try to share them, be fair, they only live in one place. Tom has been my husband's favourite since we wrangled over breastfeeding. Frank has been and will always be overlooked, near disowned, by his father. Even thinking about favouritism makes me feel grubby, tainted by being somehow complicit in a ghostly pattern sewn into an age-old blanket.

'I've lived here eighty-five years, eighty-five. They shouldn't have built these houses, you know. What with the river. Sandbags won't help. One of these days we'll need boats not blumming sandbags.'

We shake hands, she comes up to chest height on me.

'I'm sad to be leaving now, I'd have liked to get to know you.'

'Oh, you go on now, lass. You get on and get off. And good luck to you.'

'I think I need it. Thanks.'

'We all need it, we all do.'

'And good to meet you.'

'Aye, that's it now. Off you go.'

Bradford is bigger, is not twee and touristy, is full of everyone from everywhere. I know a poet and a saxophonist there and that's it. Tom will start primary school in London and come North in the holidays.

In Bradford Frank and I walk round the lake in Lister Park. There's a waterfall pouring down from the Botanical Garden, it's a dark grotto. Every time we walk past it I say, 'Have you got the shampoo?' And Frank is surprised and we laugh, and imagine him washing his hair there under the waterfall, rinsing it from a great height, unmoved by people, geese or ducks. We linger there in the sound of the water falling, it's an echo, a poor imitation of another place in another world. There are fag ends and cans, there's dog and duck shit. There are the fossilised roots of trees. In the Botanical Garden there's a stream to paddle in, borders full of herbs and flowers, shrubs and trees, there's an Indian bean tree, there's grass to picnic on. It's a haven.

Two things will happen here in the future. I will come and sit on the grass alone with a flask of coffee and a book to read. I will bask in the sunlight lying between the flower beds on my jumper. I will doze. I will glance up and notice an odd bouncing movement in the shrubbery, and realise that there is a man looking over at me and wanking. I will have to leave. The second thing will be when I am learning to meditate and the children are climbing up the tree over the stream. The flower beds will be sprawling with flowers. A couple will approach, and then jump back in surprise. She will say, 'Oh! We thought you were a giant blue flower.'

I will say, 'I think that's the best compliment I've ever been paid.'

In West Yorkshire the stone is streaked black. Bradford is a bleak industrial relic crouching over hills. The skyline bristles with disused mills, chimneys, high-rises and the silhouettes of cemeteries. There's a dirty canal, quarry heaps, and what look like bomb sites.

Yet there is a pulse, the hope of change. For the first time I really dance on a dance floor, freestyle. Maybe there is a place for me amongst immigrants from everywhere. Reggae is the heartbeat of the local pubs, clubs, and blues. Even amongst the drug-dealing, prostitution and pimping, the pool playing, the noise of dominoes clacking on tables, the slap of card games, the mood, before crack comes to town, is mellow. There are bottle fights occasionally, but this is before knives, before guns and drive-bys. There are riots, fervent political meetings and ANC benefit gigs. People clutch bottles of Pils and Lucozade, knock back rum and black, and there's every kind of dancer. From wall hugging trudgers to jazz improvisers who play their bodies like saxophones, and everyone in between. Wherever you're from, whatever you've been through, whoever you are, there is room.

Except Bradford is reeling from the shadow of the Yorkshire Ripper, and there are the seeds of religious fundamentalism in the madrasas. It is not a woman's town, but where is? The map of history here is a map of ghettoes. The Irish, the German Jews, the Poles, Ukrainians, Lithuanians, the Yugoslavians, the West Indians, the Indians, the Pakistanis, the Nigerians, the Bangladeshis, the Ugandans. There will be wave after wave, from Afghanistan, from Iraq, Iran, Palestine, there will be a fresh wave of Eastern Europeans, Somalis, Syrians. Bangladeshis will resent Romanians.

My past is over. Maybe I am hiding, because maybe I want to hide. To see what it's like when people aren't impressed, in that London after-the-show-down-the-pub way, looking over your shoulder for the next person to come in who might be more famous, or important, or grand, or gorgeous, or influential. I am an island. As though London has never happened to me.

I meet the tall man on the rebound, not the dance floor. He gets close to me by listening to my confusion about the Pakistani radical who has left me hanging when I thought we had a thing going on. Maybe it would have been simpler if I hadn't so obviously enjoyed the sex. Men want sex and then distrust you if you do too.

The tall man is kind, it's the beginning. When it gets to the point where he says, 'You look best naked,' I can sense the truth of this, because naked is comfortable, clothes are in the way. But I will also feel ruffled, because I won't be sure if it's a compliment, a put-down about my wardrobe or a cheesy line he's used before. Language is significant. I want to trust people, I do. I want to believe in them. And I want to believe in myself. Up to now the two haven't matched up.

CHOPPY

Under canvas in a farmer's field there will be a conception. We are in a rainstorm, at the end of the field there is a cliff. Below the cliff is an extremely choppy sea. This trip with two boys and the tall man was planned as a camping idyll with strolls and picnics, baked beans and sunbathing, cricket and football, ice creams and wave jumping. I have only been camping once before, for one night. The memory is a ghost that needs to be laid to rest. The tall man has been a Scout. He is a mountain man. There are two massive tankers out at sea, they have come in close to land, for shelter from the storm. I wouldn't like to be out there at sea. I am trying not to think how near the cliff edge is. It is hard not to imagine the tent lifting up like a kite, and soaring off the cliff. I try to concentrate on not imagining this.

We found stones under the hedge and made a fire pit, we found wood in a gully over the stile. But it was too damp, and even using the cardboard we scavenged from our provisions, lighting a fire, well, the kind of fire we all imagined would be a proper campfire to sit around singing, drinking cocoa and roasting things on sticks, lying down beside and watch shooting stars, didn't happen. We use gas to heat the beans and the toast won't toast.

There's one tap and Frank stood on the kettle without thinking and the tall man almost shouted but stopped himself in time, glanced over at me, turned away and lit another damp spliff. The tent is all hunky-dory inside with the bedding spread out snug. We could have done with more to eat, we could have done with being warmer, but we've got each other. We have. The ground is cold and there's a howling wind, so we compare ourselves favourably with those caught in hurricanes and have a discussion about tornadoes that is not entirely comforting. We are crammed and cramped. The tall man is really too tall for tents. I see Frank looking up at the roof juddering in the gale as the rain comes rattling down. He looks like he'd really like to feel safe and sound and tucked up and in, confident and sorted and full up and warm. There's a flicker of worry in his eyes. Concern passes across his forehead like an insect. He tracked the path of this journey carefully on the map in the car. From the middle to the edge, and now we're on the very edge. Or on the edge of the edge. I try to reassure him with a smile, 'This will pass, it can't go on forever. All storms pass. It could be sunny again tomorrow morning.'

The tall man says, 'This'll make a man of you, Frank, it's character-building. This is what you go camping for, it's just you and the elements.'

And Frank looks like he'd like to believe him, in a way. But the wind howls and whistles and rampages, and everything is flapping inside the tent and outside the tent, on the tent and off the tent. And from having been so happy to have found this field with such an incredible view of the North Sea, now we are all not admitting it, but we are wishing we were a lot further away from that sea raging out there. It is after dusk. The sky has gone mad. We are trying not to meet each other's eyes, in the gloomy orange tent light, but we are now all thinking about the tent being blown along down the field and over the cliff. Human existence itself feels suddenly, obviously, extremely tiny and precarious and random and pointless in the face of this gale.

'Wind and rain always sound much worse in a tent. The sound is amplified,' I say.

I know Frank can tell by the tone of my voice that I feel wobbly, that I might start panicking. In my mind are all the easy places we discounted and drove past on the way. In daylight, when it was dry and light and could have turned out sunny. The proper campsites, with showers and games rooms. We are in a field with a tap, there is no one else in this field. The farm is further inland in a dip, surrounded by trees. I notice that the tall man is clinging to the door-end pole of the tent, his knuckles are white with clinging.

'This is an adventure. Er . . . like Tintin.'

No one answers. He nods to the other pole at my end. And so I cling to it, trying to keep it steady, while the weather batters us. The tall man has a small bottle of brandy and I wonder how long it will be before he opens it. In an emergency way.

I sleep. I don't know how, but I lie down and sleep. When I wake up again the tent smells of brandy, and he gives me a slug from the bottle. I cling to my pole again, because the tent is behaving more and more like a sail.

'We don't want it to rip. That's all we need. Good thing I banged the pegs in right. Proper forty-five-degree angle.'

'At least they're asleep.'

'I don't know how.'

'Neither do I. It's a tempest out there.'

'Let's hope it's not a tornado.'

'Or a hurricane.'

And we say these unlucky words out loud with dark humour, and sip brandy intermittently until it is light. And finally the storm starts to die down, to abate, to leave us bloody well alone. And we've survived it, the tent is wet and leaking, dripping, sopping in places, but it's still here. We haven't been blown off the cliff, we're not huddled in the car with no tent, which could have sailed away towards the two tankers, to the horizon. We're not sodden, bereft or bedraggled, with our bedding and boots and bowls and spoons and bean tins strewn over the whole field.

'Character-building I suppose.'

And we let go from gripping the poles so tightly I got cramp. We lie down finally in the dawn light. We peer at the boys, safe in their compartment. We seek each other for warmth, for heat. And much later I realise this was when our daughter joined us, lodging in my womb. Out of the storm.

HUBBLE BUBBLE

Hubble bubble, toil and trouble. I should have known, like I know all the old nursery rhymes, but knowing isn't understanding. The water pipe with the hubble-bubble sound never sounded good to me. The tall man made it, DIY, from a chunky cut-glass vase of his mother's. The small Chinese bowls, semi-translucent, sat on top of the fire holding 'the mix'.

Inside your gut, liquid rumbles, it's the place of instinct, insight and intuition. The place of foresight and foreboding. I should have listened to my stomach rather than to him. I should have known better. I thought I deserved better. I want to be in the past tense, because the present is too raw, the present is broken. I should use a wide-angle lens, employ a retrospective point of view, recall, relate. Even if I risk being an unreliable narrator. I was there, I am there. And it's not happening any more. I am living a different life. Inhabiting a different reality. I watch the ceiling and dream of somewhere else.

Hope, vitality and naivety are definitely bait for a certain type of animal instinct. Let's call it what it is: vampirical. Simply, the vampire seduces you, to then fall on your neck and bite and suck and drain. His walk is a bold barefaced swagger, he mumbles sweet nothings in your ear in the hallway. Dressed in dark velvet, with an aura of power, the vampire has charisma. As far back as drinking my own mother's milk, it began, I drank the story of falling in love. The fairy tales I heard from forever ago pre-programmed me to believe and inhabit the paradigm. Conditioned to fall, I fell. I fall, over and over. I fall over, blinded, hoodwinked, deluded, hypnotised, I am charmed and put under a spell. As though drops have been poured into my eyes, as though my heart is not my heart. A character emerges to fit the plot, and so it goes. I am once more aboard the merry-go-round. There is the familiar push-me-pull-you tension, between what's happening and what I think is happening. Hubble bubble.

I washed out his water pipe, I couldn't stand the smell of the old water. I soaked it, scrubbed the brown ring off, rinsed it, let it dry on the draining board. The tall man was amazed that I'd even bothered. He put his pipe back together again, fitting on the length of plastic piping and the foil bowl with plasticine. There was no grace or glamour in this object, like with a serpentine hookah, no hint of the opium den in *The Blue Lotus* in Tintin. The mix of tobacco and dope was crumbled into the rice bowls. The atmosphere of an arcane ritual, accompanied by a collective holding of breath. The master of ceremonies' black locks shimmered in the flame. In the morning I would sweep dead matches off the floorboards and open the window. I would do the washing, hang it up to dry, water the plants, make and eat tea and toast, and try to be normal.

After the night the wok full of spinach curry got thrown at the kitchen wall. After months of sitting with a plant for company by the window, watering it gently, regularly, and praying, yes, praying, for another world to open up. After noticing that sour, grubby, musty, mildewy smell. A smell from under the floorboards, in the walls, a smell that cleaning never lifted. Was it mice or rats or lies or heroin or boot polish in the resin, or sweat, or deceit or despair? After taking deeper and deeper breaths in the bath with that grating fan on, my chest palpitating and thinking it might be the end, my heart feeling like it was giving up. After those days when I couldn't locate my keys or my purse, and felt frantic. After being in the trances of Miles and Sonny Rollins and Ornette Coleman, and travelling to the many valleys and bridges and castles of the mind, but in the morning feeling cold and frazzled and poor and lonely. Noticing the dust and ash, the endless slate roofs, the three wives across the road in full hijab with the metal nose guards, the brothel down the road, the kerb crawlers edging along like slimy crabs, slower and slower, closer and closer, trying to read my walk, asking for the time, asking 'How much?', when I had a pint of milk in my hand

and a long coat and wild hair, and nothing about me could be saying 'I'm for sale'. I loathe them. And the tall man laughs. Laughs that I'm desirable, that I'm angry and affronted. After he throws the lipstick out of the window, shouting, 'You're not wearing that.' After he swears at my friend who's like a tiger and fronts him over the kitchen table. After all that . . .

I throw the water pipe out of the window. We're on the second floor, and I throw it as hard as I can, because I want it to smash, my teeth are bared like an animal. And he and his sidekick, the pianist, run downstairs like little boys to check if the glass has broken, if the stale musty water, like plant water gone slimy, has spilt. Because it's the best pipe he's ever made. Perfect. And I'm a killjoy, and everyone in the street can hear this, I'm 'a fucking killjoy'. And the glass is so thick it's only chipped, not smashed, and he holds it up in triumph. He can see me looking out of the window.

We flee to the Botanical Garden and peace. Yet he still comes to find me by the stream where I am trying to find my calm, my toes soaking, breathing out, in the water. Still he comes to apologise and win me over again. The baby has started kicking. I believe in the future, I have to. And my son hugs me, then climbs the tree over the paddling stream. Until he's taller than the tall man, taller than anyone we've ever seen. He disappears, then his head pops out the top, and he's taller than the tree.

FLUID

It's not a water birth, but otherwise everything is perfect. I have a bath in my own bath and lie on a futon in the front room by the gas fire, watched over by the cheese plant. Frank is cycling, doing laps of the flat, his bike still has stabilisers on. In and out, in and out, in—

'Isn't it born yet?'

'Er, ah, not yet, not quite.'

'Taking ages.'

Out. And he rides off again into the kitchen, bemused. He is balancing well on the bike. The stabilisers could come off.

Sonny Rollins is on the tape recorder as you come into the world, and out of me. Wet hair, viscous, delicate, a girl. The next time Frank rides in he nods and lets you hold his finger. The midwives are asking for clean towels and sheets and I feel I'm the one in charge, in my space. The tall man cries. That night we all sleep together in a row, you nestling on me, Frank in his clown pyjamas.

But the next days are unbelievable. Within twenty-four hours you start going blue. The doctor is dismayed. There is consternation and kerfuffle and fear. The sweet home birth morphs into an emergency situation. There is an ambulance, an admission to the children's hospital round the block. There is monitoring, lots of blood tests and hospital clothes. It's hot, I'm on a camp bed beside you in your plastic cot. I feed you and talk to you. I lie in the half-light with my eyes open, thinking, *Surely I'm going to wake up, this is a dream, this can't be real, it's too extreme.*

There's a spinal fluid test, it's meant to be watery, but it's stained with blood. And there's the phrase 'blood to the brain'. The words are worst-case-scenario words, and I feel I know nothing about what is going on inside your body except you've been inside mine. I lie thinking about all the liquid inside bodies. I lie and wait and watch and listen and look at you. So they hardly notice me, the night staff. I watch and listen as the Irish male nurse tends to the other babies in their cots. There are big windows ceiling to floor, it's boiling in here, the heating's on full blast.

'Come along now, let's see what you've got. Here we go, you little darling, you little angel.'

The blonde baby has a nappy change and a cuddle before going back in the cot.

'Let's tuck you right in now, angel. Lovely little one. Right, who's next?'

I wonder if the nurse remembers I'm even here squashed between the window and your cot. Or if I've turned into another baby.

'Now then. Let's be having you, Mohammed. Wonder what you've got for me. You little devil.'

The nurse continues nappy-changing. Blithely unaware, he talks softly without malice, but it is there all the same. From the very start of their lives these babies are labelled, angels or devils. I don't think he knows he's doing it. Racism's blind to itself, so built in. I shift in the bed so he turns and sees me and he is silenced. He knows what he's doing. It's in his words and his thoughts, it's in his hands. This is the world you are born into, with your mixture of bloods. I lie watching, I lie waiting. I lie happy to be next to you.

And it's all about the fluid in your spine. They shine torches in your eyes. They take blood from your tender heels. The enormous tag round your wrist institutionalises you. We are moved to the infirmary for monitoring in the special care baby unit. I am on the fourth floor and you are on the ground floor. Amongst the tiny babies – the 'prems', as they call the premature babies, wrapped up in doll-size woolly clothes, they look like small birds, splayed and rigged up to monitors – I feed you. It's all I can do, my milk is all I have to give you.

So I arrive on the ground floor every three hours, coming down in the clanky lift and into the unit to sit on a plastic chair and feed you and change you and sit with you and talk, murmuring, singing, humming. The nurses begin to call me 'the cow'.

'Here she comes, milking time again, the cow's here again, grub's up.'

One of them takes me aside and whispers, 'You don't have to do this, you know. Why don't you just get some sleep, take it easy? No one will mind if she has the bottle.'

I will mind, and you might mind too. This is why I had you at home. I know it would be easier for them if you had a bottle, they could measure and weigh and sterilise and monitor. I wouldn't keep cluttering up the unit with my presence, with my chatter, with my smell, with my swollen breasts.

Up on the fourth floor the ward sister is called Sister Savage, and she is brutally well named, she's cruel. She clicks about the ward in high heels, a cinched belt at her waist. A girl locks herself in a bathroom with a hand breast pump to try to stimulate her milk, she wants to feed her baby herself. However Sister Savage decides this is not possible. The door is forcibly unlocked by a porter under Savage's orders. She drags the pump off the girl, who wails and yells, 'Bitch, you fucking bitch. Just because I have a social worker doesn't mean I can't feed my own baby. Frigid fucking bitch.'

There is an atmosphere of fear and scuttling. Sister Savage manages the ward with an abusive military precision. It is not a fair playing field, with the new mothers hormonally charged, their stitches healing, so even going to the loo is painful. I am almost glad you are in the special care unit where they have a gentler approach, even if their sense of humour is peculiar. When Savage challenges me I have to breathe as deeply as is possible, speak levelly to her, while my mind's eye plays out a terrible cartoon featuring a large hammer. We have an altercation in the lift. Fortunately for me this plays out to my advantage, I am tearful about being separated from you and I get a room to myself. The tall man visits, picks you up and calls you his sunshine in Serbian/Srpski. Frank comes too, wearing someone else's tracksuit, which upsets me more than is rational. I cry easily. I don't know what's going to happen. After five days you are allowed to come up in the lift with me to stay on the fourth floor. I am ecstatic.

My father appears bearing a sheaf of flowers from his garden. Lupins, peonies, daisies, late lilac, roses, lavender, irises. He treads softly around your cot, his voice is gentler than I have ever known it when he speaks to you. Petals float to the floor. He has brought the smell of outside in. Real flowers, from clumps your grandmother once stood amongst smiling. You still have no name, it feels like there hasn't been time to find it.

And Angie comes, my friend like a tiger. She is unafraid of the tall man, of savage sisters, unmoved by visiting hours. We sit for five hours talking, laughing, drinking tea, looking out of the window and smelling the flowers that aren't 'arranged', and seem to outgrow the vase, they look windswept and untameable. We go through names and look at you very carefully as we say each one out loud. We look at the flowers and we say the names of all the flowers we know, and there's one flower name we say over and over again, we keep coming back to it. And the name settles on you.

There is always someone kind in hospital, someone who remembers what they're doing. Here it's the nurse who found the vase, who brings us a jug of water and glasses, and biscuits. She jokes, she doesn't scuttle or rush. And she overlooks the fact that Angie sits on and on, from one visiting time to another, breaking all the rules. She offers us coffee. We say your name. When she brings the coffee in on a tray, she nods and says, 'Yes, that's right, that's it, she's Lily. Not an Iris. Rose was wrong too.'

The consultant talks of a 'shunt to drain the blood from the spine, the brain'. There's talk of 'an operation in the specialist hospital in Wakefield, in a month's time'.

I can't look at you and hold you close and smell your fresh baby's head milky smell, and absorb these words at the same time. For now we are allowed to go home. It's June. The first thing I have to do is take you to the park and let you lie in the grass. There are daisies, it's still a bit damp from the dew.

'This is the Earth, welcome, this is your world,' I say.

MEDITERRANEAN

We develop the habit of driving to a beach or a river or a lake, and just turning right to find somewhere to park up for the night. This works remarkably well. The orange VW van cost £40, the tall man put windows in it, and it became a camper van. I made black corduroy curtains and covered the cushions in shades of red. Recycling, before the word was coined, the corduroy was from a jumble sale, the red material from the old dining-room curtains in my father's house. The windows, the seats that folded out to a bed, the table and bits of the engine came from skips and scrapyards. I suppose we were recycling ourselves too.

At six weeks old Lily was anaesthetised on a gurney like an ironing board, and her tiny body slotted into a gigantic round steel eye like something from a space station. I sat in an observation booth next to another booth with a computer in it, sobbing. The nurse at my elbow tried to steady and reassure me. The man at the computer looked over towards us, annoyed, as if to signal to the nurse, *Get her out of here.*

'Try not to worry, love, it's not going to help,' she said.

'Sorry. The thing is I don't understand. I don't understand what you're doing. I can't take it in, all this machinery . . .'

'Well, we're just taking thirteen sections of the brain, you know.'

I frowned, I sniffed. 'I don't understand.'

We had been reclaiming her babyhood from hospital and stress and worry, with music, with picnics and waterfalls and flowers.

'Thirteen sections. I can see that's hard to take in. Think of it like a bacon slicer.'

'Sorry? A bacon slicer?'

'Yeah. You know.' She looked at me encouragingly.

And I realised that she had said the worst thing, the scariest possible thing. And the incongruity of the thought of a bacon slicer from a grocer's shop, here, in relation to my daughter's brain, and the idea that the nurse thought she was being helpful, made me laugh. It was so macabre, it was funny. I tried to explain through snotty tears and laughter. She considered me with her head on one side, the guy in the booth was signalling to her again, I suppose the unspoken word 'hysteria' hovered by. My laugh was an incredulous laugh, at the absurdity, at all the shiny surfaces, the fire doors, the clipboards and graphs and printouts and disinfectant, the well-meaning-ness from total strangers, and the enormity of the possibility that my daughter may be hydrocephalic, with water on the brain, brain-damaged. For good.

However, Lily was a miracle baby, she scored the highest marks in all their development tests. She thrived. No shunt was needed, no drain, no operation. She sat, she crawled, she prattled, and at ten months she was discharged by the consultant and given a clean bill of health. So we decided to travel.

The tall man's roots are in Yugoslavia, there is a strip of land in the mountains above Knin. So we packed the Tintin and Asterix books, the nappies and all the clobber we thought we'd need and drove off to Europe. Stopped off in Leicester to say goodbye to my grandmother of ninety. She climbed up into the van, and looked very comfortable sitting at the table, and had to be gently persuaded that in fact she wasn't coming with us on our adventures. I led her sadly back into the home, she didn't appreciate it.

'It's not a home. They're all women, and they're all old. And they wake you up to give you a sleeping pill. Idiots. Are you sure I can't come with you, where did you say you were going?'

It was in Leicester that the starter motor on the van gave out, but this did not deter us. We did not go back to Bradford. We had a screwdriver. We had a journey to go on. For the next few months we would be looking for places to park with three prerequisites: a slope, somewhere for the children to play, and water. If there was no slope I had to take the steering wheel, and the tall man would lie under the van with the screwdriver to start the engine up. 'There are always ramps on ferries,' he pointed out. 'It's no problem' was his mantra.

Driving South, what joy. A clean bill of health, thank God. A piece of land in Yugoslavia, how exciting. And so we drive through and down France, shopping in markets, washing out nappies and hanging them on the wing mirrors to dry as we go along if necessary. We are fine-tuned to find sources of water, taps in garages, rivers, streams. We are improvising. In a van, life is stripped down.

In the Camargue we park beside Roma in Saintes-Maries-de-la-Mer, where the black Madonna, Sara-la-Kali, is worshipped. We dance in firelight, witnessed by the small stocky Camargue horses, one of the most ancient breeds. On the lake there are thousands and thousands of flamingos. I have never seen such an exquisite sight. Movement and colour, pinks, water reflections, the black of their underwings in flight, all synchronised and singing the sky. My baguette is untouched. I am aware of a brush on my shoulder of momentous, timeless perfection. I am drenched in the moment, it is inscribed in me to keep for always.

On the Mediterranean shores Frank creates his own morning routine. He goes to the edge of the sand by the sea with his black towel, has a splash wash paddle short dip in the shallows, and then, after arranging the towel meticulously straight, aligned with the sun, he lies down for a while. He repeats this routine until he looks over at the van and surmises that breakfast is ready.

In Italy one lunchtime Frank says he is starving, so the tall man cooks a whole packet of pasta.

'You don't know what starving is,' he says.

They look at each other. The tall man winks and then serves Frank some pasta in a bowl and he watches.

'Get stuck in, then. Go on.'

Frank shovels down the spaghetti, forkful after forkful, sprinkled with parmesan and olive oil. He empties the bowl and peers hopefully at the pan.

'Bloody hell, you are hungry. You may as well eat the lot, then! I can always cook some more for us.'

The tall man looks over at me and winks, sure that Frank's appetite will stall. He watches, he smokes and looks into the Italian valley, at the village on an outcrop, he looks back at the boy still shovelling spaghetti up efficiently.

'Bet you can't eat the lot, can you?' He is challenging Frank now.

Lily is chewing a banana, oblivious. There is male daring, male electricity in the air. I watch them, while making out I'm not watching them. I stonewall the tall man's glances at me, his need to ridicule, to egg on, to beat, to win. The spaghetti is now being eaten straight out of the pan, it is easier. Frank eats slowly now, tidily, properly. There is a whole hillside between them of culture, of years, of parenting styles, of expectations. The pan is empty. The spliff is smoked, the banana is finished. The tall man's eyes widen, he is amazed.

'Well, I never thought you'd do that. I suppose I'd better make some more now, for the rest of us.'

I am proud of Frank. He has bested the tall man, despite being a small boy.

In the starlight, in the layby on a slope that is our home for the night, the tall man talks at the toenail moon.

'My dad used to hit us with the belt, with the buckle. For the simplest things, sometimes for nothing. When they went to work in the mill, I was tied to the table with a bit of rope, like a goat. Me mam has never settled in England. She buried two of her children on the mountain in Yugoslavia before she left. On her own. She waited for me dad to send for her for seven years. Everyone on our street was from Yugoslavia in those days. It's all Asian now, except us, the others have moved on and out.'

I've seen his mother standing at the end of her street staring towards the moors and the Pennines. This is how I think of her. We continue the journey. The nearer we get, the more nervous he is.

We compare and share good coffee and wine under the stars with other people in vans, mostly Germans. There is a couple in a Mercedes with a shower. The men talk about vans and mileage. I want to talk about Europe and the war. The tall man suddenly has a vaulting Basil-Fawlty-like panic, and tries to pull me away, hissing, 'Don't mention Hitler, or the war, they're fucking German. You just can't, for fuck's sake. Just don't.'

But I do. We swap notes, we are the generation raised by parents who never mentioned the war, trying to grow up in the aftershock. Carrying it in our blood, in our cells, in our bones, in our DNA. We know we remember, however little we actually know, however much our parents have decided to forget. The tall man keeps trying to change the subject but no one notices. The sea is black, except for the trail of dancing yellows that leads to us from the moon. I watch him smoking, silhouetted against the sea, angry, full of tension and trying not to be. I see him as larger than life, as a graffiti cartoon character. A man at war with himself.

The Well

In Pula the toilets are sprinkled with lime, there is no water. In the mountains bread is rationed, they sell us half a loaf. And the tall man keeps waxing lyrical about his heritage and breaking into Srpski, lying diagonally in the back as I drive. He equates these limestone mountains with Yorkshire, they are both 'God's country'. When we get close to the village he barks at me to stop and let him drive. I brush my hair, and button up Lily's best cardigan.

The village isn't on a road just a bumpy track, there aren't many cars about, but there are horses. In the kitchen there's a washing machine, but no plumbing. There's no running water, just a well. The animals' stable is beneath the kitchen. There are tall men, women in aprons, there are guns hanging up, washing hanging out, broken glass in the grass, pigs, bedraggled chickens and a cow. When I ask to go to the loo, they gesture it's out the back on the mountain, and I discover it is the mountain. There is no loo.

So this is the land, this is where we have come to see if we could live. The bottle of slivovitz is banged on the table, the men watch as we drink their plum brandy, and coffee so thick and sweet the expression on my face makes them laugh when I swallow it. We're halfway to the East. I don't speak Srpski, so I have to guess what's going on. I imagine the tall man has told them we're married because it's simpler. He always said he was a peasant, and I realise this is true now. The slivovitz softens the strangeness, the being stared at, the being watched every minute, whatever you do-ness. I feed Lily. No one here seems quite sure how to treat me. Frank has crayons and paper. We have to sleep in the house, they insist. I know I'd be happier in the van, with some privacy. The women are in the back room, behind a curtain in the real kitchen. I am expected to sit with the men, who are loud and snappy, I don't feel comfortable around them and they don't feel comfortable around me.

Marko appears off the mountain, riding bareback on a brown horse, he is the tall man's cousin. He has gentle eyes, he is ten. The men laugh at him. I am often reminded how glad I am that I am not a man. This is one of those times. We go outside and Marko climbs into the van and looks at Tintin and Captain Haddock in *The Red Sea Sharks*, turning the pages slowly, like it's a holy book. Frank and Marko mount the horse, Frank sits behind, and they ride off together smiling. The tall man watches them get smaller, disappearing into the landscape, and says, 'They say Marko knows every plant here, every animal and bird. They're proud of him. But they think he's a bit soft in the head.'

When they return, Marko, in his green cable-knit jumper and too-big trousers, strokes Lily's head. A mute woman comes, we are told she's been struck by lightning. She sits Lily on her knee and smiles inwardly. The men and women barely speak to each other here, communicating in nods and gestures and barks. I feed the baby, I feel exhausted. I can't understand why they have a washing machine in pride of place, when there's no piped water. 'Why?' I ask. They laugh at the sound of English, and imitate it. The tall man explains it's a status symbol. I still don't understand. The mother fetches water from the well, there's a toddler with sticky eyes. I'm fighting myself, trying not to judge, to sit and accept and embrace it. At the back of my mind is the broken glass in the caked mud, is the harsh bitterness of the language, the neglect. These things keep creeping to the front of my mind. I am served food at the table with the men, they insist. The men eat at the table before the women. The women sit and eat in the real kitchen.

The swaggering teenage son takes a gun off the wall and cleans it. We are taking his bed, he and Marko will sleep with neighbours. The toddler stays up and up, it's late, I'm shattered. Eventually he falls asleep spread-eagled on the floor and then his mother lifts him up and takes him to her bed. She goes out to the well to bring more water and check the animals. She looks at the tall man, but not at me. Sticking out from under the mattress I find a porn magazine, the tall man tells me to shut up about it and put it back. He's become more patriarchal here, and louder. I feed the baby. I drink the water, she drinks the water.

The mountains of Bosnia are beautiful and bleak. On the way back from visiting a relative in town (low-rise block, slivovitz, coffee, chain-smoking), the tall man points out the hut where his father's cousin Gavrilo Princip was born. It looks like an old garden shed. Princip was a member of an anarchist group called the Black Hand. He shot Archduke Ferdinand in Sarajevo, an act which kick-started the First World War. He is a local hero here. In the future a park will be named after him in Sarajevo.

We cleave to Marko. He sits in the van drawing with Frank, they are both solemn children but they laugh together, and they go off on the mountain. The men make a great big deal of going hunting in the forest. They laugh and jeer at the tall man when he says he doesn't want to go.

'They're saying I'm under your thumb.'

'Really? Is that even an expression in Srpski?'

'And that you wear the trousers.'

'So what? We both wear trousers. I wear dresses too.'

He goes. There's a posse of them. They kill a deer and rabbits and drink a lot of plum brandy. They are gone a long time. We can hear gunshots from the forest across the valley. The women prepare lamb with roast potatoes for when the hunters return. They are reeling drunk when they do, but insist I sit with them at the table and eat the meat. When I go into the real kitchen against their wishes, I see the women are eating soup with beans, sitting on the floor. They say they don't need, they don't like, they don't want meat and potatoes.

I could never live here. The land, the property that we came to look at, is a long thin strip of the field next to the well with broken glass and rusting metal strewn everywhere. The tall man whispers to me quietly one morning, 'Me dad would be sick to see the land come to this. This guy we're staying with, his cousin, he's a turncoat, he's a liar. He's a thief, he's taking the piss.'

Our vision of a vibrant smallholding evaporates in the forest mist, and floats away over the mountains. And Lily is vomiting. After twenty-four hours we decide to go to the hospital. Everyone shakes their heads. 'There is no need,' they say. We go anyway. I'm frightened. We drive up and round and down and up and round, the tall man drives like a lunatic, he's frightened. The hospital seems deserted, abandoned, except it isn't. This is how the hospital here in Banja Luka is, dilapidated, with lime strewn in the loos and corridors. It is hard to appreciate that this falling-down, leaking, rattling building can really be a hospital. There are buckets catching drips, there are ceilings falling in. It is filthy. She has dysentery.

'Has she drunk well water?' asks the doctor. 'Did you boil it?'

We look at each other. I stay with her. Frank and the tall man go back to the village and his relatives. I asked them about the well water. I remember them nodding and smiling and saying, via translation, 'Very good the water, sweet, good mountain water, we never boil it, no, no.' Later I will hear that their toddler almost died from the well water only last year. When Lily is well enough to leave the hospital I refuse to go back. As in the past, in the future the valley and the tall man's family will be broken by war.

We never cross the bridge on the River Drina. I end up driving the van along the mountain hairpins in fog and hail. The tall man lies diagonal and slivovitzed in the back, blaring at me for shaming him and his family. I experience terror. He chucks stuff at the windscreen. Eventually he conks out, passes out, so I pull up and we all sleep. In the morning, the blessed morning when I wake, I think, *Thank God it's over. With daylight everything will get better.* But when he stirs it's still there, the family honour is shredded to tatters by my behaviour, and the ranting continues. I cannot understand what I have done wrong. My quiet voice within realises that he's been desperate for some dope to calm himself down. He's replaced it with plum brandy. The effect is bad. We're parked on a main road and the police pull up. And I think, *Good. Bloody good. I can get home. I can get out of this farce, this tragic venture that sank at the bottom of the well. They'll help. I can fly out of here and leave him and his relatives to it.*

At the police station they talk to the tall man in halting English and rampant Srpski, they listen to him. They offer him a glass of slivovitz and a ham sandwich, they look askance at me. They listen to me and offer me a glass of water.

'You must leave now,' they say finally, pointing at the road. 'This way. You go Italy. You no go Sarajevo.'

Showers Like Mushrooms

Lily learnt to walk on a beach in Spain. Maybe it was the coaching round and round the campfire, Frank holding her hand, with woolly brown bulls looking over the fence. Maybe she got sick of getting wet crawling in puddles. Probably it was because she got distracted from the idea of walking, because her dad was flying a kite. She just stood up and walked with her hand outstretched for the kite. Only when she heard us all exclaiming did she look down at her sandy knees and feet, realise she was walking, and flop onto her bum. Frank gave his boots to Marko, he never liked them. He didn't like his espadrilles either, and he doesn't like flip-flops.

'That little thong bit is silly. Like ties are silly, you know.'

'I don't agree – flip-flops are one of my favourite inventions. Like wheelbarrows, hot-water bottles, tents, flasks, and bicycles.'

'But don't you think ties are silly?'

'Probably.'

'Dangerous,' said the tall man.

'Are people who wear ties silly?'

'There is no answer to that.'

We chose mountains and lakes, or the sea, we asked the map. There are *embalses*, gorgeous deep lakes, in Spain. I swim suspended by hundreds of feet of water. I'm in the belly of the Earth with all her blessings, and feel scared, elated, and humbled.

With the help of gesticulation, the tall man has found a second-hand starter motor in a Spanish scrapyard. He is overjoyed, and sits with it on his knee wearing only a pair of black shorts. He's cleaning it and fiddling with it as I drive round a roundabout. The passenger door flies open, the starter motor slides, in slow motion, off his knees and onto the road, straight into the path of a black Mercedes. The Mercedes drives over it. I stop the van. The tall man jumps out to try and recover the starter motor – it's crushed, it's unusable, he rants and raves, he jumps around all over the road, he swears in three languages. No one stops. We continue to use the screwdriver method to start the van on the flat, as before.

I walk into a lake at evening with the washing-up bowl in peace. Being domestic outside soothes me. We stay on one beach in Spain for ten days, there is just beach, dunes, shrubs, and four showers like tall mushrooms – that's all. We don't even know where we're going any more. There is just us, the beach and the sea. In the night we hear another camper van arrive in the dark, in the morning Jean-Claude, a footballer from Cameroon, is running along the shoreline. Nicole, his wife, and two children are sitting on the steps of their RV. That night we share a fire.

'So. You can go anywhere you like in this van of yours. Why don't you come with us, come to Cameroon?'

Jean-Claude is beautiful, super-fit and super-strong. The tall man can't decide if he likes him or thinks he's a wanker.

'We were thinking of Morocco.'

'Of course you were thinking of Morocco. Everyone thinks of Morocco. But think of Cameroon. It is *magnifique*.'

Jean-Claude has some powerful weed and soon the men are very stoned, imagining a windmill-like machine to wash the nappies in the river in Cameroon. Their arms spin in the firelight. The weed is too strong for me. Nicole is smoking Gitanes quietly, I cannot tell what she is thinking.

In Algeciras people are camped out, waiting for the ferry to cross to Morocco.

'You wait. Africa is something else. You will be changed forever.' Jean-Claude smiles toothily.

He runs his eyes down my lean brown body. Nicole gives me a spotty T-shirt to wear. The tall man whispers to me in the dark, 'Take a look, in the morning, take a look at the back of their camper. It's covered in stickers from everywhere, you name it, in Europe. But under them there's something else.'

'What else? What are you talking about – don't you want to go to Cameroon? What are you saying?'

'Looks like a stolen van to me. How can they afford it, for one thing?'

'He's a footballer.'

'Is he? How do we know? I reckon it's stolen, it's a hire van and they've put all those stickers on to cover up the hire company lettering. I tell you, they're probably wanted by the police. I bet he is.'

'For goodness' sake, you're smoking too much. You're paranoid.'

'And how do we know we can get visas on the way? We don't. Have you wondered what he really wants from us?'

'No. I like to take people at face value. And what about Nicole?'

'Nicole, she's a dark horse, I'm telling you.'

We cross the Strait of Gibraltar heading for Africa. We land in Ceuta, it's full of apartment blocks – it looks just like Spain. We follow Jean-Claude, the stickers and what might be underneath the stickers right in front of us. At the border we wait for them, and Jean-Claude waves us on, they've been stopped.

'Meet you on the road to Tétouan,' he shouts, smiling that charming smile.

And now we're in Africa. Women walk along with carefully balanced piles of wood on their heads. Children grin and shout and wave at us. There are camels and donkeys and the sky is red. For the first time in a long time we pull into a campsite. I watch the road, watching for the RV, I feel bad we left them at the border. I can't settle. I fetch water to wash, I boil water in the kettle for drinking. Night comes like a blanket over your head all of a sudden, I can't tell if their RV goes by or not, on the way to Cameroon. By morning it is clear we've lost them, I don't know if we'll find them again.

I map-read. I wear a long nightie. When I drive, people point and stare. In the mountains of Morocco women don't drive. At night we pull onto a farm track, and I wake in the morning to the smell of fresh flatbreads. The tall man is up first for once, up and out of the van. I find him in the company of two men drinking coffee and smoking a water pipe with a blissful expression on his face. There is a woman half hidden away in the background making flatbreads rhythmically.

'Morning. You'll never guess where we are.'

I know we got a bit lost, our map is not that detailed and I haven't got used to the way night falls here, in a trice. He doesn't wait for me to answer anyway.

'On a draw farm. This is it, this is heaven. It's where they grow it, acres and acres of the stuff. All my dreams come true.'

I have to smile, I'm not a killjoy. He looks triumphant and peaceful, sucking on the hookah, the men smile with satisfaction.

We do not keep track of time, of days or dates. So when we need money in Fez on a Sunday we end up in an escapade that involves mint tea, croissants and a man in reflective sunglasses. The tall man guards the van and the children while I (with my French) go deep into the medina and end up buying a rug, after being introduced to the weavers at their looms. I drink more mint tea. I leave with some cash.

On the coast a man carries fresh doughnuts in a basket on his head and we eat them for breakfast and ride camels. Clinging onto Frank as we ride along in the heat, I wonder if I'm happy. I wonder if it's possible to be happy and know it at the same time.

Across the estuary from Larache, we join a beach full of people from the old town camping, it's too hot there in July. There's a ferry across the river to the market. We sweat silently inside the van, it's so hot outside you need shoes to walk on the sand. I carry Frank to the sea and we dunk and float. Fires are lit at dusk to fend off mosquitoes, chickens prowl, sardines grill, pots and pans and plates and sticks are beaten, there is dancing. A big square canvas tent is put up next to us, and I look at it enviously from the hot metal box of the van. We are only cool at night or in the water. A white van pulls up first thing in the morning and two men get out and unload hundreds of watermelons. They fill the tent right up, until it bulges out, lumpy, crammed full to bursting. Watermelon juice is on everyone's chins, running down everyone's arms and there are black seeds all over the beach, the chickens peck at them. The tent gradually de-bulges and empties.

I swim alone in the wide estuary, laughing. The word 'joy' hangs over me as I hang in the water looking at the date palms leaning, at the cactus flowers, the sky and the sea. There is nothing in the way, everything is simple. Me in a body, in a body of water, lapping into a bigger body of water. All beautiful, all full, all true.

We are travelling in a wide loop, and cross back into Europe, our hopes and dreams altered. In the very middle of Portugal on a hilly *quinta*, as I reach for blackberries from the hedgerow to go with my muesli, a brown cow walks by brushing my shoulder. I bathe in a naturally pink pool, with tiny fish and water boatmen. As I squat to rinse out our clothes, in the bowl of the field opposite the maize plants rustle, and I hear the voice of a woman singing. She walks down into the maize, continuing her song.

On the north coast of Spain it rains, it pours. The windscreen wipers are not fast enough. Frank lost his espadrilles long ago. He kept leaving them outside the van, hoping he'd get rid of them, I kept putting them back in. They were yellow, and one day they'd disappeared for good. I carry him over streaming wet pavements and gurgling drains into a shoe shop, we are completely soaked through, he hasn't worn shoes in months. The assistant purses her lips, in the mirror I don't recognise us. We look very brown and worn and wild.

We drive past fields of sunflowers, their heads bowed down, grey, they look like thousands and thousands of hungry people. Like figures on the move but caught in freeze-frame, in a drought.

Dyeing

After Morocco I decide I need to learn to do something with my hands. I don't want to live in my head. We hang the rug from Fez on the wall. I go to the community arts centre to learn how to weave. A Scottish woman, Violet, greets me and says, 'Well, lassie, there must be some mistake, we're not doing weaving today. You want to learn something? You'd best do batik. You'll be good at that.'

Violet is aptly named after a colour. There is a crèche, there is tea and biscuits, there is a whole art studio with people bustling around in it. This is my introduction to dyeing.

The tall man has promised me, 'Now that I'm back, I've made a clean break. I'm never going to dabble, never ever again.'

In heroin. Apparently that was the source of the unbearable tension that caused all the aggro. The mood swings, the fear, the violence. Now it was going to be just ganja, pure and simple. He was back mechanic-ing. He had put the drama in Bosnia down to slivovitz and the culture, hunters and patriarchy, stuck-in-the-Dark-Ages stuff.

'I've learnt my lesson, I'm sorted, I'm going to make it all all right. Promise. I swear on my mother's life. Honest.'

The very word 'heroin' is frightening, is deathly, edgy, short of breath, it stings, it cuts, it aches. I hate needles. I never see the tall man 'use'. I don't think I've ever seen him smoke heroin, 'chasing the dragon', either. But what was in that Chinese bowl, what was in 'the mix', really? What did he smoke with other people? I have been living strung out with tension, with the pall of longing. I've had a cobweb cloak of suspicion draped over my shoulders. Lying and the idea of lies, always there in the air. I don't want to inhabit this razor-blade edge, or be anywhere near it. I can't tell when I'm being lied to. He says it himself, he has a silver tongue. Sometimes I think I'm living with ghosts circling in on me. Sometimes his pupils are pinpricks, his eyes all darkness, his voice whiny. Is that it? I don't know. I can't bear those times. I can't bear to be near him. I am never sure if this is the presence of heroin. An energy in the room like a rushing vortex disappearing into nothing, like a black glove wrapped around and stifling your heart. Like a possession with no exorcist, only craving, more lies, and more craving. The truth – where is it? What is it anyway? The degradation of this heroin hunger is total. Merciless, cold-blooded.

I can't think these thoughts. To be with someone you think you know, you believe you love, who's in the room with you and they're empty, vacant, they're not there, is beyond loneliness. I can't compute it. I plead, I reason, I harangue, I threaten, I weep. I hide. I soak in the bath pretending. I lie in bed in greyscape. I become good at putting on a good and smiling face which doesn't reach my eyes. I accept the spliffs proffered as olive branches. I clean up, sweeping up ash and opening windows. I am frightened of finding scraps of charred foil. Disturbed in the night by him scratching up and down the lengths of his arms, up and down. When I ask him about it he says it's nothing. I wonder, *Am I addicted too?* To this darkness, to living in this shadow, to meeting each fresh drama, and being the one who keeps clearing up and trying to make it all right again. To being the nice one, the kind one, the friendly one, the sensible one, the one with food in the cupboard, who pays the bills. In the future the terms 'co-dependency' and 'enabling' will be common usage, not yet.

The tall man tells me that when we were in Bosnia he visited a house in the next village, and placed some garlic there to reverse a family curse. He believes he's cursed. I remember the air in the mountains, thick with emotion you could cut through. This heaviness, in the water, in memories, in people's eyes. A fog of bitterness, a clenching, even in the sound of the language, that made me stroke my passport gladly, that made me relieved to be British. But now I wish we'd never come back, I wish we'd never gone away, I wish we'd never met. I can't get a handle on what's happened to me, to my life, to myself. And I don't know what to believe.

I am ready to start something new. I want to look on the bright side. I want to believe in forgiveness and compassion. I brew herb tea blood-red with hibiscus. I work with colours, I connect with people. The art studios are inclusive, for freedom of expression. Lily likes the crèche, Frank is in school and Violet has a sense of humour. We dip-dye. Drawing on cotton cloth in hot wax, then dipping it in the first colour. Often yellow. I fill the yellow in with hot wax before dipping the cloth again in a bath of red, to make orange. Then the same, filling in with wax over the orange before dipping again in red to make red, then a dip in green to make brown. You can get to black. I dye blues, then yellow to make greens, I dye purple and pink and turquoise. The yellow is sunshine, sunflower-yellow. I hang the batiks up with pegs on a line to dry between dips. I am in the process. Looking, thinking, planning, researching, talking about colours, dipping, waiting for things to dry, drinking tea and eating biscuits, chatting and laughing. I don't like the smell of the rubber gloves. But who does? I love the smell of hot beeswax.

I love the way the hot wax in the tjanting (copper pen) runs out of the little spouts so fast you have no time to think. You have to go with it and go for it, you have to let it happen. There is planning, and then there is what happens, there are drawings and drafts and ideas, but then it's live. It's alive, we all are, and I feel this in my veins, as I mix up dyes in old jam jars. Adding salt and urea and soaking waxy cloths in bowls full of colour, keeping an eye on them, moving them about a bit, waiting. And then hanging them up on the line to drip and dry. The sound of the taps running is pleasing. I hate ironing, but ironing the wax out again after the final colour is dry, letting it melt into newspaper, is exciting. A batik has layers and a life of its own. I scour charity shops for 100 per cent cotton sheets. I thrill to the sound of tearing cloth and being amongst people concentrating, producing extraordinary things, sometimes great, sometimes mistakes, but there are no mistakes, no one minds. We are explorers. I go and dye twice a week. The tall man is not impressed, he doesn't like me talking to people he doesn't know. I stick Lily's artwork from the crèche on the kitchen wall.

The people the tall man doesn't want me to know include Les, leaning over a light box designing funky T-shirts for screen-printing. Julie, batiking from a photograph of her garden meticulously, even though she has a frozen shoulder. And Ronnie, who has a face like a hawk, smokes Senior Service, and is basically an amateur Egyptologist. He's making a full-length painted door cloth of the Sun God Ra. He does hieroglyphics with precision. I borrow a book and decide to copy Egypt too. I summon up Thoth, the God of Scribes. The wax melts, smoking a little as I trail a full tjanting onto the blank sheet on the stretcher. My arm tingles all the way up. My arms tingle when I soak the cloth in a yellow bath. And when it comes to green, turning turquoise, the tingling happens again. It happens when I trail the wax, and when I soak the colours. At the sink Ronnie and I talk in low voices. He speaks out of the side of his mouth, a cigarette behind his ear, his quiff greying.

'Ronnie, this Egyptian stuff is something else, isn't it?'

'Oh yes. That's why I bother doing it.'

'I'm going to dark green next, and then I want to try and get a black.'

'Mmm.'

'Ronnie? You know when you're doing yours, do you get a kind of tingling up your arms?'

'Like electricity? Oh yes, in me legs too sometimes. That's why I do it.'

'Like you have to, in a way?'

'Well, nothing else comes anywhere close. I mean, I could do stuff with birds or animals – I mean, I do. I have done. But it always comes back to the Egyptians with me. Like it has to. As though it's just using me, my body, to get this stuff out. You know. There's some power in it anyway. Now I'm off for a smoke.'

I get to almost black with Thoth, dip-dyeing five times. Next I find myself in front of blank squares and faces emerge from the hot trailing wax. They come out of nowhere, out of the air, out of the heat, they are the faces of the wise, women and men, they just appear. The wax cools and hardens, the cloth is ready for colour. Dyeing is saving me, telling me I am really alive.

DITCH

John knocks on the front door, it's late, and I'm in my pyjamas. He's the tall man's oldest friend, a pianist, jazz. I open the door, I don't know where the tall man is, but he may be here soon. John is shaking, he looks crestfallen. He always looks almost clean and smart, except for his plimsolls. I offer him coffee, he hates herb tea. Last time I saw John I was wearing my red Viyella dress, he was playing at a club with his brother on drums. The music was watery, clean and wacky. The tall man has a photograph of him and John, aged eleven – a school football team photograph. John has tried to destroy it on several occasions. There are corners missing, used for roaches, but the tall man clings to the photograph because he looks handsome and cocky, and John looks, well, weedy and small. They fight over it still, in a play-fight way. These two know each other so well it's too well. I have heard the tall man say, 'I have thought sometimes it would be much easier to be gay. And if I was gay then it would be obvious that John and I would be a couple. When we lived in Mill Road it came close, didn't it, John?'

'Wasn't meant. And I like women too much.'

'True, true. Me too.'

The words 'Mill Road' carry the weight of all the worst bachelor scenarios imaginable. It's a grim punchline to the grimmest stories.

John is drinking coffee. He doesn't put the mug down, he's warming his hands around it. He's still shaking.

'To be honest, I came round to see you.'

'Oh?' This has never happened before.

'I'm in a bit of trouble.'

'I thought you looked a bit shaky. What's the matter?'

'You're the last person I wanted to ask, but . . .'

'What is it, John?'

The trouble with me is I like the idea of being both the last person and the first person someone might ask for help. I like the idea that I am not the one in need of help.

'Well, I owe this guy some money. I've been stupid.'

'Right.'

'And he's a serious guy. I don't have the money.'

'How much do you owe him?'

'Sixty quid.'

'Can't he wait?'

'No. And the time's up on Friday. This Friday. The thing is, this guy, he's different, he's not making idle threats.' He shifts in the chair. 'You remember Chris, the bassist? You know, long curly hair, tall guy.'

'Vaguely. Thin. Sensitive-looking.'

'Yeah. Light-skinned, airman's jacket, really good musician, actually. Went off to work in Spain about a year ago. You know, to get away from here, and er . . . certain people and substances . . .'

'I've met him. But what has he got to do with . . . ?'

'I didn't know if you'd heard.'

'Heard what?'

'About Chris. He'd only been back a month. Clean, healthy, talking about going off to Berlin, had made some good contacts. Unfortunately he got straight back into it, the smack. Owed this guy forty quid. Forty quid. Went missing, no one had seen him, thought he was laying low, you know. I know the guy was threatening him. No one could prove anything.' He paused. 'Police found him in a ditch over Thornton way. Drowned, they reckon, but it wasn't.'

'In a ditch?'

'Been dead for three days.'

'And you owe money to . . .'

'The same guy. Yeah. Said if I don't pay him he'll cut off my hands.'

'For fuck's sake. Cut off your hands?'

'So I can't play, can't make any money. And it's a signal,

203

you know, to anyone else. Who thinks they can cross him, fucking macho man. I've never been scared like this before. I know I've been stupid.'

'Sixty quid?'

'Yeah. I thought you'd get it . . . you understand about music. You know what it means.'

We both look at his wrists, they are delicate.

'You don't want to end up in a ditch.'

'No.'

I barely have sixty quid. Let alone to spare. But he begs me. He actually says, 'My brother won't help, I don't want my parents to know. I've got another gig coming up. Please. I beg you.'

The tall man comes in then, rubs his hands and hogs the gas fire. He rattles around looking for Rizlas, and says, 'John. Did you ask her then?'

I think of the electricity bill I agreed to pay because there'd been some mix up and they were threatening to cut the supply off up at his mother's. Was that true? I had got the money back, eventually. I think of my friend who owed Yorkshire Water £21, but couldn't pay it, so she was sent to jail for two weeks. I think of Chris, who had seemed so elegant and cool in his airman's jacket with his long fingers playing bass. So in control. I look at the fire, and I look from one to the other of them, and back again. I can't imagine either of them playing football these days. I think of the ditch, and Chris lying face down in inches of water. I look at John's hands, small for a man's hands, dainty. But he has long fingers, long enough to reach over more than an octave.

The two of them go out after a while. I'm still in my pyjamas. Femi comes by looking for John, he comes in but he doesn't stay long. The tall man is suspicious of him, Femi always flirts with me – he's a beautiful man, he flirts with everyone. He's a talented photographer, a journalist, a radical. After a brief chat, he opens my bedroom door on the way out, pretending he's made a mistake. I am whispering because the children are asleep. I almost have to push him out the front door. Going down the steps, he turns and looks up at me and says, 'I didn't realise it before, but you're pretty normal, aren't you?'

I can't decide if this is a compliment or a put-down.

When I try to get rid of the tall man and he loses it, he destroys photographs. Or he steals them. I will have less proof that the good times ever happened. He smashes glass. I shout and scream and then collapse afterwards, taking days to recover. My record is scratched and stuck on repeat.

FOG

Ali reckons Aleister Crowley said a dragon landed on this part of Bradford. Not a friendly one, but a malicious reptile, a beast with bad intentions. We are living under its wing, lurking in its shadow. Perhaps we cannot help what we do, how we live, perhaps we don't have the control we think we do. Drive a mile or two out and it's manicured. Cross the valley and it's white and windswept and brutal. But this is the ghetto, undrawn lines define it. Riots erupt in it. No one outside understands it. There is a mournful beauty in the rotting grandeur, in the cobblestones, the derelict creaking mills. It sings from the dives and dance floors, ululates when there's a death. It smells of damp and spices, and sinsemilla straight from Jamaica. Old chapattis clog the gutters, put out for the pigeons, but drawing rats up from the sewers. Coriander, onions and spinach crowd out tattered rose bushes. Home-made tandoori ovens replace middens. It yells, the sounds of Bollywood yearn and screech, shehnais wail from passing taxis. It thumps with reggae and the beginnings of rap. The waves of immigrants fled here, knelt here, were trapped here. Escaped to the suburbs or stayed on staying on. When the BMW garage is looted and trashed, the police start to build a fortress.

There's mildew climbing the walls, the boiler's broken so there's no hot water. The council say the rat problem is endemic, all along the row, so there's not much they can do: 'They get everywhere'. The previous tenant saw her son pick one up like it was a toy. She snatched it away as he lifted it to his mouth.

I want to escape to the park and the lake, or to the woods beyond with the red and white streams. To my allotment that looks out to the moors beyond. There's privacy, a privet hedge, space and a tap there. I want to get some sand for a sandpit. I want to grow vegetables, weed and water them, I want to get my hands in the earth. I collect kitchen scraps for the compost heap. I live in library books and through the eyes of my children, they see hope without struggle. We stand at the top of the road by the phone box for a long time, just watching a small steam roller, steaming, moving backwards and forwards. The tarmac is soft, like flapjacks being rolled flatter and flatter, the steam mixed with the reek of bitumen is soothing.

I walk along the cobbled snicket lined by dustbins and sense there's something under that sodden carpet in the overflowing skip. I feel spooked. I'm taking the shortcut to the post office. And I remember being just ten, trying to get used to being motherless.

Walking towards the wooden bridge on the way to school, taking the shortcut. I hate going round the long way with all the traffic, the shuddering lorries grinding over the girder bridge over the railway tracks. My usual stalwart companion, my little brother, is ill in bed at home. The au pair will look in on him, he has a stack of Asterix books on his bedside table. There is a white cloudy thick fog. There is the muddy bumpy puddly footpath, with one lonely lamp post. The path gets narrower and narrower, it's called Lover's Lane. I am still struggling to comprehend exactly what lovers are. I can't see if there's anyone coming the other way. I think I am alone. But as I get nearer to the bridge I can see there's someone standing still in the middle of it, leaning on the side, maybe a trainspotter. I walk on through the fog, holding my breath. When I breathe out my breath adds to the fog. I feel anxious. I will become used to walking alone and feeling anxious for the rest of my life. I am growing into being a woman.

I walk as evenly and as calmly as I can. I count my footsteps silently. I'm brave, I'm looking forward to English – I should be getting a composition I wrote about living on an island back. We're making a map of France with papier-mâché mountains. The Massif Central, the Jura, the Pyrenees – was there one more? I love French, I have a French name, Marie-Louise, on a name card on my desk. I like drinking the third pints of milk with a straw, it'll be frozen today. Mr Cronin the caretaker leaves the crates out on the step. It's December. I need to do some Christmas shopping or make things to give the others. The man on the bridge is not looking out to the tracks, so he can't be trainspotting. The rails click and twitch, so I know a train is coming. I hope it's a steam train because I like to walk through the steam that comes up through the cracks between the wooden boards, it gives me the giggles. I like to scream when the train is directly underneath. But today I hope that it'll be a diesel, because I don't like the look of this man, I don't like the feel of him standing there. The steam is too all-embracing and cuts you off from the rest of the world. The fog today is bad enough. But I go on walking. I walk up the steps, and I walk along the bridge to go past him, and I nearly don't even look at him. But I do. I look at his face and I see he's looking down, so I look down too, and see that where his trousers are there's something red and swollen and open. And I gasp, my face flushes, I don't look at his eyes. I've seen them already. I shout out and I run.

I run over to the other side of the bridge, I run down the steps, I nearly fall down them. I run into the cul-de-sac, past the garages, I run into a girl in the navy grammar-school uniform going the other way. She catches me. I'm gasping.

'Don't. Don't go that way. There's a man on the bridge. There's a man and he's got his thingy out.'

I feel sick. And she shepherds me into my school, even though I protest she'll be late for hers. I keep apologising, another habit adopted at ten. She promises me she'll go round the long way, the lorry way. I never tell anyone at home. There's no one and no way to tell.

And now I have that same creeping shame-making fear. Walking down the snicket to the post office to go and buy some stamps. Is this one of the places the Yorkshire Ripper dumped a woman's body? It feels like it. I turn back and go round the long way.

Last week I found a flowery silk skirt in a skip. I looked round to see if anyone was watching, held it up to the light, and took it home to wash and wear. I had to mend a small tear in the seam. It floats, it's lovely. One voice in my head said, *What are you doing? You can't wear stuff out of a skip. It's rubbish. You can't.* The other voice says, *Why not? Who knows? And who cares?*

STEAM

The street is named after a spring, but it's been swallowed up by tarmac long ago. Sometimes I think I can hear it, rushing and gushing under the pavement into the drains, but maybe not. The street is two dour, soot-stained stone rows. The house has been empty for two years and neglected for decades. It's a bargain. My grandmother, my mother's mother, would have approved. She was a great one for the sales. She left me some money. You can sense the floaty shadow of the woman who used to live here alone, in the peeling wallpapers, the brass stair rods, in the musty lavender smell. At first it's hard to realise the empty square back room is a kitchen. There are no units. The flat stone sink is behind wooden doors inside a tiled cupboard.

The tall man corrals people to help, with the chimney, with the cellar, with Acrow props and an RSJ when a wall is removed. The old cast-iron bath goes up to the allotment, where it sits, stately, awaiting sandy soil and carrots. At the moment I have no time for gardening so it fills up with rainwater, reflecting the sky. There is a new bath and a new loo coming. There is dust. For three days we can't flush the old loo. The dust keeps multiplying however much I sweep it up, I can't win against dust. There's a skip, loud reggae, wheelbarrows, rubble, scaffolding boards. The house echoes with calls, there is the scent of ganja. There is a pile of heavy old lead pipes lying in a heap in what will be my bedroom, like the fossilised remains of a creature, a museum exhibit.

Owen is doing the plumbing, he is usually a burglar. He is extremely polite and markedly quieter than everyone else tramping up and down the stairs. There are bundles of copper pipes, and a new boiler. The old water tank will go up to the allotment. I am witnessing the innards, the organs and intestines of the house, being extracted and replaced. I notice how delicately Owen works unravelling pipes, threading new ones through under the floorboards, soldering, and how the tall man is more abandoned, and how Neville always wears gloves. Men working or at war, each with different styles.

I make lunch. I make cups of strong tea and stronger coffee. I buy crap biscuits and white sugar. I turn the stopcock of the water mains on and off, a lot, on Owen's instructions. My father appears from York twice a week in his spotless Astra, with a thermos flask and sandwiches. Tata insists on eating separately, he is obsessed with 'Preparation, it is all in the preparation'.

He brings Polyfilla and his own tools. He smooths his palms over the surface of the walls in the front room, like it's a giant map. He is retired from the bookshop and has no one to order about now. Although he is troubled by the tall man, he also likes him in a way he never liked my ex-husband. It is a Slav thing, in fact there is very little they have in common except me and football.

'Are you really sure you want to strip all this wallpaper off? Why not paint over it? The surface is very lumpy already. Good grief. I think these were gaslights.'

I want to strip everything: the walls, the windowsills, the mantelpieces, all the doors. I want everything bare and clean and fresh. I will have all the doors and a chest of drawers dipped in an acid bath, drawers my father once painted over with white gloss.

When the plumbing is done with the pipes all joined up and soldered and the boiler connected, we can flush the loo. It is my father who notices that when the loo flushes, steam rises.

'Is someone now using the hot water?'

'I don't know, Tata. They might be.'

'Are they using the sink in the cellar? Is there someone down there?'

'I have no idea, Tata.'

I don't want to think about what is going on or has gone on in the cellar. I don't want to have suspicions. This is meant to be a new start.

'You need to keep a handle on these things, get a grip.'

'I am doing my best.'

It's hot and sticky, it's summer. I would rather be in the woods with my feet in a stream.

'No need to be touchy with me. It seems to me that the plumbing may be a problem . . .'

'There's nothing wrong with the plumbing.'

'Well, how do you know? You're not a plumber.'

'Neither are you.'

'There is something not quite right.'

The tall man has made the mistake of explaining to my father that Owen is a burglar, and that this is an opportunity for him to do some 'decent honest' work. It makes Tata suspicious, our suspicions are twining around each other.

The big sign of life in this street is the enormous beech tree down the road, where the boys play cricket relentlessly, running up for lunch, eating as fast as they can, running back down again, so they can carry on playing. The tree is majestic, its bark is like elephant's hide, eye markings run up its trunk. It is the only sign of real vigour here, maybe it grows over the spring. Attempts to incorporate its ever-bulging trunk into the fencing of the doctor's garden at the end of the road are doomed. It is lawless. I feel an affinity with beech trees, I need to know where the nearest one is wherever I live. I will collect the beech leaves and masts off the pavement for my compost heap.

They are concreting sections of the cellar floor, leaving the flagstones around the old range. I am not allowed to go down there until the concrete has set. I don't like the guy, another John, who is helping the tall man. He smells acrid, I don't like them being down there together. I wonder if I am being paranoid, I wonder if I am a horrible person, jealous and unreasonable. I notice there's steam coming up from the boiler flue – why are they using hot water down there? I am looking forward to claiming the cellar as my own. Lighting the range fire and dyeing down there. There's another big stone sink. There are shelves already, I've been collecting buckets and baby baths and jars. I have plans to investigate natural dyes with blackberries, beetroots, onion skins, and indigo.

The concrete sections have dried now. The house is empty of men. I light the first fire down in the cellar with the children. Flames flare up the chimney in tongues. I don't know where the tall man is, and I don't want to know. I don't want to know what has been written in the wet cement around the chimney stack that seemed to cause such hilarity. I don't want to think about the tall man and the other John down here. What they were doing apart from concreting. I have stopped asking, stopped voicing my suspicions. I don't believe anything he says.

'Are you going to do dyeing down here, Mum?'

'Yes, I am. And you can help me. We'll get small rubber gloves, or cut some down for you,' I say brightly.

When Frank goes upstairs to the loo, the boiler on the wall fires up as Lily and I stare, squatting, looking into the fire. Steam floats up outside the window. Frank comes back down the steep stone steps.

'That's weird,' I say.

'What?'

'Well, there's no one else in the house but us. Did you wash your hands upstairs?'

'Oops. Not really.'

'Did you flush the loo?'

'Think so. Yeah.'

'That's really weird. Go and flush the loo again.'

'What? Why?'

'Just do it, will you?'

We flush the loo several times. I go up and feel the cistern and it's warm. And I realise that Tata was right, there is something wrong with the plumbing. Owen has piped the hot and cold the wrong way round, so the loo cistern is filling with hot water every time it flushes. Owen comes the next day, very apologetic, to change them round. He refuses the spliff the tall man proffers. 'Nah. Too strong, man. That stuff, it's lethal.'

The tall man happily smokes it all himself.

ICE (AGAIN)

In winter the lake in the park freezes over, the ice is thicker than I've ever seen ice. Tom is visiting and we walk round the lake twice. I wonder if he's happier with his dad, he wanted to go and I let him. His dad's begun another family now. A girl in a red bobble hat is ice skating. There's no sign of any cracks. We throw bits of ice gouged from puddles on the path across the icy lake and hear them sing, high and screeching. The boys hold hands and step down onto the ice, and walk together out towards the duck island in the middle. They turn round and come back for me, holding out their hands.

'Come on, Mum, you can do it, it's fine, it's really thick.'

In my mind I can hear shattering. But they're right, the ice is thick. So I walk on ice. We all do.

HYDRA

I'm jumpy. I flinch at the guy wielding a video camera outside the art college filming me and the tall man arguing. The tall man threatens to wrap the camera round his neck. I feel ashamed. On a long scroll of paper tacked onto the wall of my studio space, I am drawing something in charcoal and chalks, filling it in with inks. I don't know what it is, it just needs to appear on the paper. It's taller than me. I have depicted the tall man before, in a batik called 'Man Hiding Behind Blue', but this is not him. The main thing is I'm here and lost in the process, barely finding time for tea breaks. I have to go earlier than the other students, Lily's nursery finishes at 15.15.

I worry that my father is worried about me, with his high blood pressure. He wants me to go on holiday with him and my stepmother. He comes to see me.

'Don't worry about me, girl. My blood pressure only goes up when I play bridge!'

'I see. Well, you are competitive.'

'Are you sure you don't want to come with us, to the coast?'

'I don't know.'

I don't fancy the twee hotel he has been frequenting, I've seen the photos of him playing mini golf there with my little brothers. We are walking around the lake in the park. He is stout these days. The lean young man he once was is completely disguised – his skin is marbled, he strolls with hands behind his back. He won't go into the museum to see the Textiles From the Subcontinent exhibition.

'Not today. No.'

He is not interested. I have begun to hope that my father might begin to talk to me as an adult. About life, about his life, about my mother. But he can't, he won't. We walk round the lake a second time. The silence between us is emphasised by the sound of the traffic on the main road, and by the ducks and geese. As we pass the waterfall I try to explain the hair-wash joke. Tata looks away as if he is somewhere else. As if he is wishing I was someone else.

Studying for a degree in Art is strange. The tutor and I are standing in front of the picture of my creature tacked to the wall. With clawed feet, a haughty profile, with legs, arms and wings. I like the textures and colours I've achieved on the body. The eyes are very strong too. I like the vibe of the thing. I feel better for having made it appear. The tutor sighs. He says nothing for a long time, then, 'You know what this is, don't you?'

'Er . . . I think it speaks for itself.'

'You should read Jung.'

'Oh.'

'Well, I'll tell you what it is. It's an archetypal image. The Hydra. The monster who lives in the swamp, she's half-bird. Cruel. It was one of Heracles's tasks to kill her.'

'Is, was, the Hydra female? I thought it was just a monster. With loads of heads – if you cut one off many more kept appearing.'

'Just a monster.'

'I think you might be thinking of the harpies.'

'Harpies. Hydras. Harpies. Hydras. Shrill female birdlike creatures who torment. Read your Jung. And by the way, I don't know what you're doing. What you think you're playing at. Do you?'

And he walks off to criticise the next student. Later he comes and leans on me, and whispers, 'And by the way, just a little word. Don't get any ideas about goddesses, will you? We had this girl who was obsessed with Isis, did little else in her time here. Got quite stroppy with me. Let's not have any of that. And, I was talking to Patrick, and I hear your last essay was not up to your usual standard. Something to do with "the spirit of the space that exists inside the pot". Forget it. You're studying Ceramics, not religion. Hmm. It's powerful, though. From here.'

'What?'

'Your harpy, Hydra, creature of the swamp. Whatever you want to call it. Ha ha. Bit like a swamp leaving home today. So much rain in the Dales this morning, surprised I got here at all.'

None of the lecturers live in Bradford, they drive in from picturesque moorland villages to teach us.

I have learnt a new batik technique using wax crayon from a Senegalese artist, extra-curricular to college. I've been using indigo. In my mind I'm in Kano where they fire big clay household pots in huge heaps, where there are acres of indigo vats. My latest batik is in shades of indigo with black outlines. There is a church spire wilting, a mosque crescent in a cracked sky. There is the face of a veiled woman next to the gutter. Another, in yellow, orange, red and brown, with black outlines, shows a factory with figures like insects trooping in, a molten hillside with one dead tree in the foreground, and a solitary crow. There's no water anywhere. Only one person, another student, has ever made any comment about the content of my work. Now this tutor has his harpy/Hydra Jungian hypothesis. College teaching talk is of texture and colour and form, squarely in the European tradition. It is as if I am not really here, alive, now. In the flesh, blood pumping.

'Can we discuss your dissertation? I can't quite get a handle on it.'

'My subject is Cartwright Hall.' The museum in the middle of the park, above the lake.

'And? I don't quite see . . . where this is leading.'

The theoretical tutor (a surreal and ironic title, I can't help thinking as I look into his ice-blue eyes) looks uncomfortable. Patrick becomes animated when talking about Walter Gropius. He has the uncanny habit of making every conversation revert back to his pet subject, the Bauhaus. He stares at me, glares at me. I feel grubby, my fingernails are clogged with clay, I have the shopping to do on the way home, balancing the bags on the handlebars of the bike, Lily on the back collected from nursery. It's all uphill. I have a batik class to run with single parents before that at Gingerbread. I have library books to return, new ones to source. I think the children have nits, and they've only just got over impetigo.

'I went to an exhibition at the Serpentine Gallery in Hyde Park ages ago.' (It feels like in another life.) 'They had imported people, craftspeople from India, as exhibits, for the duration of the show. There was a potter with a millstone on a pivot, sitting making pots, kicking the wheel round with his foot, turning out utility wear. There was a weaver . . .'

He interrupts me, looking at his watch. 'I don't quite follow. What has this got to do with your dissertation?'

'You know I've been focusing on crafts. Textiles, pottery.'

'Ceramics.'

'Did you know there was a grand opening of Cartwright Hall in 1901? It was a huge display of imperial pride. The lake was used for naval demonstrations.'

'And? How is this relevant?'

'Forty-seven people from a tribe in Somalia were installed in an enclosure. They did spear-throwing demonstrations twice a day. This exhibit was organised by a Viennese zookeeper. Several Somalis died, because of the climate. Stoneworkers building the museum died too. The thrust of my written work will be to link imperialism with our distinctions between art and craft. And demonstrate how these distinctions still operate in the art world today.'

'Oh God, do you have to? Well, I have to say that I don't advise you to pursue this.'

'No.'

'The library is not equipped . . .'

'I know. I've noticed.'

I can't wait to be amongst people, sitting around the table at Gingerbread, making pictures, shaking up colours in jam jars, washing out buckets in warm water.

ROWING

When the blows come it's an ordinary day, a dull day. An after-the-tail-end-of-the-holidays day. Tom is due back at his dad's in London. The tall man is not with us any more. I am at college. I have stopped smoking weed, I do yoga instead. I am still a bit jumpy, but I hold workshops and am learning to meditate. I go up to the allotment. We ride our bikes. We go swimming on Wednesdays at the old baths with the cubicles round the sides. We always stop and buy some chocolate on the way home, even with wet hair, even in a thunderstorm. We don't need the tall man. As far as I know, he's on methadone now. I have been through the mill and back and upside down and inside out and it's over. And I don't realise that this is the most dangerous time, when it's over. When I am simply getting on with my own life.

He rings, I have said I don't want him to ring. He's whiny.

'I've got a van. I can put Tom's bike in the van and get him to Leeds Station easy. Save you the bother of changing trains with him and all. I only want to help. I'm fond of him.'

'No thanks. It's fine.'

'No trouble.'

'No,' I said. 'No thanks.'

I don't want to ever be let down again. I don't want to be lied to. I don't want to see him. I don't need him, he's the one that needs me. We are ready, we'll cycle into town, leave my bike locked up at the station, get Tom's bike and him on the train to Leeds, and it will be harder for sure, but easier by a long way. Better.

It is Arshad's mum who rings the police, she saves my life. Arshad plays cricket at the bottom of the road with the boys. The tall man comes, he is magnetised to come. I don't want to let him in. I repeat through the door, 'I don't want you to take us to Leeds. Just go away. Please.'

Is there something in my tone of voice that signals that the end is here? That he is finally fully thwarted? That he can no longer control me? Tom is upstairs. The tall man is threatening to smash the windows, break in and smash the place up. I am terrified. He goes round the back. He is ranting, bellowing. I really don't want him to come in. The mistake I make is to go out to try and reason with him. Terror does that, you don't know what you're doing, you are not yourself. You're behind glass, you're in a film, you're not you, except you are. Arshad's mum sees the tall man yanking the metal washing line pole out of its concrete base in the garden and wielding it, shouting. I run. He has longer legs and runs faster.

I am lying on the pavement halfway up the street, I think I might be about to die. His hands are round my neck squeezing. Everything is in focus, the focus is too clear, zooming in on the cement in the wall, the garage door handles, the kerbstones. Tom is a long way away in the house. My throat is seizing up. Does the tall man stop himself from smashing me, strangling me, killing me? I don't know. A police car comes.

At the station, I sit in a corridor with people walking through while an officer takes photographs of my neck close up from several angles. There's a grey photographer's umbrella. No rain. A friend has made sure Tom gets back to London.

'Is there somewhere you can go?' the officer asks.

'Go?'

They tell me he'll be released from the cells after one night. I will be prey to a wild animal on the rampage. I will not sleep.

The only place I can think of to 'go', a fortress, where he won't think or know to follow me, is the manor house with the swimming pool. Where I first learnt to swim. I make one shaky phone call. I wrap a tie-dye scarf round my neck three times. On the train I keep adjusting it as we travel through the unreal peace of just fields. We stay in a newly converted flat above the table-tennis-room dungeon. We row up the Thames to go shopping. We drift back down, we steer and take turns with the oars. The rowlocks make a kind and reassuring jerk sound. Lily has a purple dress with a matching hairband. Frank rows easily, straighter than me. The water is green and gentle. The current is something we can work with and move through. We chat, we laugh, on the river there's no one to hear us. The sound of us is small, but spreads into the waterscape, ripples onto the fields, breathes out into the trees.

The swimming pool is covered now, there's a building on top of it. It seems small and echoey, no longer itself. I see I have outgrown it. The children muck about with the cherub fountain, but we keep ending up in the rowing boat. Being on the river. Moving.

RAINBOW

Some of the best conversations are also the worst. I am with my little brother, sitting either side of the bed. We are the only ones out of Tata's eight children who live near enough to get here in a hurry. The nurse has said that hearing is the last sense to go. If he has any senses left, my father can hear us. So we talk, we talk to him, for him, at him, over him, with each other. Our second stepmother comes into the room wringing her hands.

'They've given me a bed, just down the corridor. I'm shattered,' she says. 'You'll be with him. I'll just snatch a couple of hours.'

'That's fine, you get some sleep,' my brother says.

'It's been a long day,' I say.

And the phrase sounds hollow and meaningless. It's after midnight.

She sighs. 'He just went upstairs to lie down with a cup of tea. Straight from the garden. He didn't even drink the tea, it went cold. Look. He's still got earth on his hands. He hadn't even washed them. Look at them. You'd think they might have, you know, washed his hands. Look at his nails.'

'It doesn't matter. Don't worry about it,' my brother says.

She is looking around vaguely. Is she looking for a cloth, a basin, soap, a towel?

'He might like having earth on his hands. It's OK, I'm sure,' I say.

She gives me one of her looks. It says that my father and the man she is married to, her husband, are two completely different people.

'I am so exhausted, if I don't lie down for a bit I will fall over. You'll let me know, you'll call me, won't you? The nurse knows where I am, if . . .'

We all leave the sentence unfinished. We look at him lying there, pale, a bit blubbery, barely breathing. We nod at her solemnly. She leaves.

'I think he would have liked to have earth on his hands, even if it is just English earth.'

'Do you remember the box?'

'With little yellow ducks on?'

'An Easter egg box, I think.'

'A Polish Easter egg box. God, I was scared of that box.'

'So was I. Do you hear that, Tata? We were scared of the box with the Polish earth in it.'

'"For when I am buried," you said.'

We keep talking to him, over him, with him, including him.

'Where is it now?'

'It'll be somewhere. He wouldn't have let her throw it out.'

'Recycle it. I can imagine her trying to.' We grin, we are able to laugh a bit now she's not in the room.

'Do you remember looking in it?'

'Course I do. I seem to remember it was a bit of an anticlimax. Very dry like grit. Hey, I got the evening paper, thought we could do the crossword with him, he might join in. You like the crossword, Tata, shall we start with the quick, and move onto the cryptic? How about this, one down . . . ?'

'Get the old brain cells going. Although the quick ones are sometimes very cryptic actually.'

'Let's not get philosophical.'

'Yet. Do you know he was trying to improve his vocabulary, with crosswords, the dictionary and the thesaurus? He told me it was so he could write his memoirs. Properly.'

We don't say he might not get round to that now. The crater of loss is yet to open. My brother reads out crossword clues. We have adopted a jovial tone, jovial and calm. The night shifts to absolute quiet outside, street lights gaze on emptiness. I don't want Tata to die in hospital, but he is. We talk as the rain drizzles in the orange light. There is water and glasses on a tray, we share it, sip it and then offer him some, knowing he can't drink, I think we know he will never drink again. Noticing each breath inflating and then deflating his

231

chest, we are breathing along. Holding our breath with his. Each miniscule movement we note, even if it might not be an actual movement. I hold my father's hand.

We talk about us, the old times, death, life, television, religion, food and Tata. And our voices are the same to me as they've always been. We are back in our old bedroom in the dark. After he's come in with apples and oranges cut up on a plate, after we've cleaned our teeth, after he's popped his head round the door to turn off the light. We are back listening to his footsteps on the stairs first thing in the morning, the sound of him opening the porch door to pick up the post and the paper off the doormat, the sound of him doing his exercises, aahhing and puffing, the sound of the milk cupboard opening and closing, coffee percolating, porridge blurping, newspaper pages turned abruptly, the sound of brushes briskly polishing shoes, the lawnmower stuttering, the hosepipe. We run round the garden with the water spraying a rainbow. We eat chocolate squares from purple foil on Filey Brigg, we peer down the iron steps at the mirror of the Emperor's Pool. He takes out his hanky and spits and wipes at our grubby faces on the way into church, tutting, we wince with disgust and embarrassment. He swears as the car gears won't cooperate. He can't hear when my sisters play 'Young girl get out of my mind' on full blast, to put him off marrying S. One of his little fingers is bent back permanently from a game he played in Poland, he trapped it in a door before the war. He watches *Doctor Zhivago* yet again, and when it gets to the bit when they break the sheet of ice on the outside of the cattle truck, he says, 'I was once in a cattle truck like that for five days.' He plays the piano haltingly on Christmas Eve, picking out Polish carols. He hid under a sheet in the snow to escape from a concentration camp with a Moroccan. He is tall and thin with a sheen to his hair, he moves like a streak playing football. He is flabby and grey and mottled and slow. He prays in Latin sometimes, and I want to pray too.

We behave as if he is listening, if he stirs the slightest bit we take it as an acknowledgement. When the light changes to pre-dawn pink I feel a contentment, there is a happiness in the room with the three of us. My little brother is easy to be with. No one else in the world could or would do this, gentle joking, genuine affection. No one else could share this vigil. I have missed his companionship so much, I cannot understand how we have been so separate. He says things I am thinking. My father is listening. We let him know that if he's going to die now, that we don't mind, if it's time. I cry a bit but not in a desperate way. The tears just seep out of me, making my cheeks wet and salty, running down into my neck. I think, *I don't know if I can bear being an orphan*, knowing that this is a silly selfish thought. I think, *He must have been so worried about me, if only* . . . But the calm in the room soothes these feelings, strokes them out. Within the tears, laughter is still possible.

It rains at the graveside, it's a horrid day in April. Frail daffodils are bullied and buffeted by the wind. My father is buried on top of my mother. There is room for three, a stacking system, but a decision has been made to close the grave with just two. There is a Polish flag on the coffin, it's just two bits of material sewn together. Red and white. The soil here is brown. The Polish earth looks like gritty ashes. Hard to imagine anything sprouting from it. It is scattered on the coffin, which is then covered with shovelfuls from the mound of clayey brown cemetery soil, sticky in the rain. We carry umbrellas. I cannot believe that I am not visiting my mother's grave here, with my father standing beside me. How can he be dead and in a coffin, and not scrabbling about with a trowel around the rose bush he planted? How can he not be going off to fill up the watering can and throwing the old flowers and rank flower water onto the compost heap? I cannot believe that I will never walk between the yew trees with my father again.

In the future, I will visit this double grave. I will sit and feed my youngest daughter here, I will bring peonies. I will sense both of my parents here, but mostly my father. As I walk along between the yew trees, he will say, 'What on earth are you hanging around here for? Get on with living. Live. Just get on with it.'

The year he died, the year I nearly died too, I was ripe for folly. In the future I will have the clarity to see the ripples, the reactions, the causes and effects, placidly. In grief, in shock, tremored, raw and skinless, I just wanted to be lapped in balm. I had no fight in me. The flight option crept up behind me, presenting itself so smoothly, so sneakily.

Soap

There's a water pump. It's a stiff and clanky contraption and hard work just to fill up a bucket, there's a knack to it. Water is stored in earthenware jars with little metal plates as lids, in the kitchen, where people squat to cook. They are scrupulously clean, they have to be. There is a word, *jutta*, that means dirty, polluting in a religious sense. I reckon the Bengalis here in the ashram think that white people are *jutta*, full stop. We are not careful, we don't wash our hands enough, or properly. Given water to share from a jug, we put our lips straight to it and drink, while they hold it up above their tilted mouths. Their lips never touch the jug, the water falls in a liquid ribbon, straight into their mouths. So they keep an eye on us, when we're using the pump, the squat loos, and when we eat. There's no cutlery. You're meant to use your right hand to eat, the left is for cleaning the other end, with water poured from a jug – there's no loo paper. You have to keep washing your hands with soap, or you get ill. I suppose because of us they wash even more than usual, and have to throw water away if we taint it. We make more work for them with our thoughtlessness.

The first morning we all file along to the river clutching towels, changes of clothes, soaps and shampoos and conditioners, brushes and combs, like offerings. There are British Indians in the 'English party', but most are hippies really, an ex-bus-driver, therapists, an artist, teachers, a smattering of children, soul-seekers, dropouts, would-be visionaries. Some are more annoying than others. Most live up beaten tracks in the sticks in the UK. They don't know what to make of us from inner-city Bradford, or Pramila, a Gujarati from Wimbledon. There is an unspoken hierarchy in play, and the city is low. Here in India it's the other way round. There are tall date palms like Arabic script against the sky on the way to the river. Old men lounge on string beds under mango trees, monkeys watch with vicious teeth and vacant expressions, scratching themselves. There are carts and bikes, mange-ridden dogs in packs, skinny cats. There are no cars – it's too sandy. It's a fifteen-minute walk over makeshift plank bridges, avoiding slimy cess ditches and hairy black pigs. It's early morning and the sun is faded, the air balmy and a bit jaded. It's January and I am wearing a sari and cardigan and sweating. Pramila showed me how to wrap a sari, lent me a petticoat and a purple blouse. The children run on ahead. There is mumbling and grumbling from the adults, out of their comfort zone, competitive, condescending, complaining, 'We could have had a shower quite happily back at the ashram.'

'But there is not enough water for all bodies. For bathing. Clothes-washing. This is better. And so, so holy – Jamuna River. You are very lucky.'

This is Rashmay, our chief herder, explainer, encourager, who shepherds us with too much enthusiasm. I see from the frown that flashes now and then across his brow that he is exasperated and incredulous at some of our foibles. And I feel embarrassed by my Britishness. I don't belong to this herd, do I? Half of me is delighted with the scent of the air, the soil, drinking in all the differences, and the other half has an inward running commentary, asking myself, *How the hell did I get here? It's OK to meet an Indian guru, sure, I get that, natural curiosity, but you're here now for real, it's real. And what is this actually?* And, *Who are you kidding, if not yourself?*

When the river opens out in front of us beyond the long grasses of the dunes, quiet, expansive, curving, full of the sky's yellow pink light, everyone shuts up for a moment. Then, while listening to instructions, I nod, I grin, I attempt the side-to-side head wobble without wishing to cause offence, and then extract myself from the pack. I sidle away with my children, upriver, well away from them all, as nicely as I can, humming and wearing a small intolerant smile. I can still hear them at a distance arguing about shampoo and conditioner. I can't bear the idea of bathing in this beautiful river with them, and I know this is an ungenerous and unspiritual feeling, but I can't help it.

A man with a stick walks across from the other side of the river at the shallowest point, trailing two immense water buffaloes. Their curly horns and wide rumps are outlandish and infallible. A woman on the shore stands up from the stone she seems to have been pounding with cloth, hefts a basket of wet washing onto her head and then stalks into the dunes, looking back at the circus of us as if she's never seen acrobats before. On a rise in the dunes she proceeds to drape her washing out to dry carefully, over the shrubs and long grasses. Her drying saris catch the sunlight, each one is an outrageous song of colour. There is defiance in them.

I have been instructed by Rashmay to bathe modestly, wearing both petticoat and the tight, too-short blouse. Upstream I can see a woman, blouse-less, with a floor-length petticoat hitched up under her armpits, soaping, then dunking herself thoroughly in the water. I glance downstream at Rashmay on the bank wearing his white dhoti, like an ankle-length sarong, a baggy T-shirt and his *gamcha*, a thin red gingham cotton towel slung over his shoulder. The *gamcha* is multipurpose, practical, for drying, wiping, for shading, and to stash or carry stuff in. (Women use the ends of their saris.) Rashmay is guarding the English party, protecting them from themselves. He eggs them on with smiling. He is clean, his hair coconut-oiled, after a bucket bath earlier at the ashram.

I unwrap myself from my sari, wriggle out of my knickers,

undo the petticoat and do it up again under my arms, taking the blouse off with relief – it's so tight and sweaty – and I wade into the river. Lily is sitting in it already. Frank has the soap. I didn't bring shampoo, we can do without it for today. I just want to swim. I want to float far out in the middle of the river. I want to feel I have arrived in India. Properly. I want to feel India in me. I want to lie back with my ears below the level of the river.

I swim elegantly, the petticoat is like a giant petal. I float for a while, and try to inhabit a carefree headspace. I get the soap and hang suspended in the water and wash my private parts at last after the long journey. I lob the soap back to the shore. I emerge from the river in a drenched clinging petticoat and dutifully perform a peculiar shuffling dance. Which entails trying not to be anywhere near naked, at any point, trying not to show my legs or my breasts. I rinse my clothes out, and get dressed in clean undergarments. It is quite a carry-on. I rewrap the sari. Pramila told me in London, 'You will need to put on the sari in the dark, you know. In the jungle when we go to the villages. Just practise. And practise again.'

I remembered being seven and walking around with an encyclopaedia balanced on my head, climbing on and off the furniture, practising 'deportment'. It was a game, it was the 1960s, it was ironic. Yet we played it seriously.

We can't find the soap. And I worry because in London when we were chock full of her puris, chutney and chai, Pramila also said, 'And buy English soap to take with you. Palmolive is best. In India there is export quality and then everything else, rubbish, falls apart, or you know, adulterated. Not pure. You will need to bring your own soap.'

We can't find our soap in the River Jamuna. It stays there, 'export quality', somewhere on the sandy bottom. I shake out my hair, and realise the comb is back at the ashram.

'Oh. You bathe like a peasant woman. Ha ha,' Rashmay says with his dazzling smile in place.

He is younger than me, shorter than me, much more beautiful than me. I refuse to react to his disapproval of peasant women in particular or women in general.

'Did you say a prayer? To the river?' he asks.

I nod and shake out my hair again. We plod back through the sand dunes, listening to the other English children moaning and talking about pizza and fish and chips.

HOLY WATER

Everything is holy. Everything is blessed, offered to the deities before we eat or drink it. When I venture into the kitchen to try and help, and see the lethal-looking blade embedded in a wooden block for cutting and shredding vegetables, I feel, for once, out of my depth in a kitchen. Perhaps my help would be more trouble than it's worth. I am scrutinised by the cook, Radha, and feel ungainly, too tall and like a child at the same time. Although I am freshly bathed with my hair oiled and obedient in a plait, wearing a new sari, it is difficult for my inner voice not to question it all, the brass figures that live in the temple and get bathed and dressed and fed and watered, worshipped and put to bed at night. I smell some cloves and ask for the Bengali word, and the cook frowns and throws them out. Even smelling is polluting, she laughs as she says '*jutta*', and points me towards the flask of chai on the threshold of the kitchen. She doesn't want me in her kitchen. She points to the roof with her eyebrows, puts a lid on the roti dough she has been kneading, then pours out and hands me a steaming steel cup.

'Gurudev chai.'

So I take it up the steps onto the roof for him. Radha calls me back to hand me a cup of water, he always drinks water first. I don't know what I am becoming, I don't understand the role I am cast in. I feel naked, like I've shed a skin and not grown anything back in its place. And that everyone knows everything except me. On the roof he is deep in conversation but nods for me to sit, so I do. From up here I can see the cows, languid in the heat, fly-flicking and chewing cauliflower leaves. The sun is in a haze. A woman squatting on the step of her one-room brick house feels a long way away, and not entirely real. There are wrought-iron gates on the ashram. A shiny white estate car, new, is washed and polished and put to bed under a cover at night.

He doesn't look at me but has left some water in the bottom of the cup.

'You drink.'

He carries on talking in a mixture of Bengali and Hindi to a young man with a moustache wearing chinos and a stripy shirt, with broad bare feet. His second toes are longer than his big toes. There's a green comb in his shirt pocket. The guru is slight, with long black hair and Mongolian-looking eyes.

'This is Shyam,' he says slowly.

Then he gets up and goes to the edge of the roof and shouts for more chai. There is a flurry from the kitchen and two cups of chai are delivered by a boy in a dhoti. I drink the remains of his water.

'Good,' he says.

Pramila has told me this is the best and quickest way to advance spiritually – to eat or drink guru's leftovers. I have nothing to lose. I am in another world, there is a mesmeric quality to everything here, and a sense of simplicity. Being here is like being stoned, but without so many laughs.

There is an Englishman who has made all this happen, who translates, who speaks Hindi awkwardly. I prefer the unspoken, the non-translation version. I want India unadulterated. I wonder what my father would think, have I become a heathen? It has seemed like a natural and inevitable process. From the meditation class in Bradford, to a camp on the Welsh borders, meeting the guru, and him looking into my eyes and simply saying to me, 'You coming India.'

Like it was already a fact. Like he had a perfectly ordinary way of seeing into the future.

I don't know what he and Shyam are saying, but Shyam's eyes twinkle at me. We sip our chai. In the garden below I can see where the marigolds and spinach have been watered, like sweat marks on the earth. A brahmachari in a white dhoti swings into the yard on a bike with a bag of yoghurt, chiming the bell. Frank is sitting on the back of the bike, side-saddle. At first I don't recognise him, his hair is so short. He's wearing a purple Greenpeace T-shirt and a dhoti.

I wake from a nap in the late afternoon to the sound of slow strokes mopping the yard. Radha has a bucket of water mixed with cow dung. She is coating every inch of the yard with this dark soupy mixture, it's flecked with straw and grains. It looks like fudge. It dries into a light soft surface. The pump makes its clanking noise, Radha is washing her feet.

In the evening a conch sounds out, as if from ancient times, the drums pound and then fade into a watery heartbeat. Burning camphor leaves little traces hanging like question marks in the air. And water is thrown over us, as if to make us clean. *Washing away our sins*, I think, like a Catholic. We have wooden malas for mantras like rosary beads. I think, *Hail Mary*, and laugh to myself. Munching bits of blessed fruit, for a split second I taste communion wafer and smell frankincense. Guru meets my eyes in the cloak of the night.

SINKING

We are halfway there. Although it is unclear where 'there' is, just 'MP', they say. And Madhya Pradesh means simply 'middle country', it is huge. This morning I bathe in a river sitting in a bowl of pinkish rock. There are lizards and snakes, this is apparently tiger country. The water is clear and cold and deep enough to swim in, and I am past caring what is done or not done. I rebel and swim with only my sari tied around me so I can float free, do a few strokes of proper crawl and get puffed. Then I return to the inevitable stone by the shore, don a fresh petticoat and pound my clothes on the stone.

I haven't seen another woman swim, unmarried girls wear floor-length nighties and dip under the water politely. Of course the men and boys do, and charge off rocks, splashing and shouting and mucking about. Rinsing out my sari has become a small ritual. Wherever I am, it is always the same and always different. I wade out shin-deep and throw the sari out like a net, so it floats on the surface of the water. I watch in the stillness of time as the cloth absorbs the water and darkens. I steep myself in the moment so it stretches. I watch the sari frittering on the surface, the colours wrinkling and shapeshifting. Then I haul it in, all crinkled up and dripping, and squeeze and rinse and squeeze and again, and throw it out again, and haul it in, until it's done. It is a chore but it is satisfying, it is doing the laundry, but it is meditating.

Prashant puts his and guru's dhotis in a bucket to soak in the sun. He sprinkles Ariel powder from a sachet, and the bucket froths up to the brim. Wearing a sacred string and underpants, he soaps himself vigorously all over. Then rinses and ties his gingham *gamcha* round his waist while he deals with the underpants. Detergent bubbles float downstream. I worry about water pollution. The space around guru seems to swell whenever he is close. He asks me to see these Indian youths like Krishna, the god of the universe with ten thousand milkmaid attendants. The god of the Rasa Lila, those moonlit riverside dances. The god who lifts mountains, dances on the head of a many-headed snake and has the whole universe in his mouth. He plays a flute, he's black. His reality is the only real reality, everything else is an illusion, maya. Here in India, this is quite seductive.

I am getting my head round the everyday stuff as we travel. It's like camping or being on tour. My personal space has shrunk to my sleeping bag. It's the bowing, foot-touching and all the brass deities that still give me problems. In my head I don't buy it. Yet I'm here and everyone around me behaves as though I do buy it. I have previously encountered Hare Krishna drummers in Oxford Street and kept a very wide berth.

Very possibly we are being love-bombed and brainwashed, and I know this vaguely at the back of my mind, but don't think it applies to me. I can't. Frank has been adopted to sing, and learn ragas. Lily now has brass Radha and Krishna figures given to her by guru. She looks after them with great concentration, they need rose water in their bath, they need fresh flowers, and bananas if possible. Every day. They have sets of clothes that need changing. I didn't let her have a Barbie – is this any different? Is it better or worse than Barbie and Ken? They have a special brass pot for their bath water. I don't believe in it. Except that everyone around me does, there are grown adults with figures they look after too. Really. In fact this is a mini version of what goes on inside the temple. And in the back of my mind is the smell of frankincense, statues and saints and purple cloths, my brothers in cassocks and lace surplices, the monstrance, holy water, communion hosts and feast days and sin. This is the same but different. When we get 'there', maybe I will work it all out.

Five people have diarrhoea, so I need to concentrate on being clean, on staying well. I may as well say the mantra guru whispered in my ear. Yesterday I fell asleep on a palm-leaf mat in Prashant's mother's front yard with my sari end over my head, despite all the comings and goings. Later we sat beside a huge mango tree and sang under the moon. We had to wait until afterwards to eat. I was ravenous, rice and dhal never tasted so wonderful.

The Bradford in my mind is a very, very long way away, and it's just grey. Suspended in mist, in ether. I wallpapered my bedroom in white flowers. I pumped myself up with yoga daily, to clear the tall man out of my life. And keep him out. He managed to get a prison sentence converted to time in rehab. Addicts find so many ways not to change, sadly. He doesn't. Each morning I woke up, and within a minute, there it was, that awful remembering. My father is dead, he's not here, he's not anywhere. The body clothed in a navy suit and tie, the body wearing brogues and buried under the earth was not Tata. I can't get used to it, I keep thinking of him – he's always been there. And now there's nothing.

They call it the jungle, bamboos, jackfruit, and mango trees, dry rice paddies, wattle and mud houses with deep verandas, grain in baskets, rats in rafters, cows. At the village pumps, brass pots and plastic buckets, the women and girls do all the water-carrying. They seem to do all the work. We have been told to say we are married women with husbands working hard in the UK. We are told so many mixed-up things, both practical and incredible. Frank is picking up Bengali. I am picking up a mixture of Hindi, Bengali and English, a group language which sounds childish. Nothing is as it seems.

The jungle means the country, it's not like the jungle in my mind. But my mind is confused, the problem always with English minds and English bodies, according to Rashmay. Everything is so very beautiful and at the same time ugly. So profoundly true, and patently false. When the five-day-and-night non-stop singing of gods' names, with drums and ragas, bells, and passion breaks out, the Bengalis respond with ululations that ring round and round the cow-dung floor we sit around. The sound of ragas day and night builds up until people roll around in the cow dust, wailing and weeping, and I find myself hugging fragile widows in white, as frail as paper, wiping away tears and snot, calming the shaking. It's catching. And I sink to the ground drowning in grief. I can't tell whose grief is whose any more. Later, refreshed by the collective catharsis, with the ragas still continuing, I drink very strong chai on a wobbly bench and find myself laughing loudly, cackling. I can hear my father's voice: 'This is group hysteria, pure and simple. This is dangerous, you are wading in deep waters.'

'You are just afraid of the Bible,' I say back.

'Nonsense. Absolute nonsense.' His voice fades.

Towards dawn I go inside the makeshift temple. Behind the celestial lovers surrounded by lotuses on moonlit waters, garlanded with white jasmine flowers, is the shining black goddess of destruction, of everything and nothing. Kali: her red tongue lolls out, her many arms are fully weaponed, she has a necklace of skulls. Despite appearances, the vibe reminds me of Mary, Our Lady, the Queen of the Oceans, the Queen of Heaven.

After five days and nights the music stops. The silence is disconcerting in the early morning. Shyam, kohl-eyed, does a comic mincing dance, imitating a girl balancing a clay pot of curds from the temple on his head. Then he smashes it on purpose. Everyone rushes to taste or smear curd on their foreheads. And then people start chucking water at each other, the holy cow dust floor turns to mud, and we are shrieking and shouting and laughing and smearing mud and slipping and chasing. We process down to the river with people playing samba rhythms with spoons on tin plates. We plunge into the water together. It's over.

Springs

I am in India in my head, it never goes away. Except I'm not, I'm in Bradford. My allotment is getting a new addition, a James Grieve apple tree that Z is giving me because it wasn't doing too well in her back yard. Before Eid, a goat from her next-door neighbours' yard got out and chewed away all the bark down one side, and chomped the leaves and shoots. It was a big goat, oblivious to its fate, and it had given her quite a turn when she saw it out of the kitchen window. Z's neighbours joked that the meat would taste even better.

I've got help to plant the apple tree. It's Boxing Day and it's hailing. I have fingerless gloves and cold earlobes. Tariq and his family are leaving town soon, and this is the only time he has, and he knows about trees and roots.

'This weather. We must be crazy, but it's worth it. It should survive if we're careful.'

He gets the tree out of his car, he's clipped some straggling roots already with his top-of-the-range secateurs. Tiny white hail balls lie about everywhere, but the ground's not frozen. We dig a wide hole and plant the apple tree, I hold it upright while he covers the roots. We water it, then stamp around on the earth, and then water it again, each of us pouring. He places his hand steady on the trunk.

'I'm sad we have to leave. But it's just too hard for us here. This community.'

Tariq's ballads on guitar have antagonised some of the elders. He is a sweet and thoughtful man, with a round head and a soulful voice, but is seen as too radical, too Green, here. We decide the roots are well covered, and despite the cold the tree is settling, it looks happier already, up here on the hill with the view of the moors, next to Paradise Cemetery wreathed in brambles. We walk out of the allotments and stare at the woods below us, the valleys beyond, the mill chimneys, and sigh deeply before we part. We have both wished to feel at home here, to put down our roots and belong. I am not water being easily absorbed into the earth, but more like mercury. Slipping and slithering and unable to settle.

I haunt the woods with the children. If anywhere, I could belong here, with the great beech trees that cling, their roots rippling like giant grey fingers. Trailing through the mud, we stamp loudly across the troll bridge, to scare them. We wade in the water in wellies. We sit and ride the fallen trunks beside the confluence, where the two streams meet. The iron water of the red, and the white stream that flows clear through the bluebells in May.

We make dams, play pooh sticks, chase a ping-pong ball up and down the stream. Watching the routes it finds through the rocks and sticks and mud banks, we concentrate, lost in play. The sound of the water churning and chattering massages the inside of my brain. The sound of the city is a faint etching here, a peculiar thought. We decide to build a fire next time, when it's dry.

Where the two springs meet, the red trickling out of a mini cave in the earth, the white confident and stately, there's a backwash, as though the springs don't know how to take to each other. Don't know what to be. I touch the water, and then anoint my forehead. It's not a stoop of holy water in church, I'm not genuflecting or crossing myself. Lily collects the pink water, because 'red and white make pink', in a jam jar to take home for the bath of her small gods. Cars screech round and down the hairpin bend that runs through the woods. In the layby at the bottom, people torch cars. So when you skip over the stepping stones to cross the stream and walk up onto the road, there's always a crusting of soot, ash, charcoal, and broken glass.

Riverbed

I came back to India after hearing guru is dead. I suppose everything ends in death. I'm on a kind of pilgrimage of my own. It's just the three of us, me, Frank, and Lily, in the foothills of the Himalaya visiting a cave by a river. There was a train, then a bus, then we rode through the woods on horseback, there's no road. Coming into the valley felt weirdly like we were riding into a pop-up book. The river is held in pebbles. There are driftwood islands and two shacks squatting on the riverbed selling chai and hard biscuits. You can see the monsoon high watermarks on the sides of the gorge, the level is way over our heads. We sit here in what will be, and what has been, several metres of water. It's the dry season, we dunk biscuits in sweet gingery chai. We are sitting in the middle of a dry river. Later we can go into the cave. You can see it from here, it's not big. Just a black hole in the bank a bit like a keyhole.

I suppose prophets are ten a penny in India. Saints, sadhus – anyone can don an orange cloth and wander about. The prophet that appeared in my head before I met guru emerged from this cave. Meditating on a windy, chimney-pot-rattling night in Bradford, a young man with long hair and thick eyebrows reached out and gave me a flower. When I opened my eyes the flower and the prophet still felt more real than my gloomy kitchen and the sputtering gas fire. I can see now that that was the beginning of this whole odyssey, and wonder if meditation can be dangerous. There is a fire on the opposite bank to the cave, it's never allowed to go out.

The shiny white estate car was in a head-on collision with a lorry. Two killed, then laid out on the side of the road on white cloths. Someone took a photo of guru and Prashant, now just dead bodies. In the ashram, after enormous outpourings of collective grief and desperation, was the inevitable jockeying for succession between Rashmay and the tall Englishman. I went to look into their eyes. And saw something unhinged. A frenzy buzzing around their heads. There were factions and rumours. Guru and Prashant were buried in lotus position covered in salt, next to the little mud temple in MP. Since their deaths several villagers say they have met them walking on the path to the river. He was never really a man, they say. In the ashram there was no sense anywhere. Not even by the river, where I used to meditate each morning sitting on an old jute sack. By my favourite tree where I once saw a snake dance in rhythm with my singing, there was a pile of human shit, and fruit bats squawking, swarmed overhead. So we came away, back to the beginning, to another river.

When we enter the cave it's very small and very dark. The temple on the other bank of the river holds the prophet's samadhi place, his grave, in marble. We are sleeping in a room behind it with lots of windows. I have been given karma yoga to do in exchange for staying. I collect dry mule dung from the riverbed in a basket. And then pound it up into little flakes to put on the flower beds round the temple. For three hours a day.

'This is strange work. Weird. It doesn't seem like work. More like punishment. Like breaking stones. Why didn't they ask you to help in the kitchen?' Frank asks.

I pound dung clods with a round stone. The people here move about slowly, like clockworks, like they are underwater. I try not to think of *The Prisoner* or *The Wicker Man* here. I presume there are reasons why I have not been asked to help in the kitchen, despite the fact that this prophet's teachings eschew caste, race and pollution laws. I like being outside anyway, combing the riverbed. It is easier with the children too. So I try to embrace my task.

'I bet you, Mum, when the rains come all this will be washed away anyway. All this donkey shit. It's pointless.'

I try to resist my children's indignation. They have both been having nightmares in the room with seven beds we share with no one else.

'It's like the seven dwarves.'

'Maybe.'

'It isn't, though. Not really.'

Lily has made a little altar for her figures on the windowsill. She picks flowers for them behind the temple. At first our room looked like a luxury option, with its big windows and river view. With real beds, not floor mats. However, each night is an ordeal. One wakes then settles, then the other wakes. I don't feel like sleeping or waking, myself. I dream of snakes, I dream of complicated situations in railway stations, I dream of being pursued and captured . . . I don't want to dream.

Wherever we wander along the river it feels like we are being watched, and not kindly. Only sitting on the bench outside the chai shack in the riverbed do we seem to blend in. I ask if there is another room we could use. It feels like I have collected and pounded enough dung to cover several allotments now. And I'm tired. There's a skinny German guy who calls himself Hanuman, after the monkey god. He tends the fire that never goes out. He's the only one that meets my eyes and talks to the children softly, the other people here ignore them. It is Hanuman who explains, 'I heard you asked for a transfer. You know, actually, I'm not surprised that room is freaking you out.'

'Oh? Why's that then? It's got the best view.'

'Yes. I am sorry to hear you've been having nightmares.' He ruffles Frank's hair.

'Do you think there's something funny about the room then?'

'I wouldn't sleep in it.'

He sleeps next to the fire, in a shack that looks like it might have been washed away and then put back together again. He takes a long in-breath, and we wait.

'You see, the thing is, there was this group here recently. They just stayed too long.'

'Oh?'

'Well, it was only after about ten days that we realised they were using, you know, heroin. It was all a bit heavy. People got upset. Understandably. That they should be doing that, here.'

'And when was this?'

'Just recently. No one has used that room since. We didn't realise at first. People have strong experiences here. You can imagine. It's a powerful place. The room was really properly cleaned after they left. They didn't want to leave. And we found stuff, you know. I suppose you may be picking up on the vibes.'

'I see. This is what we have been trying to get away from, back home. This story, those vibes.'

'You know then. There was a bit of a split actually. Because some people thought that they should be allowed to be here, that it would do them good. If not here, where? You know, where can people go? What is a refuge or a retreat? They were Italian. Anyway a lot of people got angry and upset, including some of the villagers. Everything goes downstream. Personally I came to the conclusion, sorry kids, but I thought they were taking the piss. Just taking advantage, you know.'

'Yes. Your English is very good.'

'Oh, I've been in London. A lot of people come to India to get away from things. But in this life there's no getting away, is there? Not really. Might look different, but it's all the same.'

'Yeah. Maybe.'

I like Hanuman, even though he's hiding behind a name. I still don't know I'm part German, no one ever mentioned it. My father certainly didn't. In the future I will be able to own it, know it. And guess why it might have been left out.

LEVELS

These were the lake lands, the Somerset Levels. Burrow Mump, Glastonbury Tor and Wearyall Hill were three of the islands. One could be Avalon. The lake people island-hopped and fished in long wooden boats. There are still channels, dykes, flooding fields, orchards and the River Brue.

First, there is the field with the outdoor kitchen. Water is collected from the tap by the farm with a hundred cats, carried in containers in a wheelbarrow, for washing and washing-up. I have agreed to cow-sit and learn to milk. It's high summer. Sitting on a crate, my head resting against

Lavender's flank, I finally grasp the technique before the cowman goes away for ten days. Squeezing, pulling, coaxing, squirting, aiming, using bread-kneading muscles, my arms ache in new places. Half filling my first bucket gives me a real thrill. Except Frank is practising driving in Lavender's field. The car crawls up behind me. I am shocked and jolted from my meditative yet pleased with myself state, Lavender flinches and kicks the bucket over. I watch the milk being swallowed up by the grass. Back where it came from, so laboriously, via Lavender's four stomachs. Still, I know how to milk now and the worst has already happened. It is calming, even blissful, sitting on the crate milking under the oak trees with my head resting in Lavender's coat.

Milking is quiet, is a contributing task, but it's also an excellent way of getting away from people. From the circle of tents and the tipi and the aftermath of smoky evenings, away from people's halva recipes, porridge, and bad chai. Examining the stars and listening to the guy who lives in a bender in the thicket playing his didge, are high points in the field. It would be hard to explain why I haven't left them all to it. Surely I've finished with this charade, these people? They hang round my neck like a raggedy family. I am not scared to go back to my own life on my own, just reluctant. I am a spectator, going through the motions. I am flotsam, left by the tide. And then the ninja appears.

After the field is the house. Too many people in a house is far worse than in a field. We escape with the ninja into Glastonbury, to chomp hot pasties from Burns the Bread. If it's fine, we go to the River Brue and swim. There are willows bending over the water, with branches an easy height to jump off and lean on. We hang our clothes up and sit in the clefts of the willows and nestle on the grassy banks, relishing the quiet. Away from the collective madness. I wade amongst green reeds, loving the feeling of them caressing my skin. I lie on my back looking at the clouds as they drift by above us. This is the best bath available. Standing up in the river, we see we are all coated and draped around with green reeds and willow leaves. We are the gods and goddesses of the river. We start laughing and can't stop, setting each other off again, so we can't even remember what's funny because everything is. The ninja does a handstand, his feet wave, waggle and wriggle, and he disappears. When he surfaces the hair under his dreads is sheeny. He's an otter. His eyelashes twinkle with water.

Then we fill up the water containers from the white and the red springs by Chalice Well. The red iron water comes out of the wall of the gardens in a thin pipe. The white calcium water we collect from the other side of the road by the cafe, where the trees are strung with blessings and wishes, and the air is full of ganja smoke. We mix the red and the white together, it's like drinking gin.

We make the detour to Wearyall Hill, which is Pisces in the zodiac landscape, the fish. We stare at the Somerset Levels all around us, at the town and the Tor, which the Tibetan monk says is rose quartz. With half-shut eyes that defy time, I see lakes everywhere, dotted islands, a boat culture. We light coconut incense from the Africa shop by the holy thorn. Some people think this tree is a descendant of a staff planted in the hillside by Jesus's uncle, Joseph of Arimathea, when he landed. He was a tin merchant. People believe Jesus came here too. There are prayer rags and ribbons on the iron railing round the thorn. It flowers every year at Christmas. A relative of this plant thrives in the churchyard on the high street, the Queen receives a sprig from it every year.

In the future, Lily and I will climb Wearyall Hill and the thorn will look stark dead, slain by a chainsaw, lopped limbs akimbo. Ribbons will have multiplied tenfold, wishing it back to life. On the undersides of the Tor, next to the Egg Stone, we will visit another thriving thorn, laden with prayer rags. Around its trunk someone will have tied a tie and left it there. It will need untying.

PISSING IN TRIANGLES

The ninja, Lily, and I have opted to stay in the hut by the river rather than in the main mud ashram. It may be mud, but it looks like a barracks. I don't know why we've come back to India, except we have. Frank decided to stay in the UK and I miss him. The ninja is deeply disappointed by the jungle, it is not up to scratch, compared with his idea of jungles. The hut is a wooden frame with palm-leaf mats tacked on and we have a small veranda and a two-brick fire, so we can make our own chai. I have bought two buckets in the market. To walk to the river I go past roots and knobbly shrubs and rocks and dry bays of stony beaches. In monsoon time the river is a huge body covering all this. Now it is an arm, green and quiet. Adivasis, the indigenous forest people, walk about silently on the other bank. They make depressions in the shingle beside the river, and water pools into them, filtered by the shingle. I wash in the river and carry my wet clothes up to hang in the trees that lace around each other like entwining limbs that surround the hut. We crush peppercorns and ginger for chai with a stone on a stone, and boil up water in a pan, as if we aren't really part of it all over there in the ashram.

Shyam visits and looks at all the dead leaves lying around, and without explaining, just sets fire to them. So suddenly we are in a circle of fire, he enjoys the shock on my face. I glance over to the buckets of water. He laughs and squats on his haunches and stares at the hut, at us, at the dying circle of fire changing into ash, then he looks at his watch, and stalks off.

There is a latrine at the ashram, but we piss into the earth, outside. It's too far to walk. Lily has fed and bathed her figurines, we have fed and watered ourselves, drunk our chai, and we all feel the urge at the same time and go out under the tall trees upriver and squat down. The men piss squatting here, and the ninja has adapted and adopted this style, after being stared at once too often standing. And although we are all at some distance, and in private, he calls out, 'Do you realise we're all pissing at the same time? It's nuts.'

'That means we're pissing in a triangle,' Lily calls.

'Yes. I suppose we are,' I say, watching the ground darken beneath me.

'Pissing in triangles.' I hear the ninja laugh.

He and I walk downriver to the rocks that look like elephants crouching. Rock slides run into the water and there is a bubbling cauldron of foam which the English have christened 'the Jacuzzi'. We are alone. I can feel tigers, this is their place, not ours. For a moment I feel as though I am seeing us through tigers' eyes. We are the animals, we are the strange.

The next morning has a peaceful rhythm to it – we have been for a walk upriver, Lily has tended her god and goddess, the clothes are drying – but I am not happy. I am itching, I am itching all over. And the word 'itch' does not do this sensation justice. It is unbearable. I cannot imagine not itching, I cannot imagine it ever ending, I cannot imagine the time before it started. There are no bite marks on me whatsoever, but I can hardly bear the feeling of hundreds of tiny darts constantly pricking my skin. This has been going on for over half an hour. I am in bits. My body has been taken over by pain. I am in agony. I'm wailing and ripping at my clothes. The ninja leads me to the river and lowers me into the water, I am shivering all over. I can't control my lower jaw. I am apologising for the fuss I am making, but I cannot imagine a non-itching state any more. The ninja speaks calmly and slowly and lowers himself into the water beside me. I have no more strength for wailing. I judder. We're both in the river. I am stark naked. There is no one around, but this feels deeply subversive, to be a woman in India naked in a river. I make sounds of great relief, gasps, panting. I can't control my own body. I relax, I shit out a long turd and feel really terrible. I'm polluting the river.

'Oh no, what have I done?'

'You can't help it. It's OK, it doesn't matter. You didn't mean to do it. Shh.'

Rolled up at last in cloths, I dry out. I stop shivering. The itches fade. The ninja freestyles a rap about our day, the walk, the itches, the river, the fire. It makes me laugh. He puts the chai pan on the two-brick fire.

GANGA

In the dim light there are few people about. It's dank in Kashi, Benares, Varanasi, city of light, a tirtha, where the two worlds meet. The Ganga is the river of heaven. Its flow down from the Himalaya is slowed by the dreadlocks of the blue god Shiva. The myth is hard to resist here. The steps down to the Dashashwamedh bathing ghat aren't wet yet. Today's funeral pyres are yet to be lit at Manikarnika Ghat downstream. Up the steps in the B&B the ninja is asleep, and I have come out with my towel to bathe. Although there is a perfectly good shower indoors. I asked him to come, but he wasn't up for it, just slurred, sleepy-eyed, 'I'll jump in the shower later. Count me out.'

'Sure?'

'Completely sure.'

I've got into a rhythm I don't want to break of going to the river first thing. There are Brahmins in starchy puffed-out dhotis, sitting under huge bamboo parasols on platforms above the water. They have trays of rice, sandalwood, and turmeric pastes, red sindhur, and solemn expressions. Widows are starting to flock down to the ghats, shaven-headed and fragile in thin white saris. They sit in lines and beg outside the temples, they move like birds. They carry small brass pots to the river to collect the holy water.

The steps are getting wetter now as more people appear, to make their prayers and ablutions. I dip one foot into the water, it feels oily. Leaf boats with nightlights float downstream under the girders of the railway bridge. Discarded necklaces of squashed marigolds and jasmine drift past like amoeba, or used-up messages. There are wooden rowing boats tied up, and the dhobi-wallahs are coming out, taking back their territory where boys played cricket last night, with washing, piles of the stuff. They grunt loudly as they pound it. The laundry of middle class Varanasi will be laid out in long lines to dry.

The water is colder than in the jungle, and it's not clear, more like soup. Logs float by, and unidentifiable objects. Lumps of stuff you don't want to look at too closely. I know the poor can't meet the costs of cremation, so bodies are likely to float by. Giant painted plaster goddesses are ceremonially sunk in the river at the end of festivals. Everyone wants to die here. Especially if they don't want to come back again in another lifetime.

The far bank is just sand, hazy with lazy morning sun. It stretches out into nothingness, so the sense of a crossing point in a myth, or in reality, is strong. It is not far across the river from here, but it feels far, there's nothing there. It floods in the monsoon. On this bank there is humanity, steps and temples and walls, houses and courtyards and alleys, bikes and rickshaws, only in the distance is the noise of motor traffic. A train rattles over the bridge. I'm in the water now and swim a few breaststrokes, not far out. I haven't brought soap with me, I vaguely rub at my body, and decide to immerse myself completely three times. Everyone here is performing a rite which has continued for thousands of years.

I try to imagine the scale of humanity at Allahabad upstream, when the Kumbha Mela is on, with millions in a tent city, bathing and being fed. Afterwards it all reverts to sand and water again. Like the coloured sand mandalas created meticulously over several days, and then in one gesture swept aside. There is everything in all its grandeur and glory and precision, and then there is nothing once more. Nothing. Sopping, I trail out of the water in yesterday's sari. I climb out to find my dry clothes, and perform the awkward hopping, shifting on the spot dance of getting wet clothes off and dry ones on, without offending anyone. Men bathing do not have this problem, they soap themselves vigorously all over in loincloths or underpants, making loud accompanying noises, huffing and puffing.

I wring out my wet clothes and squeeze out my hair to tame it into a dripping tail running down my back. Then a Brahmin, the one with the least forbidding look, nods and beckons me. So I climb onto his platform and bend towards him as he anoints my forehead. On my return the ninja says, 'Do you realise you've got grains of rice and some yellow and red stuff, the red stuff looks like dried blood, stuck to your forehead? I don't know about you, but I need to find some decent coffee.'

'The monkey has huge teeth,' Lily says.

'Yeah right. Careful where you put your washing. A monkey reached through the bars and pinched a banana.'

'And knocked over the coconut oil.'

'And it tried to make off with your blouse. Long fingers. Honest.'

I look over the ramshackle roofs and see a monkey holding someone's bra and looking a bit puzzled.

I want to sit by the burning ghat next to the enormous bell, near the cloth-wrapped dead burning in the open, meditating on the experience of being in a body, on leaving it. On death and dying and grief and loss and freedom. Death here is not taboo. The ninja is more interested in lassis in clay cups, scented with rose water and cardamom. He is resigned to being refused entry to the Shiva temple next to the big mosque, the path between the two bristling with barbed wire and armed soldiers. Most of all he enjoys eating apple pie and lasagne.

'I don't think they should call this lasagne,' Lily says. 'It's not right. It's got cottage cheese in it.'

271

'At least they tried,' says the ninja.

It feels like we've escaped, we didn't realise how much weight we'd lost in the jungle. We order thalis with exquisite curries and rice and puris, creamy raitas. We drink glass after glass of water, but can't finish the food. There are people here from all over the world, travellers, stoners, just plain tourists. It's restful, but I also feel like I've lost something. Perhaps the ninja is helping to free me from a fake family of misfits, sheltering under the umbrella of a dead guru. Freedom feels daunting. What is beyond the other shore, the mist and smoke, beyond the waves and currents, lapping? Beyond wet feet and sopping saris, the action and dramas of life? Just space.

THE TAP

We're in the greenhouse up on the allotment. The view billows out over the woods to purple Yorkshire moorland, beyond the chimney stacks and empty mills. One good thing about Bradford is you can see out of it. But the high privet hedges need clipping down and back and we haven't got round to that yet, trying to secure a pane of glass that's been loosened by the wind in the greenhouse. I can hear the voice of the next-door gardener. He's a Labour Party stalwart who uses old election banners made of corrugated plastic to line his compost heap and raised beds. He uses a spreadsheet to assist with his crop rotation. He's at the gate.

'Hey, hiya. Hi there! Is the water off?'

'I don't know. Is it?'

We share a tap with eight other plots. A barrel fills with rainwater diverted from the gutter of the greenhouse. We usually barely exchange greetings, because this man is a serious head-down gardener, and a very busy person. But he's in my allotment now, looking at the gooseberry bushes, at the cold frame, at the sandpit, at the 'weeds'. My hedges sprawl, my seedlings are under threat from slugs. I am not on top of it.

'Goodness, you've grown a baby in your greenhouse.'

'I suppose you could say that.'

It's Amba sitting aslant in one of those bouncy chairs that look like mini deckchairs. She's quite happy, and makes it very clear for one so small that she prefers by a long way being at the allotment or in the woods, outside, anywhere but in the house. She looks tiny and wise.

And I feel a little better about the state of my allotment and my compost heap, which is harbouring vermin in the middle of its sweet fermenting morass. I feel like my neighbour's plot is not quite as productive as I thought it was a minute ago. The ninja is introduced, Amba is introduced. She had to come, we could feel her willing herself into a small body from the firmament beyond. I still don't know if I'm right about the ninja, during the pregnancy he kept disappearing. But he's here now. Amba has a fetching stripy suit on, bare feet and a fringe. She is a delight. Now I have two daughters twelve years apart, both tigers. I am thirty-nine.

'Great up here, isn't it? Got it all. A garden, a shed, a tap.

What more could you want?' The ninja is trying some male bonding, pushing out his chest.

'Except for some reason, only known to them, Yorkshire Water have turned off the supply.'

'Sure to be temporary. Maybe mending a leak, or a burst pipe, who knows?'

'Yeah, I suppose so. Who knows?' Pause. 'Well, I've got a couple of new barrels and I brought my hose so I was going to fill them up, and now . . .'

'Typical,' the ninja says in solidarity, squaring up his shoulders.

'Sometimes you get more than you planted. You'll never guess what I found up here last week. A harvest of sorts,' I say to our allotment neighbour.

The ninja is laughing now. The neighbour has an 'I don't know what to think' expression on his face.

'No. What?'

He still looks cross, annoyed that his water storage and time management plans are undone for today. I take a beat as I wonder whether to tell him what I'm about to tell him. I have never worked out how developed his sense of humour is, pitched against his sense of righteousness. I take the plunge.

'I cycled up here the other day with the compost bucket from home. And under that hedge there, see, the one that's trying to take over? I found a whole case of lightbulbs, and two portable music centres, brand new, still in their boxes. Tucked in out of the rain.'

'What did you do then?'

'Well, what do you think? Took them home in the bucket.'

'But . . . you should, I don't know, take them back.'

'Back where?'

'They might have come from the school. It's just there.'

'Well, but what if they didn't? Be a bit weird, wouldn't it, strolling in there,' the ninja points out.

'What about the police? Report it?'

Amba makes chirruping sounds from the greenhouse.

'I'll need to feed her now.'

'Fancy a cuppa?' The ninja wields the flask.

The gardener shakes his head and makes a shuffling backwards movement. The gate squeaks and then clangs shut after him.

'Places to go, people to see, eh? I feel like Robin Hood or, I don't know, a pirate. The way he looked at me.' The ninja loves being at the allotment, he says grandly, 'This really is all I need. Space. Shelter. A tap. A view of the world.'

He takes his notebook out, where he writes lyrics. I wish he was a bit more involved with the gardening. I think of the 'decorating' of the small bedroom he did, his tagging days have had an influence. When we leave, the tap is gushing, splattering, making a stream down the path, thankfully skirting round a heap of dog shit, and carrying old leaves and debris along down towards the steps to the woods.

'He's such a professional, you'd think he'd have checked it, made sure it was turned off. Lucky we were here to notice.'

Back at the house the ninja mixes, he samples, he records odd snatches over tapes. I will discover these sudden interruptions in the flow of my favourite music much later.

YNYS ENLLI

Amba is in a sling attached to my front, facing out so she can see. It's bulky, I feel like a Michelin Woman because I'm wearing an orange life jacket as well. The three older children stand on the slipway and wave me off, they are spending today on the beach here in Aberdaron, North Wales, without me, with a generous picnic.

When he arrived from London on the coach, it was clear that Tom's heavy bag was bulging with beer cans. I noted it as a rite of passage. I wish he wasn't at boarding school trying to fit in twenty-four seven. His voice is very level, his world very closed these days. Yesterday evening I made the mistake of getting carried away playing with seaweed on the shoreline after we'd eaten. High on the crashing waves and brine, we ran along attacking each other with seaweed ropes and rubbery ribbons. I didn't realise Tom was angry, not at all enjoying himself, until it was too late. And he sulk-stalked back up the road to the campsite ahead of us, on his own. When we all got back he threw the washing-up bowl around the field, swearing loudly. I shouldn't have found it funny. He probably finds us, and camping here, mortifying and uncool. Later he will be proud of the photo that depicts him in his swimming shorts strolling the beach like on a catwalk, or the one where he's posing in front of Snowdon in shades, his hands making V signs. I try to reach him in these holiday times, my eldest boy, the high diver, the piano player. He likes the ninja, but it's not enough. And now the ninja isn't here, and no one can say what kind of a family we are, or what will happen next, and it's all too much. The beer has nearly been exhausted. They'll play cricket, eat and laze.

Anyway, I'm having a day out, the others didn't want to come. I'm having a day to myself with the baby. I am going to Bardsey Island, Ynys Enlli, off the end of the Llŷn Peninsula. The island is shaped like a crouching dinosaur, a T-Rex. It's the resting place of twenty thousand saints, Merlin has a cave, or an invisible glass house with thirteen treasures – Bardsey is a pilgrimage destination of many layers. The boat rocks, the boatman is dependable-looking, dark and Celtic. We are spoken to about being stranded, rations, sitting out storms, trade winds and the like. I'm grinning like an eight-year-old. After all the talking, we leave swiftly. I watch the wake skirts trail at the stern, and keep an eye on the mainland changing shape, now I'm away from it. The church is a detail, a tiny model. Aberdaron shrinks, the humpy bumpy hills like a serpent's back writhing along the peninsula align with the raffish clouds and the sound and swell of the sea. Inlets and cliffs and rocks and shallows all look more complicated from here. We're at sea. I feel an umbilical tug as I sense the children getting smaller and further and further away.

The day before yesterday we all crowded into a burial chamber and, apart from the patterns on our jumpers, looked like an ancient race with glittering eyes peering at each other, and out towards the light of our peculiar world. Today, while they play at the beach, I have four hours, four precious hours. Without being so much of a mother, marshal, mediator, consoler, counsellor, caterer, cleaner, nurse, improviser, expedition leader, delegator, etc. etc. ad infinitum and long past bedtime, available in the small and the early hours, on call twenty-four eight. We are camping with a spectacular view of the sea, it helps. Even though we risk the wind battering the tents, so far it's been OK. The view is green and blue, mostly, green and blue is enough.

Amba is dozing, although the wind is blowing into her face. I can feel her body utterly relaxed hanging against mine with her legs dangling down. She has an all-in-one red suit, with padded feet, it's like a portable bed. We round the rump of the island and I can see the lighthouse striped red and white like seaside rock candy, like a barber's pole. The island is a rock with grass on top, there are a few houses, but mostly it is grass and it is rock. There is one beach in a curve at the waist of the island. On disembarking I walk along to look at the church, trying to get away from the other people, their binoculars and conversations. I want to be as alone as possible, with the island.

We end up on the beach in the sun, the sand is nearly as white as salt. And strewn with seaweeds like strange creatures, humped, slumped, splayed and freeze-framed, lying in drifts. The rock pools feel more holy than the church. I breastfeed Amba sitting on a rock, munch my sandwiches and eat an orange and then a banana. She sucks at a tiny bit of the banana with her gums, dribbling. She looks sleepy, and I lay her down in the nest of her coat in a pad of seaweed, cradled by the rock, it's a soft bed. She looks sublime, still and easy, eyes shut, surrounded at a safe distance by miniature worlds in pearly pink pools. Mussels and limpets stud the rocks, barnacles and red anemones cling. Amba makes small grunts as she sleeps, like it's a well-fed pleasure. The air has gone quite still and the sun quite hot. I am sitting in a hiatus, and I start to wonder if I could get away with having a swim. I weigh up all the reasons not to, but I can't resist the thought of being in the sea. It is so peaceful, so utterly quiet I can hear myself breathe. So I divest myself of my layers, undoing buttons and zips while realising I am towel-less, but what the hell? I can easily dry in this sun. And there is plenty of time until the boat goes. Hopefully I will escape the eyes of the fully togged-up, map-carrying fellow passengers.

Amba is safe, well off in her nap and too young to move by herself. So I hop into the sea. It's as warm as a cooling bath, and knee deep in sea I swim in a kind of doggy paddle of bliss. There is no one watching, there is just this moment and being in the water. It's warm enough to get my hair wet and not worry about it drying, so I float on my back and dip my head in fully and drink in the sky. This is my pilgrimage, being with my small self. I glance over at the tiny shape of Amba in her red nest in the rocks and it's a beautiful sight and a beautiful day. When I float back onto the beach I feel blessed, somehow saved. Even after everything that has happened or might happen. Even though ostensibly my life has gone completely wrong, love has not delivered, and I've been a complete idiot. Here I am myself, the person my mother listened to and loved. The quiet lulling sea is a benediction, the island has somehow allowed me into its heart.

Skin dries easier than anything, and I'm sitting in my pants, angled at the sun and reluctant to get dressed, as Amba starts to stir. She looks up at me and I look back. We communicate with notes of music, sounds of reassurance. I look up and there's a seal come in close, staring at us. Its head has come up out of the waves like a periscope, a meerkat. It stares while owning the curve of the bay.

This is when I think I will baptise Amba. I am feeling very much cleaner and clearer than I have in a long time. Catholics can christen, you don't have to be a priest – it's all about the intention. Frank was baptised with a cup of lemon tea by a Welsh writer in the cafeteria at the National Theatre. But this isn't a Catholic thing, just a small ceremony of welcome into life. An honouring of the peace and beauty all around us. So what if I am maybe alone yet again? I am tired of the tug of hope and promises, maybe I'm meant to be alone. I anoint her forehead with rock-pool water. The softness of this moment stretches time right out, it's always. Until the seal, still staring at us, makes a seal noise like a hiccup then disappears underwater. And so I dress slowly, and we wend our way along to the harbour to wait for the boat back to the mainland. The boatman mentions that the Bardsey saints are sometimes seen wandering along the shore. On the seal's beach, at the waist of the island.

LOCK

Amba can walk now. The Five Rise Locks at Bingley are nearby, but five locks is way too many for her, so we come here, to the lock at Hirst Wood. There is something fascinating about watching people in boats negotiate locks. Nowadays I observe the relationships of strangers coolly. The person on the boat has all the power, hand on the tiller, steering, revving the engine and creating a stink of diesel, and the one on the bank, locating the metal lock tool, skittering across the wooden footbridges, dealing with ropes and posts and passers-by with dogs, is the lackey. It is like watching late arrivals on a campsite with a brand-new tent they've never put up before. The stark relationship dynamic is played out graphically. Few relationships appear truly collaborative.

The very worst sight for me at the moment, the one I can't bear to see, is good dads, kind and thoughtful dads, playful dads, easy-going dads. Not that sepia memory of my father stalking the beach, brandishing one cricket stump and yelling at my light blue sister. No. The sight of any old middle-of-the-road dad, playing ball with his children, running along with a child on a bike with stabilisers still on, laughing, a dad comforting them if they cry, picking them up if they fall, feeding them, listening to them, makes my stomach clench. I am filled with the steam of rage. Rage that keeps the tears and the ranting inside. If I cry I cannot stop. The sweet sight of a father's commonplace care, a mere inch of tenderness, makes me feel uncontrollably angry. I know it is unreasonable. I am recovering, apparently, I've had post-natal depression. I've never had it before.

The ninja has gone for good now. Frank says we are better off without him and he's probably right. He had to stand up to him, when he lied. He won't be back. It was all too much. Everything. Perhaps it was OK when he felt he was being a ninja, but this now, here, it's almost ordinary. From being my friend, my companion, lover and Amba's dad, the ninja shifted into skunk-smoke psychosis. From basking in the rock Jacuzzi upriver in the jungle, joking, rapping, splashing, he was ducking and diving in the smoke from the riots, dodging looters, black BMWs and lobbed fireworks. He was on the hunt for the best ganja, any ganja.

When the fires died down in the light of the morning, there were melted traffic lights, and you could see the sky through burnt-out roofs. From water to fire.

The night of the riots the ninja came back scared, and scary.

'It's madness out there. There's no fire engine going to put that out.'

And in his eyes I could see that haunted had triumphed over soft. I didn't want to admit it to myself but there was no way to go on together.

Depression is a crater, a sink. I've sunk. There is nothing glamorous about sadness, it is not friendly or interesting. It does not make a good story, even for a person who relies on stories. I can only zoom out. Perspective comes sitting in a circle of women at the Isis Centre. We are asked to imagine water, a river, or the sea. And Nadine can't.

'I can't see nothing. Not with my eyes shut. There's nothing there. Nothing.'

'Not even a small stream?'

'Nope. I can't. Not a bloody drop. Just grey, like. Like interference on the telly.'

'Well, maybe it needs some practice. At home, when you've got some quiet time . . .'

'Chance would be a fine thing.'

'Or, perhaps you could start with light, imagine a little light. A candle? Give it a try for homework. It might help.'

Nadine nods both dutifully and doubtfully, like a pupil who will never be convinced by school. She is a small and stocky woman in slacks with dull eyes and a quiff of silvery hair. Her husband is an alcoholic, her son an addict.

'I can give it a try.'

The other women are all on drugs, medicated. They nod. I shift in the community centre plastic chair and glance at Nadine. I am embarrassed by the torrents, the tempests and oceans behind my eyes, the deltas and fjords I have at my disposal, anytime, anywhere.

I walk slowly along the towing path with Amba, holding hands. Thinking of the days of real horsepower, when people lay on the top of their boats and walked their way, step by step, through the arched stone tunnel roofs of the canal. Even round bends, when daylight was all in the mind, they walked, upside down, to make their boats go along. The horse was led around outside, meeting up again after the tunnel on the towing path. There are moments I feel like the person lying on the roof, back in time, with my feet in the air. Not the one at the lock on a footbridge, fleet-footed and clever with ropes, obeying orders. Or the one with a steady hand on the tiller, in control and revving the engine. Not even the one leading a horse gently around outside the tunnel, letting it snatch at the grass.

I am in grief, adjusting to loss, and not like an accountant. Although maybe I could tally my feelings and experiences more efficiently, mathematically. Ration them, compartmentalise, and thus live a more orderly life. And is this all my grief? Or am I feeling feelings denied or stuffed to the back of the drawer by others? I wonder if I have ever not been in grief and that's why I always return to water. To wash it away, flush it out, rinse it clean. Cleanse my soul, I've been wading in the water, a motherless child. Soothed and pacified by the sound of the rain.

In the future, I will go to Llangollen alone and visit the aqueduct. The canal sits in a thin trough suspended ludicrously high above a deep gorge, over a pounding river. Amid Chinese selfie-takers, and intrepid kayakers, I will cling to the railing that is only on one side. The other side of the thin trough is open to the sky, to the fall. Even on the safe side and clinging to the railing, standing on two feet on the dry land of the thin concrete path, I will suffer a terrible surge of vertigo, and feel that it is all wrong. The idea of putting water above water, of making a thin shallow channel bestride the glorious breadth of the natural gorge and come to be the destination, the world heritage scale attraction. While the river itself, the rocks and rapids, has come to be the destination of suicides, flinging themselves out from the railings at aqueduct level.

At Llangollen I will sleep in the car behind the breast-shaped hill with the ruined castle on its summit. I will sleep hiding from the town, facing out in my sleeping bag towards the folds of Snowdonia. I will use rainwater and dew to wash in the early morning.

Amba and I walk away from the canal over a concrete footbridge, across the flood plain and through the council houses, past dog-shit bags caught in trees. There is an angry brown bubbling weir, and then finally, fields, a hill and, thank God, space. We walk alone on a path made by feet, mud smooth and rooted. It is all green river and riverbank now. Except for one man sculling up and back again, in the quiet before the weir breaks it. In this forgotten zone with no particular name, where in the future they will nearly build a bypass but don't, because a man making the decision likes rowing. Where beyond the next bridge and the bend, sewage sits and festers and bubbles in circular tanks. We walk. We walk by the river.

At the next session Nadine is a bit breathless, like an overexcited child.

'You'll never guess. I'll just have to tell you. I did it. I couldn't get a candle. But guess what? I shut my eyes and I saw a light switch and I switched on the light. Just like that. And it came on, it shone.'

Her eyes are bright, her shoulders not so slumped. We all sit up a little straighter.

'I'm off to try seeing water next. You just watch me. I'm going to keep at it.'

RESERVOIR

They have decided to cover the reservoir at the bottom of the road that's like an eye to the sky, a bird haven. I feel the walls are closing in. I go to the community choir in the church and sing, it's a way to be with people but not. Homework from the Isis Centre is making a collage from magazine cuttings, the title is 'Your Dreams'. Not the nightmares.

Amba has a wooden duck on a stick. She can't get enough of it, walking it up and down the pavement. It bears little resemblance to the mallards in the park, but that doesn't seem to matter. It makes a satisfying clicking noise as she pushes it along. The clicking sound pierces time. Backwards, mourning the life of the street filled with children playing and adults talking, and forwards, to when the wooden duck will be given away, burnt, or just rot. I take a photo. I collage as Amba sticks tissue paper scraps on card as if this is very important. Perhaps she is right.

There are no fathers in our life now. Not hers, not even a birthday card, and not mine. If Tata had met the ninja, I can't imagine what he might have thought, or said. When Amba is eighteen, she will say that she feels she's been living with my father, she knows him so well, even though he died years before she was born. At the moment I feel he is freer than he was when he was alive. Freer, but still not easy.

I think about my ex-husband trying to get my father to like him, to notice him. In my father's house, my ex-husband lifted up the entire hallstand, coats, scarves, umbrellas and all, and placed it in front of the closed kitchen door. When my father opened the door, he just peered through and said, 'Food will be ready in ten minutes,' ignoring my ex-husband and the hallstand completely, and then shut the door again.

When my father first met the tall man, they sat in the garden talking about Yugoslavia, then my father suddenly leapt to his feet and saluted. The tall man responded immediately in kind, although he was not a saluting person. For a second I saw them both quite differently, two tall dark men standing to attention. Saluting each other, daisies at their feet in the grass. As they sat down again, they both looked over at me like I could never understand them. Like they understood me.

It is easy to collage with my small daughter. She has spurned the round-ended child's scissors.

'No good,' she says. They're not, they barely cut.

I pick out the colours and images I want as the wallpaper of my mind. Lily points out later that they're all green and blue, and outside. People swimming in wild places, underwater worlds, clouds and sky, and sea. Women crossing a wooden bridge. Water buffaloes. Bicycles, fields, hills, mountains, waterfalls. This is how tragic I am now, my hopes confined to an A3 mish-mash from second-hand magazines, stuck together with lumpy flour-and-water glue. The sky outside my window is blank and faintly yellow, the view is a dirty stone terrace.

At the Isis Centre we compare our homework collages. I begin to see myself more clearly now, in comparison with the shiny cars and sofas, brittle fashions, sleek steel and glass cityscapes the other women have glued together. I decide I must summon myself within, and find the stamina to explore my dreams. To investigate a way to live a healthier life. I can't see it here in Bradford. I've tried.

We stop and get out at a burbling singing stream by Glencoe, with egg sandwiches. As soon as we have sat down they come: swarms of midges, sudden as hail, black over our everything. We have to sprint back to the car, a sandwich left to the stream in our haste. I am winded and astonished. How can somewhere so majestic, so utterly beautiful, be impossible to sit down and have a picnic and a paddle in? The car glides past Loch Ness with no monster, the water shimmies in the wind, and the journey goes on and on and on.

At Findhorn, people are living in (converted) whisky barrels. It started with one caravan, meditation and giant vegetables growing in the sand dunes. The community is seeking a better way to live. The camping area here is next to a living machine. The living machine is a big greenhouse housing the sewage system which means reed beds and gravel and plants and heat. This is fine, there is a certain beauty to it. However, the other side of the living machine is a hedge and the other side of the hedge is an airfield, and this airfield is a busy airfield. It's an RAF base. We are less than fifty yards from the other side of the hedge in our tents. In the future, my helicopter brother will laugh at this juxtaposition, of the peacenik hippies right next door to the fighter jets on manoeuvres around Findhorn Bay and beyond. Findhorn folk use the deafening, scary interruptions to 'attune' themselves, breaking into circles of silence. We are right on the front line of this dissonance, in our flapping-in-the-wind tents. The aircraft look as enormous and outlandish as perhaps the giant cabbages did at first, growing in the sand dunes. They are fat and khaki, emerging as if out of the bowels of the earth, monstrous and deafeningly loud. Much too near. The scale of us people is flattened, is laughable, next to them.

On the local beach we play with driftwood and stones and dig desultorily. The sea is bitingly cold. I volunteer in the gardens, where we stand in circles holding hands before tackling our allotted tasks. I take Amba with me, she's three now. There are no other children here, and no other campers. The focus is on being 'conscious'. As I garden, I cannot help being distracted by Amba and a rabbit that seems to be playing hide-and-seek with her. Her delight and our laughter are clearly not appreciated. Nor is the rabbit.

My gardening entitles us to attend a 'community lunch'. The four of us troop into a glassy geodesic building, Frank eyes the large buffet carefully. There are maybe forty people sitting at tables already eating and wearing bright loose clothes, the men in patterned trousers.

'Do you think we can eat all we want?' Frank asks.

'Can I have a big plate?' Amba asks.

'Mmm. Do you think they've got any soup?' asks Lily.

'Probably. There's some bread there. And look at all the salads. Beautiful.'

'Will you ask, Mum? About the soup?'

'Sure.'

We are in a short line behind a woman with a plait, an orange headband and car tyre sandals.

'Hi. This looks lovely, doesn't it? Do you know if there's any soup?' I grin.

She nods and gestures with her head. The idea that I have come here looking for a better place and way to live makes me try more conversation.

'Windy today, isn't it? Do you live here?'

She shakes her head.

'Have you come far, are you here on a course?'

I get no response and think she may be mute, and feel a bit embarrassed. And a thin to the point of emaciated man with leather bangles comes over and whispers in a rather officious way, 'Didn't you see the board?'

'What board?'

'There.'

'No, I'm sorry, I didn't notice it.'

A chalkboard says 'Silent Lunch' in Gothic lettering.

'What's that, then?'

'Well it's a Silent. Lunch.'

'Oh. I did think we could come and eat today, because I worked in the garden.'

He is staring hard at my eyebrows. I know there is nothing wrong with my eyebrows.

'Do you have to have the children in here?' he asks.

I look around at all the comfortably tabled people slowly eating their salads and their soup. I look outside at the ferocious wind, at the spots of rain flitting onto the hexagonal windows. I look at the children. Frank has a fully loaded plate of quiche, baked potatoes, bean salad and two pieces of cake already. He raises his eyebrows at me.

'Could you eat outside?' the man asks.

Everyone is staring. I look at the bench outside in the teeth of the wind, at the dark clouds and I shake my head.

'We'll be as quiet as we can.'

'Why do we have to be quiet, Mum?' asks Amba reasonably, and loudly.

We eat sitting by the window watching the rain, away from everyone else. I realise this is not what I was hoping for when I sat patiently collaging blues and greens together.

In a small room in a handmade house there are six people, it is very early morning and the air is Scottish nippy. The others are still asleep in the tents next to the gurgling reed beds, next to the airbase. Eileen Caddy, who first came here decades ago and lived in the caravan in the sand dunes growing giant cabbages, holds this open meditation in her house. She is eighty now. There are china ornaments on flimsy shelving. It is with my eyes shut that I see more clearly. Amidst the peaks of a mountain range sits a great golden reservoir. There is enough to go round. Even though the sky changes from light to dark and the clouds thicken and bank up, the light is behind it all. The reservoir sits there, always available. Golden and still.

BAY

I have the audacity to believe that I can leave the darkness behind. I can move away, to blue, to green. To where the sea encroaches, to somewhere else. And it is walking on an isthmus, tiptoeing quietly away from the wailing, bawling city, to be embraced by nature. Is this allowed? I am looking for peace and safety, that's the only plan. Space and time to heal, because there is quite a backlog.

The first time we arrive in fog, it's so thick I want to get out of the car to see the road. Even though that is illogical and ridiculous. The landscape is invisible. Everything is this thick white ether, smoky, mysterious. Putting tents up is a surreal act of faith. We sleep. Before I even wake up, Lily and Frank are wading across the mouth of the river to the sea. They come back dripping everywhere, exhilarated, breathless, noisy and quiet at the same time.

There are views that are spellbinding so you forget everything. Views that unleash you from this lifetime, with your name and story. Views that set you free on the wind. You rest your hand on a stone and it goes in, and on, there is a connection. Peace. Place, no place. Time, no time. From Pentre Ifan there is such a view. It encompasses the whole of the bay. The mouth of the estuary with boats aslant in the mud sand, and the clitoris of the sand dunes. The breast of the mountain, and the shadow of the Dragon's back behind it all, backing it up, all of it, cwms and woodlands, fields and gorse, heather, moorland. There's the sea spread out, Cat Rock like a dagger, signposting Dinas Head that looks like a soft billow, a take-off and landing point to the clouds. There's the beach itself, folded rock forms, posts, cars allowed away from the quicksand.

The whole sky is open to clarity, and perspective, the whole bay is spread out in front of us. Our tents are somewhere right down over there. We have arranged ourselves in various locations around Pentre Ifan, the burial chamber, in character. Frank has climbed up, Lily is stretched out on a flat rock, Amba is under the cromlech looking up, examining it. The pimple of the mountain is framed by the stones that barely touch, yet hold the weight of the monolithic capstone. It's megalithic, it's mega. This is a place of both music and silence. We don't feel like tourists, we forgot the camera anyway. We feel as though we have returned, because everything here feels familiar. It knows us and we know it. It's two-way. Maybe somewhere here is where we need to be.

Sunset is coming on August Bank Holiday. The tide is creeping in and in, up and up. We're all swum out on the beach, our damp clothes clinging to our damp skins as we swarm around a flask of steaming chai. And then tear baguettes apart, dunking them in the jar of olives and sun-dried tomatoes, stuffing them dripping with oil into our mouths as if our lives depend on it. Today there are cars and vans parked close together. It's crowded, there are people everywhere, lighting fires in the dunes, boiling kettles on stoves in vans, eating chips from town and waiting, clustering, looking out, over to the mountain, at the first stars coming out, at the bowl of the estuary at twilight. At the moon rising. And we wait too, not sure why we are here.

With darkness the display begins. In the future, health and safety regulations and insurance concerns will put a stop to all this, but now the pyrotechnic who designs firework displays all over the world, including for the Queen, dazzles this messy whooping oohing and aahing crowd of tourists and smallholders, cabin dwellers and permaculturists, babies on shoulders, teenagers on drugs. The tide keeps coming in like a thief in the night behind us, because we are all turned the other way, gazing at the purples and reds and sprays of diamonds and trails of snakes. And it's hard to know whether to concentrate on the sky, where the fireworks explode and dart and shimmer before they dissolve, or the water, where all this is reflected as if in another world, a mirror of this one. I feel like I live here already, in both. I am not trapped. And behind us the tide creeps up, reaching the wheels of cars and vans, but the fireworks have taken over the landscape, the waterscape, the headspace. There is the scent of woodsmoke and home-grown weed.

The tide doesn't care about people or fireworks. The tide doesn't care about vehicles, the tide waits for no one, ignores everything. So when it's all over, the show, the banging, crackling, sky-shattering extravaganza, there are people arguing, children wailing, as they try to get their vehicles out while the sea laps round their ankles. The sensible people parked up on the hill by the golf club. The patient sit and wait it out: the tide, the crowd, the panicking, this weird traffic jam in the middle of nowhere. We are quite by chance sensible and patient. We look out to sea again, and back at the mountain and the shadows of the boats bobbing up and down in the water as the estuary fills up. We look at the moon looking back. Knowing we are in some kind of allegory, up to people's ankles, knowing that (for now) the tide always turns.

ESTUARY

I watch Frank and a girl called Becky standing naked outside the Medina Cafe, covered from hair to toe in blue-grey estuary mud. People drift past carrying bowls and spoons, one woman says to another, 'Wow. They look amazing, really realistic. I must check out the creative area, I haven't had time yet. I'm really knackered, Saffron had colic last night.'

'Yeah, they've got loads of stuff up there from the scrap store. I'm looking forward to doing some felting.'

I can tell by their eyes that Frank and Becky are amazed to be mistaken for sculptures. They strain to keep completely still so the moment is preserved. It's that kind of camp. As the mud dries it starts to crack, so their skins begin to look fractured. Washing off mud is harder than coating it on. A dunk in the estuary won't quite do it, there will be mud behind their ears for days.

Dark woods fringe the estuary. From the top field you can look out over the mud towards the oil refinery at Milford Haven in the far distance. The splayed channels look like a diagram of the inner workings of a woman's reproductive system, with fallopian tubes and everything. Filling up and emptying out with every tide. In the future this view will sprout wind turbines, gradually multiplying, so it will look like a distant battlefield of energy ideologies.

There are five hundred people camping here in one field. For twelve days. There are compost loos, long drops, and standpipes dotted around the edges of the field. People queue up to use them, and clean their teeth under the trees. There are buckets and bottles and barrels on wheels and flat folded containers for water. In each camping circle there is a fire, and kitchens of various designs, from those with awnings and sinks and made-on-the-spot Welsh dressers, to those with washing-up bowls sitting in the grass and empty cans underfoot. People sit around their fires on handmade wooden chairs like personal thrones, camping armchairs, logs or the ground. There is a copse of tipis, there are yurts and bell tents and every kind of ordinary tent too. It is a village arranged in circles, the circle is home. An anthropologist would have a field day, a field trip, in this field.

I'm working in the cafe, the breakfast shift. At 8 a.m. Felix, who is an anthropologist, plays his violin gently as he ventures around the whole field. Gently stirring people lying in their tents awake, with shreds of Bach, of Mozart. At first camp life feels idyllic, fascinating, stimulating. Then it is extremely annoying. I wonder why I thought, why anyone thought, this was a good idea. But this is par for the course, loving it and hating it is part of it. I return to my circle from my shift, job done. It's sunny, there's a kettle perched on a horseshoe trivet, the fire is going nicely, prettily, and there is a good stack of dry wood and kindling stacked nearby. I rinse out my mug, fish around in my tent for a teabag and sit on a log to wait for the kettle to boil. All I can hear is live music, people talking, children playing and fires spitting now and then. There are only wheelbarrows and bikes, no cars, they are all lined up in the next field. And this car-lessness is so restful and simple and freeing it is hard to convey. We are not being seen through our cars. The kettle is boiling, the steam rising. I pour the water into my mug and relax.

Lily has taken Amba to the crèche, she is working in the cafe herself now. I have for the moment not a care in the world. I think about having a sauna, but there's no rush. I watch people rushing off to workshops, clutching water bottles and blankets. The best workshop for me is right here, by the fire, in the sun, I've even got a washing line rigged up. Tomorrow it is my turn to cook on the fire for the whole circle, but I have no immediate cares today. In the cafe I have fed the foibles of early morning campers, the fussy toast woman, the site crew who want 'the works', the Native American who likes a large soft omelette. My sun-browned feet rest in the clovery grass.

In the UK it is a bit optimistic to expect good weather to hold for twelve days. Inevitably after five the sky goes dark. The clouds pile up. It is dawning on me that here I am exposed to both the weather, and the people. I packed camping food and there's a wholefood shop on site in a yurt. I packed the requisite layers, coats and boots and spare socks. But I don't know if I have the layers of skills to share like this, for twelve days and nights. Beyond good manners and acting, beyond good intentions. I look at the sky and hear faraway rumbling, and notice it echoes the knots squirming in my stomach.

There is a 'healing area' in the far corner under the trees. I venture over there shyly, it's my one day off. Amba loves the crèche so I'm free. I approach the area like I am holding a guidebook and just want to check out the lay of the land, the accuracy of the map. I am drawn in by the flowers, lolloping in tall vases and buckets, and before I know it I am in a tipi with a tall woman in glasses listening to me babble. What on earth am I saying? I don't even know. After a while she says, 'Just lie on your tummy, dear.'

I cry a bit, and judder and snot, and go beyond embarrassment out into that place of semi-giggles. Lying on my tummy gladly, I can't even see Joan, she's resting her hands on my back. It's OK. I am lying on a blanket, on reeds, in a tipi, by a wood, above an estuary, under the clouds, and I feel safe.

Afterwards she says, 'Come back if you can. I can ask Graham to give you a massage.'

Sitting around our circle fire at twilight, Felix suggests I rent his house on a Welsh mountain. I can sell the house in Bradford. The fire warms me deep inside as I consider it. Shyly, I succumb to a massage the next day, to lavender and sandalwood oils, and Graham, a soft bear. I watch my body clench. I can see him from face down, sideways, tracing the tension in my muscles, my flesh. He has few words, and uses them carefully. He meets my eyes for a moment.

'It's OK to feel,' he says simply.

And I weep like there is so much liquid inside me it will never exhaust itself. Everything blurs. For the first time in such a long time I am being touched carefully by a man, in a non-sexual way. And this very thought brings more tears flooding out. The grief is alive, is like a creature that needs tenderness, that needs a field to wander in.

Of course it rains later. A rain to clean muddy bodies perfectly. It rains and rains, and whoever decided where the fire in our circle should go doesn't know this field. Drainage is a whole thing, an art. There is a stream of water that flows relentlessly straight through our fire, like it knows the way. It is pitiless and ruthless. We stand forlornly around the remains, charred black and sopping, staring at the stream of mud. The neat stack of wood was not covered by a tarp. The wood is sodden, Lily's sleeping bag is sodden. I have to poke up the tent with a stick inside, so the pool of rainwater on the roof doesn't drip through. I dole out precious stashed dry socks.

WATERTIGHT

You could not say the move flows. 9/11 was a week ago, and it's hard to leave a Bradford still reeling with shock and knowing that being Muslim has just got even harder. The driver ducks out at the last minute, i.e. he drives the rental truck almost to our house, loses his bottle and then leaves it with what I will later learn is four hundred quid's worth of damage, stuck at an angle at the bottom of the road. We are going but we are stuck, what does that mean? I have a long silent scream on the pavement where the trailing plants are waiting to travel. I go into the house where the futons are all rolled and tied up, the chairs neatly stacked, the children expectant and confused, I go upstairs where the rooms have already shed us, and scream out loud. And at the back of my mind there is the issue of where we are going. And how it will be.

Thankfully I think of ringing Olu from the choir and she says her partner Greg will do it. So he steps in, in his matter-of-fact way, gets the truck unstuck, helps us load up, makes jokes, and drives it to Wales. We lose him on the M62, and he will be notified later that a camera caught him speeding. When we are motorway-ed out and away from them at last, the hills tease us with the very idea of traffic. Our convoy of two reunited, we stop at a petrol station after Aberystwyth, where we can see the sea at last, glittering in the distance. Greg sits on a bench that seems to have been put there especially for him, drinks coffee, chomps a ginger biscuit and says, 'That's the best ginger biscuit I've ever tasted. Let's have a dekko at the map again.'

The road hugs the sea and there are more sheep than people. It is when we have snaked up the mountain overlooking the bay and driven up the track that we notice that the doors of the barn are not yet on. The barn is brand new, timber-framed with a curved corrugated roof, it looks like a giant gypsy caravan, without the wheels. It is not quite finished. Last week Felix rang to ask if I was sure.

Sure! I thought. *I've sold the house.*

And then he said, 'By the way, I've decided you can move into the barn instead of the house.'

Our possessions will be stored upstairs in cardboard boxes for the whole winter, there is too much of us to move into the barn. The truck looks enormous next to the sugar-pink house and the toy new barn. The plants and pots and pans and camping stuff and books, the compost bin, the washing machine, the gas cooker, the hoover, our clothes, our lamps and futons and tables and chairs, ourselves, fill up the empty space far too rapidly. Chris the builder looks astonished and embarrassed, Felix looks nonplussed at Amba's blue shell paddling pool, and invites us into the pink house for chai and food his wife, Anu, has cooked.

That night Greg and Frank are tucked up on the futon sofas downstairs, Lily, Amba and I are upstairs. The whole barn is open plan, and we chat, we can hear each other quite well without shouting.

'It's grand is this. Grand.' I can hear Greg shift in his sleeping bag.

'It's a long way from Bradford. In lots of ways.' Frank's voice sounds small.

I use the camping cooker to make Greg a good breakfast before he leaves in the morning. And as I watch the back of the truck lumber down the track and disappear beyond the cattle grid, I feel a sense of desertion, a sudden desolation. The nearest house is a mile away, the bus and nearest shop three miles away. There are sheep, there are mountain ponies, there is cloud mist. There is wind and gorse and heather, there are stones. The Preseli Mountains lie curved and silent as clouds play shadows across them, like a solemn tune. The slopes are a sea of browns moving. It is hard to believe they are fixed.

The house and barn sit on a narrow strip of land planted up with rows of tiny young trees. There is a wind turbine, a solar panel and a generator by the pond. We are off-grid. There is spring water that dribbles out of the tap rather than gushes. There is a Rayburn in the barn run from an oil tank. I would not choose to be in the barn, I like to be alone and private. This is not that, I do not have a room of my own, I do not have a door to shut. The smell is of fresh wood, everything is new, is not quite finished. There is a Belfast sink in an alcove, where there is also a shower, but no tiles. The other side of the Rayburn is the smallest room, the loo, the only room with a door. Anu, Felix's wife, can't come into the barn because of this. And this is why we can't rent the house from him after all, the plan was for them to be in the barn when they weren't in India, and us to be in the three-bedroomed house. Now it's all turned around, at the eleventh hour. It would be polluting for Anu to use a toilet that is not more separate from the kitchen/living area, and a shower in the same space as the kitchen sink. She cannot eat any of our food or come in and sit with us for the same reason. She is from a small Indian town, she is young, she is also marooned up here with a husband twice her age. She likes to give Amba milk and tomatoes, in the house.

I have to make it work. I drive Lily down the mountain to get the bus to college. I cook on the camping gas stove which rests on the mains gas cooker we can't use. I only use the hoover once, on the big rug I've laid out upstairs. Felix comes running in, it's drained the batteries in less than a minute. A dustpan and brush will do. We adjust. The gardener persuades Felix to let me use the house oven, the barn Rayburn doesn't get hot enough for bread. Chris the builder carries on tinkering with the building, the barn doors are put on their hinges. I feel like I am running a teashop.

At night the wind ripples the corrugated tin roof. The curved barn end facing the prevailing weather is all windows. I will come to understand why Welsh farmhouses have small windows, as I will understand what 'prevailing weather' means. Upstairs I lie in bed with my own curved shape reflected by the mountain curves. I track the moon, there's no need for curtains.

The worst night comes just before they go to India. A storm rampages in the small hours, the roof rattles and bangs and torrential rain ratchets the volume up and up. Like hippos are up there slamming into the metal. It is worrying, then scary, then actually, it's terrifying. We have to shout to each other from up to downstairs, and the other way round. Eventually it comes to:

'I love you, everyone. Whatever happens.'

'Even if this is the end. Maybe it's not the end.'

'You are all amazing and wonderful, and . . . I love the world. Thanks for having me.'

'You're an angel. You're all angels.'

'We are.'

'Even if this is the end, I still love you.'

I had no idea we were so soppy.

Even in all the rampaging racket there are long, flat, poignant silences. After fear, what ifs and cold sweat panic, we seem all to be shouting softly in the same voice. We seem to hit a plateau of resignation as the fear becomes exhausted. I can't help thinking that Chris may not have considered putting a lightning conductor on top of the tin roof, he is a connoisseur of aesthetics. There is no point thinking this thought. There would be no reason to say it out loud. Garden furniture is Chris's expertise, I have discovered during his tea breaks. This is his first actual building. Sleep comes over us eventually, stealing into the night of the storm like thick cloud. In the calm of morning, everyone except me sleeps in and on. I look out at the mountainscape, I look gratefully around me at the still-standing barn – fragile and cobbled together it may be, but it's still standing and we're still alive. There's the familiar carpet, and the hump of Amba under the bedclothes. When I swivel out of bed and put my feet to the Stanley board floor, it's wet. It's more than wet. It sloshes. The futon base is sitting in a puddle two inches deep. The prevailing weather has prevailed.

Chris is summoned. There will be much talk of storm windows and traditional, vernacular design. I mop up water a lot, with big towels. I wring the towels out of the window again and again, as Chris tries from the inside and the outside to make the barn watertight.

SNOWBOX

I meet a few people who have lived here. One of them says, 'You'll need a snowbox up there. It can get cut off in winter. Two weeks' worth of supplies. You keep it intact, don't touch it, just in case. And never run out of matches.'

The trees halfway up the mountain are being felled by the forestry commission. There are huge lumbering lorries, there is the sound of chainsaws. This work will continue long after we've gone, it's a big block of monocrop. Noise is more noisy when you can identify each individual source of it. The silence is always being interrupted. And there's the wind. When it's bad, Amba gets blown over crossing the plank bridge over the ditch leading into the barn. I learn to make infallible shopping lists, and do everything that needs doing in town once a week. Weekday mornings we drive to drop Lily at the bus stop for college through clouds masquerading as fog. The sky is shades of pink, and we often have to stop for ponies trudging, mud-scuffed, wandering the mountainside in packs. Halfway down, the cloud might break and then there are the sand dunes and the estuary, the beach, all in glorious technicolour sunshine. Looking like a child's drawing of a different climate and country. And we might have stayed all day up the mountain in dreary grey cloud, in the dimness, without knowing.

On the days when the sky is clear and blue and wispy cirrus clouds drift, we fill up the blue shell paddling pool outside the back door. Squeezing all the sun from September, October, even November. The autumn sun is a balm, a break, a blessing everything and everyone slows down for. Frank is here and in London. He records the black plastic sack caught on barbed wire buffeting in the wind, he records the wind playing the pipes of the metal gate, and the car crossing the cattle grid. He asks me to drive over it slower to get the effect he wants. In the future this kind of recording will be hip and then commonplace. In the present, I am bemused, appreciative, but also a bit concerned. The sheep are sprayed with ownership blobs of colours too bright in the sun, fluorescent turquoise, green and red, like murder blood. At sunset we get into the habit of racing to the stile past the pond and the generator to watch the yellow orange sun sink in the cup between the outcrops at St David's.

Amba runs into the middle of the field and sheep cluster all around her in her woolly duffel, as though she is one of them. And then she gets German measles. It passes gently, mercifully and quickly, I fan her with a Tintin book. Then Lily gets it, and she is truly possessed by German measles. Her body is not her own, the heat and itching are unbearable. After a morning moaning in my bed, she suddenly rushes downstairs, two at a time, strips off her clothes and plumps into the paddling pool that's way too small for her out the back door. The cold water provides some release, the barn fills with the sound of Lily's relief.

There is a rainforest waterfall that feels like a vision, the path suddenly leads out to a pebbled cove. There is a square beach. Caves in the cliffs and in the woods, Angel Mountain and the outcrops of Meibion Owen, the giant's fighting sons turned to stone preside. Amba is always looking out for mud and puddles, streams, any paddling opportunities. Like she has been pre-programmed. She refuses to wear her pineapple T-shirt under her jumper so the jumper goes underneath the T-shirt and she strides out like a farmer in her wellies, pineappled. On the outcrop above the bog, attended by buzzards, amidst dazzling yellow gorse and spent heather, the lichen is orange. She yells. She's stuck a foot in a crevice and lost a boot. And I can't find it anywhere. It's like the outcrop has swallowed it, taken it as a totem payment, so she has to be piggybacked away with only one boot, like Mr Magnolia.

We become familiar with the mud estuary near the bus stop, with grass clumps like mad professor hair, mini inlets and quickmud. Amba carries Monkey, still in her pyjamas, and charges straight off the mad professor clumps into the mud and slides and skates and falls and is glooped in soft gluey mud that sucks. I have to extract her and then myself, and rinse her and myself and the inside of the car and our clothes and boots. Sand is easier than mud.

'Will there be snow? I mean proper snow?' she asks.

'Maybe in February.'

Half of me longs for snow. I think of my old bedroom wallpapered in white flowers. Now I wish for white everywhere and nothing else at all. Like a spell. I want the bare moorland, the full sky, I want pure isolation, don't I? I know there's no running away from yourself, I am right here, fair and square, whatever the weather. It has been pitifully lonely sharing a bed, a life, and children with the wrong people. I don't think I feel lonely now, but maybe loneliness has become so familiar I don't notice it, it has embedded itself inside me, like an extra organ inside my body. I want to shed it. But right now, I'd like a halt to the trundling sound of the logging lorries. Up here, the now takes precedence. I have been without matches or a functioning lighter only once, it won't happen again. Amba imagines a snowbox made of ice, in a cave. We have apples and flour and vegetables in sacks. The fridge sits empty and unplugged, we keep a black bucket of water outside the barn door instead. Rats or squirrels have developed a taste for tofu.

Before they went to India, Felix and Anu planted a peach tree in their new polytunnel. I dug up a new vegetable patch and planted broad beans. They're sprouting nicely, in a neat block, and I feel inordinately proud of them, and myself. Making a new life, a better life, a healthier life. Amba roams the garden confidently, we water the beans together when it's dry.

Last night there was a cat, inordinately big in the dark, paused by the lean-to where the wood's stacked for the house. There have been reports of wild cats in the area. I wonder how big they are. This black shape in the night, eyes alight, was tall, as tall as a dog, as tall as a big dog. I can feel a presence hiding, watching us. We find a sheep, eaten, behind some rocks: flies, bloody wool and bones.

'Do you think it's a panther? That's a wild cat. I like the word "panther".'

'I don't know, Amba,' I whisper, wobbled by the thought that the word might summon the thing. For Amba there is no divide between stories, myths and legends, epics, and real life. Here the overlap seems possible, even likely. She wholeheartedly longs for snow.

'We need snow. Like in *Tintin in Tibet*. Do you think there are Yeti here? Do you think there are Yeti anywhere?'

She seems to feel it is necessary for it to snow here, now, for her. I am humbled by the thought that she believes I know the answers to all her questions.

The police come on Boxing Day. In the nearest inhabited house, a mile away as the crow flies, there has been a double suicide. The man provided logs and some of the wood to build this barn. I met him. Their smallholding overlooks the square beach. The policeman says that standard phrase, 'They kept themselves to themselves.' There is a footpath that skirts their house, and through the windows, you can see leaf borders glued around the doorways. Outside, the place is beautifully tended: young trees in rows, vegetable garden composted, two wooden chairs are angled towards each other, but facing the sea. They made a pact. She was ill, they believed it would only get worse. He used a shotgun.

Ice seizes up the generator, which is the backup to the solar panel and wind turbine. The pond has a drainpipe poking up out of it to keep the wildlife alive. Icicles hang from the under-gutters, then drip, then shatter, but I never complete a fully functioning snowbox. Snow does not come, only the ice and hail and vicious winds. And half of me feels relieved, that the car has held out when we rely on it so much. But also I am disappointed, to be denied the experience of being snowed in up here and forced to be resourceful. I'm annoyed that it has been a wet winter, not a white winter. The dull bass beat of climate change mocks my whimsical wishes.

The next-door field is littered with massive lichen-speckled stones. It's unclear if they ever had any sacred significance, if a farmer has dynamited them, or if they are just innocently lying about like beached whales. Now they are being dug up and transported to make a sea barrier on the Cardigan estuary. The inevitable yellow toy-like machinery churns and delves churns and delves, there is the sound of stone on metal and an underlying vibration in the ground that is linked to my guts, which churn along with the disturbance. So now, just when I have managed to distance myself from the logging down the road, and being able to identify which sheep coughed, and mark the flight of buzzards from their calls, there is this atrocious building-site-like noise. In the next field. I try to reach deep inside myself, delving for any metaphor to help me understand and appreciate this latest development up here on the mountain. Where I have planted myself for peace and, even, healing. I have become horribly territorial in a very short space of time about the almost silence. The stone harvesting is a dreadful racket. And there are people around now, in hard hats and hi-vis jackets, playing bad radio stations loudly. No doubt the farmer is making some money out of the stones, and having his field cleared at the same time. I find it hard not to take the gouging personally, it's painful. I feel it in my body. In the spring we will move, and settle across the estuary from where they are moving these boulders. To fend off the sea.

I throw down the pegs I was carrying to hang up the washing, when I notice the broad bean patch has been decimated, the plants uprooted.

Amba explains calmly, 'Oh. But that's my graveyard. I was making graves, you see.'

I feel angry and bewildered. It is easier to be angry than bewildered.

'But we planted those beans. They grew. We watered them together.' She stares her stare at me. 'They were the only beans we could plant in the autumn. What the hell were you thinking? They're ruined. Dead, all of them.'

'It's my graveyard.'

'But . . . what? But why? Something needs to be dead to be buried.'

My anger is there in the ex-broad-bean patch, in her graveyard. I notice she has arranged leaves on the earth, like sodden old wreaths, beaten up by the weather. After a cup of tea, anger in the wind, spread out over the mountain, I have to wonder if moving out, away from the city, moving up a Welsh mountain, has been the right thing to do.

Witches' Cauldron

I am in the town library on a computer. It is one of the shortest and darkest days of the year. The weather is piling it on extra thick, there is hail outside and damp bedraggled people in here. They come in a little out of breath, puffing, as if it's all too much. Not just the weather out there, but all of it, everything else. Being cheerful would seem a bit sacrilegious, in the face of this December misery mode.

I have been observing people minutely since we moved off the mountain into the village. The first morning, I kept spotting humans going about their ordinary business, walking along, getting into cars, posting letters. I had become acclimatised to just seeing sheep and birds and clouds and weather on the mountain. I choked on my tea.

'I've just seen another one.'

'Another what?'

'A person. It feels like a shanty town.'

'Mum, this is not a shanty town, get a grip,' said Lily.

My vision is still adjusting. The village is not a shanty town, but everything is so crammed in, the house is up against the rock, it's standing room only on the hillsides overlooking the river. I have become accustomed to long sweeping views, distances, outlines, shapes, listening to a lone car, identifying each tractor, each digger, on one road. I can see a lot of human and non-human activity all at once now. From up on this hill I can see the town across the river, the boatyard and boats moored on the estuary, several roads, the ruins of the abbey and the church built from its ruins, a car park, a school, a pub, there's a car dealership, a hardware warehouse. It's all too much sometimes.

On the mountain it was all about the weather, the winds and their directions, the rain, mist, fog, clouds, and knowing the sea was skulking down there in the bay. I was in the middle of nowhere, now I am somewhere, I feel a bit lost.

Opening my inbox I see there's mail from Tom. I last saw him by the fountain near the rose garden in Regent's Park, wheeling his bike along. He was off to Australia. I open the email and it's a big photograph of massive lowering cliffs overhanging a turquoise sea, a strip of sand, palm trees. It's wild, lonely looking, forbidding, gobsmacking. I look around the library as if I want to hide the picture from the bedraggled rainswept people here. The turquoise in particular seems too gorgeous, too incredible.

This is the original beach from the book The Beach, *but not the one in the film. Have opened an Internet cafe here.* He writes, ever brief, ever pithy.

Tom is now in Palawan in the Philippines. I last heard he and his business partner were buying a club in Slovenia. Or taking Brixton club nights to the Black Sea. Then there was an opportunity in Bulgaria. This is a beach, but it is a lot further away. It's on the South China Sea in fact. The other side of the world. I can only think of James Bond, and those islands that stick up like crumbly fingers out of the sea, defying reason, islands in macabre fairy stories. Which James Bond? Is it *Thunderball,* or the one with Donald Pleasence stroking the white cat? Is that *Goldfinger?* The one with the volcano? Is there more than one with a volcano? And what about the volcano in disguise, with water in the crater? Was that even a film? I don't even know, and it seems ridiculous to google it. Like going down a mineshaft for no reason. I look at the photo of Palawan, and then at the hail falling down the library windows. Slow melting. It doesn't seem possible that both realities are true at the same time. Of course it is, but I feel it shouldn't be. Tom's Internet cafe will win an award for best Internet cafe on a beach, it will have a real monkey as a mascot, a familiar. And probably a bit of a pest.

I think of Tom when he was put in the incubator that wasn't needed, so close to my bed, but not. Just a fraction below the required weight at birth. I think of Tom in the underwater worlds, diving over there. I look up the Mariana Trench, the deepest part of the sea in the world. I think of him kayaking in the interior of the island. I think of the picture he sent me from college of himself got up as a pantomime cow, in the style of Magritte. He has a bowler hat on in it, the blotches on the cow are clouds. I think of him eating an ice cream by the fountain in Regent's Park and explaining that despite having three jobs he is living on pasta and tinned tomatoes. I think of Tom . . . and know he must be different now, but the same. I think of my father making a new life, unable to go back to Poland after the war. He first went back to visit after twenty-four years.

The worst thing about going to the Witches' Cauldron is the sign in a red triangle on a white background of an upside-down human figure plunging down, accompanied by a black exclamation mark. These cliffs might be seen as forbidding from a certain angle, the sea is jade rather than turquoise. These words are precious stones, and that seems right for the sea. Some days it is lapis with the sun dropping gold flecks on the surface.

'What is that sign?' Amba asks.

'It's just to remind people to be careful, that it can be dangerous.'

Pause. 'Do people fall off here, then?' Pause. 'Do they jump? The sign is silly – you don't fall upside down, do you? Do you? Do people die here, then? What happens to the bodies?'

'Let's just concentrate on the path, shall we? And try not to look down too much.'

'Why do people come here if it's dangerous?'

'It's beautiful.'

Amba nods thoughtfully, having exhausted for the moment her line of enquiry. We have recently watched *Far from the Madding Crowd*, and I hope she isn't remembering all the sheep that fall off the cliff, or the sheepdog that gets shot. We need to focus on the path.

Inevitably we encounter map-in-plastic-wallet, ski-pole-stick-wielding walkers, prowling and clipping along at a fine pace on the Coast Path. They are determined and supremely focused, timing themselves, calculating the undulations, the crags and precipices, the steep slippery rocky winding path, in kilometres. They pause at Viewpoints to record them, and at intervals to adjust their clothing, the map, or grab an energy bar or a slug of water.

In contrast we amble, and when we get there we set up a camp, sprawl, gorge on our picnic, scout the area, have a dip, paddle, shell and rock pick, draw, scribble, drink, and doze. I count it as a good expedition if I fall asleep outside. Better if I dream. The Witches' Cauldron sucks and slurps, wave hands claw at the shingle, creeping up and down, the sea echo-chambers itself, carving rock bowls. The cauldron is the biggest bowl, under arches of rock a sculptor would judge unlikely, unsettling and not possible. Except it soars, it holds, it encloses and protects and is forever creating whirling water, foam, and calm too. If there are mermaids hiding from giants, they would seek refuge here.

SWEAT

I have been invited to a sweat lodge on the slopes of Carn Ingli, Angel Mountain. Emma lives here in a handmade straw bale hut. The sweat lodge is a bubble, a bender of hazel poles draped in woollen blankets. It looks far too small for all of us to fit into. There is a fire outside, bottles of water, drums, lanterns with nightlights in them, and a shelter, where dry wood waits and where we can put our clothes. You can hear the small river below babbling.

As the fire builds up some serious heat, the big flames die down. The heat's at the heart where the stones sit

324

baking and waiting. We sing in a desultory way, Native American songs, songs about fire and water, songs of the Earth. I move from one foot to the other a little uneasily, this is my first sweat lodge. I have always liked saunas. This is different, this is ceremonial, or attempting to be. In the future I will be amused to hear disagreements in the Welsh hills about the right colours, the right directions, the right elements and the right use of tobacco. I will listen to people swapping conflicting notes on fire walks, both before and after I walk a fire. This group of people is a barely cobbled-together impromptu tribe. We will all be naked together in a few minutes.

The fire and the stones glow red. Dusk has passed and the moon is on the way up. Pete is carefully taking stones out of the fire with a garden fork, and carrying them down to place in the pit in the centre of the lodge. We begin to remove our clothes. In the firelight we take in the shape of each other. We are smudged with white sage smoke. The smell is a cross between weed and eucalyptus. We are being cleansed with smoke. When the hot stones are all inside, we snake down into the lodge. There's straw on the ground inside, it rustles. Light is now moonlight, outside. We hear the river below. Everything, the light, the fire, the dark, the water, the earth, us, is beginning to fit together, with no gaps.

'Careful of the stones in the middle. And if you need to get out, just say "door".'

We are all being very British, like we're in church, whispering, 'sorry'-ing, 'whoops'-ing. We have to crawl round to the right, shuffling up some more to make room for everyone. The sound of bodies shuffling about on straw is strangely familiar. It's the sound of a stable. There is not room to remain separate in here, knees touch as we all find the most comfortable and do-able way to sit. There is a squeaking temptation to get the giggles in the dark. Because now it is very dark. Pete, by the 'door', a thick blanket, has shut it. And there is a smoky sagey smell, some of the hot stones glow, but not much and not for long. They smell like hot metal and earth. There is the acute awareness of bodies, of limbs and feet, as we settle with our genitals nestling in the straw on the earth. Our names and identities, our narratives and personas are outside somewhere by the fire, in the folds of our clothes.

There is a demijohn of water to share, the people who feel nervous and want to be close to the door are close to the door. We are all tucked in, like the spaceship is now ready to roam. We honour the spirits and the elements and the directions, we hum Oms. The sound we make together, locked in this tight circle, reverberates inside and out. The darkness becomes restful, a break from the usual group experience. Then there is the heat, because that is what this is about, this is about heat, this is about sweating. We sing a little and we begin to sweat. The silence in this dark blanketed pod, in the night under the moon, above the snaking water, is dense. And we keep on sweating. Like we are shedding whole skins together and individually at the same time.

Like in a sauna, there begins to be to-ing and fro-ing. There is in, and there is out. There is the sound of water tossed on the fire, hissing. There are waves of scorching heat rising in steam. The heat is intense and my sweat is trickling from everywhere up, to everywhere down. The rivulets and runnels know their way, coursing down paths of the least resistance. Drinking from the demijohn is supremely satisfying. When the door is opened the night air brings a chill inside, and we can see each other shuffling round, crawling out and clambering down towards the river. The water looks black, brushed with silver moonlight. We are steaming bodies in the night air. And there are great sighs here and small shrieks, because cold is extra cold after the sweaty steamy heat. The water is icy. And we dip and slosh and duck under the trees, the river goes on streaming into caverns under roots, round trunks, over stones, worrying shingle. I tiptoe back to the lodge to crawl in again.

We go in and out three times, to steam in the night air, to slosh in the river. The stones are cooler, the others are out by the fire now drinking from mugs and beginning to get dressed. I crawl back into the dark womb of the sweat lodge alone. Now I can hear no breathing but my own. The stones are cooling, like they are breathing out and lying down to rest with relief. As I lie down on the straw on the earth and cradle myself, there's no one to witness me, I can't even see myself. Just feel my body, skins slaked, glowing from the soft river water. I breathe slowly. I breathe and I'm an animal. I never realised it before. I am four-legged, I am skin and flesh and bone and sweat and shit and blood and air and water and . . . I have arrived, even though I have been here all along. I didn't know this animality, it is a new wonder, this streaking across long grass meadows freedom. Inside the dark lodge, the beetle pod, I roam. I range.

I emerge for the last time and look back over my shoulder at the humble mildewing blankets draped over the hazel poles, held together with string, at the muddy straw, at the old, going-cold stones. And I feel gratitude.

BLOOD

I am sitting in the woods in a small clearing sheltered by oaks, holly, hazel and, weaving in and out, honeysuckle. Ivy is in the oaks. Everywhere around me on the ground is moss, the limbs of the trees drip with lichen. Stumps of trees are camouflaged by moss nests, fairy tumps. I can hear Amba out in the open talking to the ducks, she has developed a taste for their scrambled eggs in the mornings. We are house-sitting Emma's straw bale reciprocal frame roundhouse in the woodland on the slopes of the mountain.

Last night I slept long and full, the birds who live in the turf roof tapping on the window woke me. This morning I started bleeding. I washed in the stream and then I came across this small glade, as if it was meant for me personally, for now particularly. So I am sitting here on the moss, more comfortable than any carpet, soft strong springy and absorbent and I am bleeding, naked from the waist down. It's nearly summer and I am bleeding into the moss. I can feel the leaking, and of course it is not really leaking, because that implies clothes and mishaps. Blood is seeping, coming out of me in dribbles and gobbets, as and when it wants to. I do not have to control my bleeding. I do not have to control myself. I do not have to be covert, or embarrassed. I just sit here in the moss, letting my blood flow into the earth in its own time in its own way. I am unplugged of tampons, un-hampered by mattress-shaped pads, fat or thin, regular, night-time or super, with wings or without. I am not trying to get to grips with a Mooncup, or wondering where to empty it. Or hoping a sea sponge is absorbent enough, or whether it might have got stuck, and where I can squeeze it out. I am not worried that a tampon is stuck stringless inside me. I am not thinking about the width of my gusset. I am not thinking about absorbency and plastic and cotton and the adverts, where period blood is blue. I am not thinking about stains showing up on the outside and giving me away. I am not worried about lumps in the contour of my arse in trousers that make it obvious I am bleeding. I am not worried about the smell of my blood and sweat. I am curious. I am on it. I am having a period, my egg, now blood, is going straight into the ground. And I feel like a child sitting in the shallows daydreaming, sitting in simplicity. I feel like a serf with the yoke lifted, a horse let out in a field. It makes me laugh out loud how much anguish I have experienced over the simple fact of being a bleeding woman over the last thirty years. It is this simple, sitting in verdant mosses letting my blood return to earth. And it feels like the earth is loving it, lapping it up, this red stain that is not a stain but nourishment, a red gift. How twisted up it feels to think of all the blood spilt on all the lands in war, in butchery. Instead of this.

Later on I wear moss in my pants. Amba is traumatised by a greyhound that mistakes her small form for prey. We chase breakout goats off the new apple trees. Amba steps into a pond she's been eyeing up and is utterly surprised that the water, in just one pace, is way deeper than her welly. We swim in the lake among water lilies, our skins brushed by swifts and silver-blue dragonflies. We dry ourselves laid out in the grass, and wade into the water again, the clay mud making us soft brown shoes. I hold her up to float on her back and she stares at the sky. We are held by the water in the lake, by the woods, in the bosom of the mountain.

I bleed and I am happy bleeding. In the future I want this to be normal, being a woman is a miraculous thing. I am wet and sweet and bloody.

WHALE WOMAN DANCING IN THE RAIN

If there were instructions, they would read:

1. Put up a yurt or other shelter in a field, with horses in the distance. (The horses are optional.)
2. Light a fire under cover.
3. Put a kettle on if possible.
4. Make sure you have a good picnic and the wherewithal for hot drinks.
5. Be amongst people you can trust. In particular, have a solid whale woman who can dance.
6. Towels might be good.

7. The more it rains the better.

Pip is in touch with whales, you can tell when her eyes get that faraway look. She might look like she's out to lunch, but she's completely focused, listening through all the waters of all the seas to whale songs. We are stranded in the field, held in the spell of the mountain. And the rain chucks it down. We had been hoping for sun, end-of-summer sun, but sun all the same, but it's utterly wet, the grass is waterlogged, is underwater. The yurt holds up well. There is something about the sound of raindrops on canvas that can be hypnotic and hysteria-inducing, but maybe it is just us. We are tapping out rain rhythms with sticks one minute, banging a bowl another, until we drum and dance, dance in the rain for all we're worth, and more. And it is ludicrous in such rain to wear clothes, because skin is the thing, skin is waterproof, we shout at each other. It's the best rainwear. Oh, what sweet luxury to dance naked in the rain with a whale woman.

ABOARD

Keewaydin is the name of the ship, the word is mentioned in Hiawatha. Keewaydin is the north-west wind in Ojibwe. The captain is Paul. We have embarked on a voyage, we navigate the silted-up estuary with some difficulty, after loading up with provisions and people by the bridge in town. We are off to Ireland by sea. The only way I have been able to persuade Amba that this adventure is a good idea is by citing the sea voyages of Asterix. I don't think she thinks we will come across Roman galleys or pirates, but I'm not sure.

A month ago I went down to the river, round the back of the hardware place, looking out for herons and listening for curlews. They yearn, echoing across from bank to bank, then they get back to the business of hooking food out of the mud. But that day there was a rowing boat coming up the river fast, white and red, with ten white and red rowers in it. The effect was as if I had gone back in time. I blinked and blinked again, had I walked into a daydream, a film loop? (*A Man for All Seasons*.) Was Henry VIII himself about to round the bend in a gold canopied boat tossing venison bones to the fish? Would Cleopatra soon be materialising before my eyes in a pooped barge, all clad in purple and kohl and mystery? I blinked. Do I watch too many films, live inside too many books? Do I find it difficult to distinguish truth from fiction? Reality from history? Had I lost the plot and my grip on time? The boat was undertaking a re-enactment of a journey from Ireland. The men were real, they wore white leggings, and the boat was lovingly recreated from historical documents.

We are not rowing to Ireland. The Keewaydin has red ochre sails. Her mooring is by the field between the village and the town. She is a Lowestoft lugger, one hundred years old. She is wooden all over, and this is a delight. Paul bought her for a pound in Malta. The ship sleeps sixteen, there are cabins with bunks, portholes, a galley with a wood burner, an engine room, decks, fore and aft, there is a bowsprit, a tiller, rigging, and all the clobber and terminology of sailing. We leave from the quay by the bridge. The town was once a thriving port with a custom house, local house names nod to the whole world. Silt has changed all this. The estuary

335

is silted up, and the channel is difficult to navigate. Our party is slightly drunk with the idea of the voyage ahead, but Paul frowns as he concentrates on steering the correct course. The buoys in the estuary are like bollards at a cycling proficiency test: they wind. There are no straight lines. We do not want to go aground.

As we sail out to sea past Cardigan Island, more and more nautical terms and references are getting dredged up out of my consciousness. I didn't realise before quite how much I have absorbed being part of an island, seafaring race. At sea we speak differently. Ashore is full of landlubbers. I am standing on my sea legs in the stern, near the tiller, looking at what I thought was the familiar land going by from the point of view of the sea, and realising how completely different everything looks from this angle. Nothing is ever quite what it seems.

The children – there are five aboard – are crowded in the bows, cheering the waves we're cresting, laughing at the salty spray. Except Amba, who stands beside me astern, looking at this spectacle uncertainly, even disapprovingly. The boat is going up and down over the waves. The sea is spread everywhere, and we are going further out there, where there will soon be no sight nor sign of land. I don't want to think about this too much yet. But I have to stay up here on deck. I have already been down in the cabin and in the galley attempting to behave normally, organising my bunk and my stuff and thinking about making a sandwich. And, or should I say, but, a mere five minutes out, I felt horribly nauseous and shaky, really ghastly, and quite honestly struggled to climb the ladder back up onto the deck. I almost didn't make it, it's pretty steep, and I feel like death. I must look like death too, Paul notices immediately, and just nods at me kindly and says, 'Look at the horizon. You have to look at something that is fixed. Don't go down below unless you have to. You won't believe this, but I get seasick too. I've just learnt to work with it.'

'Right, Captain. Look at the horizon. OK.'

'Don't look at anything on board. Because it's all moving. The swell isn't too bad at the moment. Could be worse.'

'Aye-aye, Captain.' I feel ironic.

The very word 'swell' and Paul's explanatory arm movement, up and down, makes my very stomach swell and begin to heave. I feel monstrous and retch over the thick solid old oak side, feeling fragile as paper, then breathe in and out as slowly as I can, as if this is a completely new activity I am only learning now, this minute. I am vaguely aware of the kids at the front behaving like they are on a ride at a fair, oohing and aahing. Up and downing. Now they are riding the bowsprit. I can see that Amba is looking queasy, she looks at me with a worried pity. She looks like she should be looking at the horizon too.

I am on board with a bunch of energy workers of different kinds. In the course of the day I will be approached with various remedies for my plight. I have been properly sick over the side, and feel slightly better as you do when you've actually been sick. I think of all the provisions, all the meals I imagined, and burp loudly. The soup, bread, and deli treats down in the galley will not be eaten by me. Paul's interesting collection of grogs, the cakes in boxes, will not be sampled by me. I can vaguely hear people being jolly down there, they bring innovative snacks up on deck, walk around normally munching them, chat and laugh, and childishly I feel it is so unfair, so random. Emma is the only one who is sicker than me, and she is completely prostrated on her bunk below, with a bucket beside her on the floor. Possibly wishing she had never left her handmade hut. But maybe unable even to think such a thought, or think any thought. I lie down on the bench around the stern and shut my eyes, I am less than an hour into an adventure, and already I am longing for my own bed and duvet and absolutely no movement whatsoever. No sea, no nothing. I drag myself up to peer out at the horizon line as instructed, and see we are right out there now. The land behind us is a stripe, is a fuzz, is going, is gone.

Paul is counting the numbers of the seasick-ed out, and therefore useless, crew members. There are sails to put up and this needs person power. Most of the children except Ted are too small. There is heaving, ropes are involved, timing and listening carefully are involved, and I am a groaning jelly of a person under a blanket beside all this impressive and energetic activity. People peering at me and saying kind words is mortifying. I had pictured this so differently, I had hoped to be part of the crew. I was going to rustle up satisfying meals in the galley, help with the washing-up, sample some of the home-made wine I saw being stowed away. I was up for unfurling sails, learning new knots and climbing the rigging, swabbing the deck, personing the tiller and navigating by the stars. Everything about the Keewaydin now looks fearsome, and I feel pathetic. Hmm.

Frank, who is aboard as the mate, has brought his bike with him and is riding it round the deck, just because he can I suppose. He will be on watch on the tiller tonight.

'Do you want to go and lie down, Mum?'

'No. Don't.'

'You'd be more comfortable down there.'

'Too ill. Loo smells like fish.'

My pronouns have gone. One of the loos smells pungently of fish, from its previous life presumably. However hard it is cleaned the smell is engrained in the wood forever. It is definitively hereafter 'the fish loo'. It is sickening that Frank looks so glowingly well on board, running up and down the ladder, making cups of tea, eating, washing-up, sailing, riding his bike, playing his bloody guitar even. I am grumpy in the way I can get away with being grumpy with him, and he eventually shepherds me below to my bunk, finds a bowl in a cupboard, makes a herb tea for me in a flowery mug, tucks me up in my sleeping bag, offers to make a hot-water bottle and keeps patting me, so I know I must look really appalling. I feel about ninety-five. I think.

CUTTLEFISH

Down in the bowels of the ship, I drift in and out of reality.
Everything is wood, everything creaks, there's a whole rhythm
of creaks going on, and I am an unwilling baby rocking in
a cradle I can't escape. I'm underground, I'm underwater
underground, I can't breathe except I can creak, creak along
with the creaks that sound sinister, ominous, deathly. Maybe
I will die here. And burials are pretty simple at sea, they aren't
burials, they just weight you and slip you over the side. You
sink, it's fathomless.

Someone is holding my left wrist meaningfully and

staring into my face. Murmuring. 'I am using acupressure. The movement is difficult, and it could be one of your triggers,' she says.

This brings guns to mind, and then I think 'triggers' sound like a species of fish, eel-like and mischievous. Or are they parasites, or something . . . 'Movement' is a symphony or related to constipation but I can't remember what that means. She goes blurry, she is drifting away. I can hear Emma across the way vomiting up her guts, and more, and again, and I wonder if there is anything left of her. I see I have dribbled rather ineffectually into the bowl. I am not even that good at being properly seasick. I turn to the wall that's not a wall but the sides of the deep belly I'm buried in, no one will remember where I am.

I see a tiny white ball lost in the palm of a huge hand and a head nodding. It talks about chewing tobacco, and that this is a minute concentration, called Tabacum. I feel really ill. I sleep and stir and Amba is stroking my forehead, then she plumps herself down sighing and lies skewered to her bunk.

'I'm too sick to read.'

The Crab with the Golden Claws is open face down across her. 'Just rest.'

'Captain Haddock goes mad and sees things, fires in rowing boats and phantom giant whisky bottles. Tintin is never seasick, even in *The Red Sea Sharks*. Even when he is wearing a kilt in *The Black Island*.'

I can't believe she can get out such a long sentence when she looks so pale. I can't comprehend that there are degrees of this sickness. I think about rum. I think about oranges. I talk about oranges, I think. Someone gives me painkillers, they feel broken and bitter. I feel broken and bitter. Where am I going again, and why? And is this life, is this living, and what for? I am hallucinating, and this is ridiculous. I am making a mountain out of a molehill, or rather it's a storm in a teacup. I am on a little trip across the Irish Sea, on a very short holiday. It is no big deal. Why am I thinking dying would be easier than this? It's crazy.

Amazingly Frank appears brandishing an orange, I wonder what bartering went on to procure this treasure. Are oranges even available? In wartime? Or did I bring oranges? The efficient me is gone, is retired, is unimaginable. I hunch up and peel the orange very slowly, the scent of the skin is utterly delightful. The flavour of the orange is sensual, wonderful, the segments, the little woven-together strands are juicy and sharp and sweet all at the same time. Amba is asleep, maybe he can rustle up another orange for her later. I am savouring this archetypal orange, the most medicinal orange in history. Someone comes along and places their hands on the back of my head. I put up with this for less than a minute and shrug them off in a bluster of bleariness. I slump against the belly again and fall into my own mind and it is cavernous and I hear groaning. There are rattling rusting chains and fucking creaks, those booming beating-heart creaks. And I'm crying in a slave ship suddenly, and I can't be. There are bones on the sea bottom everywhere. I can't shit myself because I've heaved up the whole of me already. There's nothing left. I am just a pair of eyes in the dark. I am just the dark.

I have drifted back from the bottom, and there are fish. Light, sunlight even, in shafts. There is movement, there are big fish – great bus sides of them pass by. And then jellyfish squeeze in and out above me and I can see through them. Seaweeds stream out, there is yellow and turquoise, thank God there is turquoise. But I don't believe in God, I don't believe in turquoise. I don't believe in me. I don't believe in this world.

But none of this matters, because like a bustling school of schoolmarms the cuttlefish come. Squirting ink behind them they mince along, propelling themselves in ¾ time. I am not at liberty to ignore them. 'Cuttlefish,' they say, 'cuttlefish.' And I wait for them to fade out, wriggle off, before I wake up, as if I can control anything at all. But I sit up in my bunk and think. I am awake and thinking. I am thinking about cuttlefish, and their sepia ink that artists used to use. And, sucking their brushes, got ill. I think of the movement of in and out that propels them along, and my womb and stomach and the in and outing, the up and downing of the ship. And I automatically reach out my hand and open the kit and self-administer Sepia, the remedy made of cuttlefish ink. As though creatures can appear in hallucinations and speak, and advise the right cure for seasickness. It is all too much. I no longer care what all is, what is too, or much, what is real or possible. I only know that cuttlefish are my friends out there in the ocean beyond the bowels, the way out of the belly.

Paul is astonished to see me half an hour later coming up the ladder onto the deck. And even more astonished to see me singing and dancing to Ted's drumming and Frank's guitaring, and improvising my own songs of the sea. Sea shanties. To the deep, to freedom, to blue and turquoise, to cuttlefish. To peace. I can't believe it either.

We glide into the harbour at Drogheda. It feels like hundreds of years have passed, or been lost. The estuary is framed by stone quays that go on for a long, long time. It feels like miles, it feels like hours. We stand on the old deck wearing blankets, ponchos and hats, with the bike and the drum and guitar. There are lines and lines of cormorants on either side, hundreds, thousands of them. It is as though we are in a procession. We are the procession, and they are the crowd lining the way, flapping their black wings up and down like esoteric flags. It as though we are in another earlier time. The groynes are crowded with black silhouettes, wing displaying, taking us in and taking us into Ireland.

Half Empty

It starts but we do not realise it has started. It will not be clear for nearly a year what is happening. It comes when life appears to be the most normal. Secondary school is confusing and tiring and Amba tries to leap over the gulf, to acclimatise from being the biggest in the small school to the smallest in the big school. She gets a sore throat and feels achy all over. It is a duvet-on-the-sofa honey-and-lemon-and-ginger hot-water-bottle and Monkey time.

'I don't need Monkey.'

'Silly me,' I say.

'But he is a bit cold. And do you think you could mend his neck?'

I mend Monkey's neck with embroidered ribbon, he's Monkey, he can carry it off. Monkey is effortlessly cool even in his orange trousers. I have a sore throat, I have honey-and-lemon-and-ginger.

The year sweeps round, in January we are still both ill. Attending school has been a priority, but I keep having to pick Amba up at lunchtime. She's tired, she's achy, she has dreadful headaches, she's limp and nauseous. She wants only to rest and can't bear noise, or people. The doctor says, 'Just wait,' several times.

Midsummer we get a diagnosis: chronic fatigue syndrome, ME. I have it too. Eventually I see a consultant, an expert.

'It is like your strength and health is a pot. And you are sometimes empty, sometimes half empty,' he says.

'I never feel completely well, the pot is never full,' I supply wearily. I'm not here for punchlines. I am not a pot either.

'Exactly. Think of it like a bucket. You have to fill the bucket.'

'You are just talking about pots and buckets. But what can be done? In terms of treatment?'

'Treatment?' His teeth are very white. 'There is no treatment for this. Really, hmm, you are on your own.'

'And my daughter? She has it too.'

'She might recover. She is a child, they can recover.'

'And what do you recommend?'

'Well, you sound like you are eating healthily, you are

doing all the right things. We do not understand ME, yet. We don't really know. I cannot advise you.'

He is clearly ready for his next patient, but I have waited three months just to see him. It is fifteen months since the beginning of it all. Surely this is some kind of joke, surely there is more? He puts the cap back on his pen, he has finished making notes about me, he is finished with me.

'I don't need to come back and see you?'

'There is nothing I can do. As I said, really, you are on your own.'

I am inside, but the sky has fallen in.

I am angry, but it is exhausting to be angry. I am angry with buckets, while knowing it's crazy to be angry with buckets. I want to kick those red fire buckets full of sand that people put their cigarette butts in. But I feel too fucking weak. I am envious of everyone who can get up and go about their business and more, swim, cycle, run, dance. I feel like I have been punched in the stomach, and all the air is on the outside. I'm just shrivelled and hollow. I'm just tired. I tried riding my bike and had to get off and walk slowly. I was too dizzy, dangerously wobbly, faint, just pushing a bike along a pavement. We used to cycle to school together, and back. I can't balance, it is not safe for me to ride a bloody bicycle. Swimming makes me ache all over for days afterwards, gives me headaches, makes me feel drained. I am not in control of my own body. And Amba often feels even worse than me, incapacitated, exhausted, floppy. ME is like the worst day when you first get flu. And this level of ill sits there on both shoulders, ever ready to swoop down and claw you in the guts, take the heart out of living. It takes the hope out. I cannot believe there is nothing I can do. I cannot believe this is my lot. And I cannot find a pathway, even a small one. Where I am is off the map.

Amba is referred to a clinic for young people in Bath, where they are doing research. I do not yet know that this appointment will take another year to materialise. A year. Meanwhile she goes to school if she can, and is accommodated in the nurture group. This sounds nicer than it is, and consists of a Portakabin, children who can't fit in and no teaching. I fetch her more and more often after a phone call. I do not yet know that we will feel bullied and disbelieved and pressured by the school about her attendance. That they will hold meetings that are fraught with stress, coldness, and a lack of trust. Meetings that we need days to recover from, that will feel crushing. I do not know that I will have to fight, hard, with emails and letters and phone calls and more meetings. I do not know that she will have two years at home with nothing but illness and pressure before they find and fund a tutor.

I learn that certain friends are draining, even if they don't mean to be. Even kind people, nice people, wear me out. After a short time, just fifteen minutes, their presence makes me feel completely deflated and drained, like all the air suddenly farting out of a balloon, and as suddenly. I learn that some people do not believe in ME, as though it was an article of faith. I hear the terms 'lazy', 'yuppie flu', 'skiver', 'entitled', 'oversensitive'. I listen to a desperate mother on an ME helpline, wailing a pitiful litany of woe, mismanagement, and lack of care, a tale of no hope, when I rang her to ask for help and advice. I will put the phone down and realise that the doctor was right. I am on my own. He told me the truth, but I couldn't believe it.

I am juggling buckets or pots of energy, playing a hellish game with every minute of the day, every morning, every afternoon, every day of the week, like a ghastly inverted version of *The Sorcerer's Apprentice*. Except I am not slopping endlessly full buckets around trying to manage a surplus of plenty. But working with drops, drips, monitoring the onset of a drought constantly. Looking sideways at Amba while she juggles being young, growing up with this plague that perches inside your mind dribbling negativity. I arrange to do less and less, we have had to cancel so often. ME is not understood by so-called normal people. We have no crutches or rashes, no wounds, there is no trajectory, no visible, palpable end to it. I develop a dark humour, watch Bollywood films, and rely on the company of writers. I can pick them up and put them down, I can dip into them. I finally realise I do not have to read through every book to the end. I give myself permission to do what I want to do, to do what I can do.

If I manage to go for a short walk and am seen out, I think people think, *She can't be that ill.* They do not see the return to the house, the kettle immediately boiled for yet another hot-water bottle, the pyjamas re-donned. They're still warm. I take to going for short walks by the river, early, before people and their dogs are even about. I can't engage with them. I can't answer their questions about how I am or what I'm up to, how Amba's doing. What is there to say? I feel terrible mostly. The good face I put on when I go shopping is wearing thin, is wearing out. I don't have a replacement. I need a set of masks hanging in the hallway to don for different occasions. I ration every action, even going up and down stairs. I pace myself. I have to sit down a lot, I fall asleep on the sofa all the time, sparked right out. I never thought I would get into listening to the radio, it is Amba who recommends it. We listen to Radio 4, like little old ladies before our time. I think this must be what it's like to be old, to not be able to do things, to get spoken down to, and have people humouring you, othering you, whispering about you as if you're not there. I get paranoid and know it, but can't stop. The vortex of dark negative thoughts and ideas is always within reach. I am thirsty for living but can't even reach the cup. I am not half empty, I am empty. Crying is too tiring. I stare, I lie staring when books can't reach me, can't touch me, I can't hold them up. I stare into greyscape. I retreat into 'what if' country, toying with worst-case scenarios, harnessed in coping strategies and avoidance techniques.

I can't remember things, I slur instead of talking and can barely string sentences together or remember the capitals of countries I have always known. When the phone rings I can't answer it. I can't see the future happening. I am not there. I am not here. This is not me. This is a full stop, this cannot be my story.

Tank

Stirring myself out of a lukewarm bath I've been in too long, maybe I fell asleep. I still keep putting it off, getting out. Finding a way to actually move and emerge into the air. A creature from the sleep of the deep. The bath creaks with my shifting weight. The water lurches. Looking at my wet footprints on the lino, I realise that due to Chronic Fatigue bloody Syndrome I am now an expert in the micromanagement of time and energy. No one will evaluate or even notice this skill, but nevertheless it is now built in. I have it. There will be plenty of hurdles I fall at, skid around in the mud and have to go back to lying down with a hot-water bottle, reading books I've read before, recovering, resting, bloody being good to myself, listening to my body etc. etc. Anything 'chronic' is boring, it bores into your very soul. You are bored of yourself. Bored of your misery, weakness, aches, headaches, bored of eating and nausea, bored of bathing and shitting, bored of being affected by everything and everybody to such a ridiculous extent, bored of being fragile, bored of not being able to do things. Bored of people not getting it, bored of being bored. Bored of being, full stop. And as for syndromes, let's not even go there.

I miss myself. I long for the quickening in my chest. The quiver of feeling alive, alert, awake, aware, in action. I inch towards a higher plateau of energy, an inch at a time. I still can't ride my bike. If I dig I ache all over, yet Amba has an idea.

'I've been thinking. You could take on an allotment.'

I gawp.

'No really, think about it. An allotment with no pressure.'

The allotment field was the winter mooring for the Keewaydin. Between the village and the town. I know this field, I helped Paul plough with two horses, jaggedly, and plant two long rows of potatoes that came to nothing due to giant white slugs. Bracken thrives there. Now there is a new rabbit-proof fence, there is a shelter with a noticeboard and there is a tank for water. So watering is possible. The tank feeds several ballcocked troughs, conveniently spaced around to serve thirty plots, now marked out with string and posts. I remember evenings sitting beside the fire waiting for sweetcorn and potatoes to cook under the oak trees above the river and the boat. And Paul saying, 'I'd like to see people growing food here.'

Now they are. Years have gone by, time has been squished, swallowed, striated, stolen, and exiled by ME. My time, lost to the sofa, hot-water bottles and despair. Things have happened without me knowing how or when or who made them happen.

We are walking around the field where the allotments are and admiring the water troughs and the fencing, and I ponder. I wonder. I have been investigating no-dig beds in library books. Amba is talking about fruit bushes, and mulberries. She is talking about mapping it out on graph paper and willow arches and strawberries. There is a sweet breeze in her hair.

I am thinking about cardboard and manure and mulching, and playing in the sandpit when I was little. The sand was delivered in wheelbarrows every year, fresh and orange. There were three steps down to the sandpit, there was the tap, buckets, spades, bowls. Water was the crucial ingredient in every enterprise, houses or mountain ranges or tunnelling operations. My little brother was always humming or brumming his cars along. We made rivers and ponds, we made oxbow lakes. Even if they seeped away to make the sand darken. I am thinking about when that whole section of the garden was sold off, so the three massive conker trees and the copper beech umbrellaing the Speech House weren't ours any more. The first shiplap fence appeared. The meadow grass full of wildflowers that had once been Lady Guisborough's tennis court was gone, and behind the fence a brick and glass bungalow appeared, with a lawn like a bowling green. Mr Farrow, the dentist, would go over this lawn with a garden fork, pronging it at careful intervals, to aerate it. My little brother and I, with sandy hands, would peer at this foreign activity through precious gaps in the fence silently. Observing Mr and Mrs Farrow going about their lives. How ordinary they seemed, how normal, how new and shiny everything looked, how compelling this was, in contrast to what was going on at home behind us. I am thinking of the smoke from the bonfire in the Cabbage Garden, the smell of lawnmower petrol, of playing hide-and-seek crouching in the middle of the Michaelmas daisies, holding my breath and almost bursting from staying quiet, or hiding in the hollow of the bigtreeinthecorner. I am thinking of Tata poking charred papers in the incinerator with a stick. He stood next to me, but he was not there. He was somewhere else as he reached through the flames in the incinerator.

Enjoying the sun and the oak trees, I sit on my allotment. No one will notice how much or how little I do, and if they do they're just overly competitive and I don't care. Most will be far too busy with their own plots. I have gathered cardboard boxes. I have gathered my muscles and a wheelbarrow. I place strategic pallets to sit on. I wait and watch the birds with a flask and a blue mug. I am gifted plastic sheeting and an old carpet and feel disproportionately elated at these small trophies. I pace myself, and monitor my energy level like a scientist in a lab.

Gardening is like playing in the sandpit. Mulching is like making sandwiches or lasagne. I have plenty of tea breaks. I water leek seedlings on the windowsill at home waiting to go into my two new beds. I have made them very carefully. One is dug painstakingly, the traditional way. It's hard and very slow. The other one is assembled from cardboard boxes, then manure, then on top, there are wood chippings. Unwanted wood chippings.

'Ugh, leylandii! Too acidic. Nothing will grow,' the expert allotment-holders say.

In fact they make a nice warm cover on top, and help the drainage. I stick my fingers in to make holes for the leeks in both the beds. I water the roots in gently. I fill them up and pat them. I tend to them, weeding and watering them when it's dry, filling buckets up from the trough. The no-dig bed sprouts few weeds, it is always warm and wormy. The leeks in the painfully dug bed turn out mincing, skinny and insubstantial. The leeks in the no-dig cardboard bed grow fat and strong and three times the size. And luscious.

In the future I will learn more about the magic of mulching, take in the science of lignin and the slow release of minerals, the health of critters and the pitfalls of bare soil. I will hear how pesticides mess with the natural immune system of earth, and how it takes five hundred years to build up an inch of topsoil. And I will have the feeling that I am hearing a metaphor that I can almost understand about myself, my health, and the earth. That we are not separate or different at all.

I work kneeling. I fill up the old bath on my allotment, carrying black buckets from the trough. As I try not to stagger, try not to let the water slop over the sides, I hear the ballcock rising as the trough refills again from the tank. I gauge how much or how little I can do, so I don't overdo it and get ill. I learn by trial and error. I sit and breathe and stare. I make comfrey and nettle elixirs. It is possible to feel satisfied with what I can do.

At the harvest fair, awards are awarded. I do not enter, although I like to go and look at all the entries. I do not feel that we really grow vegetables and flowers, we tend them and they grow. And we grow growing them.

The Abbots Pool

The Cut, it's called, and it feels like that: it was cut. Mud like the inside of guts, mud you could drown in, in great flopping folds. Wet mud that wrinkles up and crusts, but never dries out. The river goes through the city split two ways, into the harbours and docks, and along the Cut, partnered with a railway line and a cycleway. Roads embrace the water on both sides, and there are tatty rattley trees. The river has been engineered to flow through basins, beside quays, the river has been tamed to be fit for purpose.

Visiting Lily in Bristol, I seek water. I appreciate the paintbox colours of the terraces crowding the hills, Leigh Woods sprawling above the gorge, and Ashton Court below glowing green, the trees stately. Yet today it all feels like a stage set. The gorge is a neck straining for water and air, the mud piles up on itself with no mercy, the suspension bridge is like some fantasy of a man who's spent too long in an attic with a model railway. I am seeing the city as though through a glass window. Sensibly coated and booted, even with a mobile phone, why do I feel like a ghost? I am not convinced by coffee shops. I am pacing myself, trying to keep the wolves of exhaustion and nausea at bay. I am still afraid of flaking out, crumpling up, feeling unable to cope. The memory of myself as a striding strong woman seems dodgy, blurred, and unreliable. Historic. I have tears behind my eyes, ready to flow. Too thin a skin. Thoroughly sick of working with my thoughts, trying to see the good in everything that happens. Trying and trying so I am bending over backwards so far I feel like there is a precipice behind me and the fall, the fall will be infinite.

I have been calming waters for years. There is nothing left of me, meeting and failing to meet expectations, being constantly available and being accused of being unavailable. Years like a long line of trees in a plantation . . . I walk across Spike Island to the Harbourside. The waters are unsettling. It could be, should be, so uplifting, so life-affirming: canoe volleyball back there in the basin, the dinghies and skiffs, the barges and narrowboats, kayaks and paddleboards. The chugging packet boats with Wallace and Gromit on their bows. Or the ones with shark teeth, playful, ironic even. Moored in front of the Arnolfini is a metal gun warship. I can't forget. I can't pretend. I remember. This is a world centre of slaves. These quaysides held those disembarkings. These markets sold people. And it's on the harbour bottom, it's in the wailing shrieks of the gulls, it's in my faltering breath, my bones. I am finding it difficult living in the present in the past.

Later I pick Lily up and we drive to the other side of the gorge to try to find the Abbots Pool. It's hot, the paper *A–Z* I cling to lacks clarity, there's just space where I want to go. We trudge uphill through woodland, skirting lumpy ruts on the track. The bluebells are over. And beyond up over and then through, there's a stile then a bit of barbed wire, but we still have not found any sign of a pond, a pool, a lake, or even a stream that might trickle, tickle, tease us, in the right direction. There is no discernible scent or sense of water, not even a bog. It is not swampy or marshy, there is no pond. Luckily we both have bottles of water. It is too hot, I trickle some on the top of my head and smear it round my neck. And we come to a field like a specially thrown-down blanket that beckons us to lie down. So we settle for resting – we've given up on finding the lake or whatever it is, we've had our visions of ponds and glades and fat fish and herb gardens and flowering shrubs bent over still waters. We lie down in the field that is not the Abbots Pool and relax finally, accepting that this is this. It is what it is. That expectations are killjoys. It is enough to be here in this grass, surrounded by these trees. The water is here somewhere anyway, underground, there are water tables and aquifers and reservoirs, but right here and now, water is not on the surface. This is what was meant to happen, it is OK to be lost – it is quite sweet in a way, a bit archetypal like a fairy tale with so-called grown-ups starring in it, and we find ourselves funny, chat and plait the long grasses. We ration our sips of Bristol tap water and share oatcakes.

In the future I will do early morning yoga, despite dog walkers and dog shit, beside the almost round Cheddar Reservoir. When I look up to the left I will see Glastonbury Tor. The reservoir will be very low, too low, with a pinkish rim and ducklings, and yellow flowers on the steps that should be underwater. A sign will say *This is Bristol City Water Supply*, you're not allowed to touch it.

Lying on the green blanket with Lily, I feel so very pleased with myself that I even got here, that I am this much better to go on an adventure, even though it seems to have failed. But we know there is only 'failing better'. That maps are not infallible. For some journeys there can be no maps. We both hold so much in our bloodlines, in our DNA. In our skeletons. There is so much we don't know, no one said. Or there was no one left to put it into words.

'This place, it feels like Poland,' I say grandly, spreading my arms out.

'Does it? How do you know?'

'I don't know how I do, but it does.'

'You must go. You must. You don't really know who you are.'

'God knows how.'

'No, Mum, don't. If you got here, you can get to Poland. You don't have to be one hundred per cent better. Just go as you are.'

'As I am?'

'Yup. You know how to pace yourself.'

'I certainly fucking do.'

Of course, on what I think is the way back, over a rise through a thicket, a path appears and there it is, the Abbots Pool, just over the hill from where we were all along. When we'd completely given up on it. There are dogs, there are always dogs, there are people, but not many. The pool is an oasis for moorhens, and us. There are beech trees in abundance, and I am happy.

It is not long before we slip in and swim, swim around the scrub island, brushing close to the water lilies, in a kind of foreplay of a love of a place, there is plenty of space. And I look over at Lily and know we would neither of us have done this on our own, that we needed to be lost and then find ourselves, swimming. There is the absolute pleasure of tangled wet hair straggling down our backs on the way back to pints of tea.

As we drive down to enter the city again we see a bearded man on an old bike. Paintbox and easel strapped on the back, he's making his way to the pool. We look at each other and wonder if we have seen him, we laugh – he's out of the South of France, he's out of the 1900s, an archetypal 'artist', a blip, above a city dedicated to graffiti art that's now morphed into corporate 'Street Art'. He's perfectly real.

In the future we will see him again, on the duck-shit shore of the Abbots Pool, with his easel, painting a painting in very bright shades of green. I will be wearing my green wool jacket and cerise gloves. I will stand a little way away from my daughters and greet the elements in a Tai Chi way, my bright pink gloves tracing semaphore-like patterns in the reflections in the water. When I look round, they will both be smiling.

Mountain Stream

This moment has been a long time coming, primal and essential. I am on Polish soil. Here in the wild Tatra Mountains, I am beginning to absorb what it means physically to be half-Polish. I can barely walk my feet are so blistered, I am balanced on a rock beside this mountain stream of bitingly cold water. It's freezing, my feet are plunged in up to my knees, there is agony, and there is ecstasy. We are on the way down a mountain path through dark woods after being transfixed, hypnotised up there, lying in the green meadows staring out up and over the mountain peaks, absently scoffing bread and sheep's cheese. There are signposts in Polish with images of bears. *Bears Beware*. Bears with long claws. I am unsure how big bears are. We can feel them. There is the energy of bears here. We want to see a bear, and also we don't want to see a bear. A prickling feeling tells me the bears are in charge here, this is their place, and they are probably keeping tabs on our progress right now. Have been watching us for some time. Yet, what the hell, we yelp at the crystal water, and we drink it, we gulp it down. It was very hot in the sun up there in the upper world. We've been parched. We slather water on our faces, sloosh our armpits and fill our water bottles up. This water is full of vitality, it makes us laugh it tastes so soft and fresh. It is like it has a bright and clear laugh of its own. The sound of our gaiety at the pure pleasure of drinking mountain water rings out through the surrounding trees.

Amba requires photographing, so she positions herself on the rock and I oblige. We are aware of our voices, aware we are performing as you do around cameras, and when you feel you are being watched. We can't help looking about us, both hoping and fearing to catch a glimpse of a bear. Near enough to be identifiable, far enough to be at a safe distance. The idea of a bear coming up or down the footpath, dodging roots and rocks like we do is silly, is far-fetched. Surely a bear would flit, familiar with the trees, the hollows, the caves. A bear would read the woods in ways we can't even imagine, see differently, move with absolute freedom and familiarity here. Our laughter is a little shrill, a little echoey, and there is still the hobbling walk back down to the road to come that we want to put off for as long as possible. But we know it has to happen, and then there is the likelihood that I haven't read the map or the bus timetable correctly, it being in Polish, so . . . I think Amba has now almost recovered from my New-York-style exchange with the overcharging taxi driver on the way here, when he said, 'Fuck you, lady.' We carry water down the mountain, aware of the presence of bears and feeling very little.

Our room is above the cheese market, on a road that becomes a path that horses use like humans. The house is all wooden, there is a solar panel too. When we arrived in Zakopane and got to the room I had actually booked, everything felt wrong. There was no view of the mountains, there was no socket for the kettle, the furniture was flimsy, the lampshades very dark. Worst was the man raking the gravel outside, and not in a Zen way. And then the heavens opened, the sky clapped, a storm was breaking over our heads. And I couldn't settle. When the downpour tailed off, the man reappeared and began raking the gravel again, slowly, for no discernible reason. I breathed in deeply, broke out of the trying-to-put-a-good-face-on-it mood I'd adopted, and said to Amba lying on the bed, 'I don't think we can stay here.'

'No.'

'There is something sinister about that raking.'

'Definitely. There is, I was thinking the same thing, and not wanting to think it.'

'Nothing is quite right. Nothing works properly.'

'Exactly. We can't stay here, Mum.'

'No.'

'This might be our only time in Zakopane, and this place is actually really creepy.'

'Yes.'

'It feels like the scene of a crime.'

'That man raking.'

'Why is he doing that? And looking up at the window? What are we going to do? We can't stay here.'

'I am going to go out and walk around and find somewhere else.'

'How? Can you do that?'

'I've got to. And I'm going to.'

'I just can't walk any more right now.'

It had been quite a way from the bus station.

'I'll lock you in, I won't be long. We want to be this end of town, near the market. We just can't stay here.'

'That woman on reception is like . . . a doll or something. I hate to think what is going on here. What has gone on here?'

'Try not to think too much.'

It can be hazardous to have a vivid imagination. So I found this room, our room, the right room, with this mammoth view of the Giewont Massif, the balcony, solid furniture, and a decent kitchen. Yes, you can't walk straight into the bathroom, you have to go sideways, but this is bearable. I found the right people too, who drove me back to the gravel place and picked up our stuff and Amba. As we drove away from what felt like a horror film set, a rainbow hung across the sky.

On the third day, I want to go on the cable car up to the border with Slovakia. Up to the snow. To visit beyond the skyline that I have got to know quite well while eating muesli on the balcony, while just staring out the window. The cresting curve of Giewont will always be in my head now. I can tell. To manoeuvre this expedition to up there, to travel in my first cable car, in fact, I have to take a very deep breath and employ a giant-sized helping of diplomacy. Since Amba is engaged on her device, head down sitting on her bed, engrossed in the intricate and delicate nuances of the closing scenes of a love affair.

As the cable car lurches and ascends above the treetops, Amba swears. Our fellow passengers look genuinely appalled and clutch their small children closer, further away from us as if we are dangerous. Amba is actually terrified of heights, she has vertigo, she is terrified of the jerks as we pass each post, of getting on and off, of the top, and there is also the dull fear underneath of feeling too exhausted to enjoy anything, even getting out of your comfort zone and being scared shitless. It is an act of faith to be in Poland at all, with ME. Only we know what it has cost us. But the ME years have focused my mind stringently, pummelling it, reminding me to be happy to do what I can. I am thrilled to be here at all, in my father's country at last. The trip is built in with resting, with breaks, with goals and moveable goal posts.

At the top of Kasprowy Wierch, the snow is yellowing, the path to the border is a slushy trail of black dots of people like ants, intent on their destination. We adjourn from following and get off the trail to take in the view. The snow fields and jagged peaks look celestial and remote. Other, somewhere beyond the reach of humans. The wind gusts across to us from that distant world, where no cable car or road or path can go. The sun makes all the shades of white glow like light, and provides sheer angular shadows. The view is urgent, expansive, bigger than we can take in in one go. There is exhilaration in the snow, we sit and eat some. Like we are convalescents taking the waters or bathing in hot springs, we suck the clean snow.

I have come to see experiences as either nourishing or draining, peaks or troughs. People too. The extremes of the polarity are easy to spot, it is the confusion of the middle range that is so hard. And then there is the added calculation to take into account, that there are two of us here with ME and we experience it differently. There are gains to be made by getting out of the comfort zone carefully. The baseline of duvets and films and snacks can get to be a jail. I suppose the label 'disabled' fits, but I feel no affinity with this negative word. Focused on the things you can't do, rather than big up the things you can. It reminds me of 'dishabille': 'messy' or 'undressed'. As if the present state is never enough, when it is all there is.

We know how incredible it is that we have made it up here, as we stare out at the snow fields and look at the ski lifts with their chairs dangling down like giant paper clips. I can hear two girls speaking English.

'There's some English people, shall we say hi, and have a chat?' I suggest.

'No way, don't you dare. Can't you hear them? Gap Yaar Darling types. They're just taking snaps and moving on, this is just a selfie opportunity, a place to tick off on their itinerary. Let them think we're Polish. Don't say a word.'

'OK. OK.' I whisper until the girls are out of earshot. 'Do you know my father, your grandfather, once escaped from a concentration camp in the snow? With a Moroccan and a white sheet.'

'As a disguise? Neat. Hey, try some of this snow here, it's quite clean.'

We suck on snow companionably, in silence. I used to think my father was studying, 'concentrating', in the camps he was in during the war. Then I realised, from the Ribena bottle, that 'concentrated' means full strength, undiluted. I think of the fear he experienced, with no film score, no arc of his narrative. Nothing to signify the futility, the anger, the courage, the brutality, the terror, the running, the hiding, the killing, the random loss of life. He left his homeland and his parents when he was nineteen and the war 'broke out'. Like war is always sitting somewhere jailed, and waiting to escape.

I bleed into Polish soil at the foot of the Tatra Mountains. I thought I had stopped my bleeding, Amba's menstrual cycle is the one I am aware of now. And yet when we dismount from the cable car, our legs feeling like we've been at sea, and walk off to find the sweet spot, the quiet spot, to rest awhile, I need a wee and squat behind a tree, and see I am bleeding. Although I know my father would be flabbergasted to listen to talk of blood, I swell with happiness. It is fitting that I have come to Poland and bled here, maybe finally for the last time. It feels right, like the illogical sense I have had since we got here: that I have returned. I remember it. The streets around the central square in Kraków, the river, the trees, the views. Although I have never been to Poland before. I am carrying Poland in my DNA, it's liquid apparently at body temperature. People stop and ask me for directions in Polish. Everything feels completely familiar.

Vodka

'Well, you see, the last time I saw you, you were three. You haven't changed! I remember your mother very well. The house. The garden was so beautiful.'

'I had no idea. Well, I suppose I was only three.'

'Your father should never have married S. You were so young then. How old?'

'I was nine the year my mother died, and he married again the same year.'

'I wrote and told him not to, it was wrong. How old was he? Forty-eight.'

'And she was twenty-three.'

'Exactly. He didn't write again, not for years and years.'

Renia's garden has the same flowers as our old garden: peonies, lily-of-the-valley, roses, irises, lilac, Michaelmas daisies. Her garden has the same flavour, although it is completely different. I picked snowdrops for my mother as she lay dying, and put them in a blue-and-white-striped egg cup. She could barely open her eyes to see them. She was determined to last until the Spring. She died in the night on the Spring Equinox, 1968. Nearly fifty years have passed.

Renia is my father's cousin, she's a diva. On the grand piano there is a photograph of her with her hair up, she looks like Sophia Loren. She has a photograph of our great-grandparents and their three grown-up children: her father, my great-aunt and my grandfather with my grandmother. My great-aunt's child in the foreground is an almost bald baby, perched on an animal skin. I have never seen this photograph before. She examines the corners, the back.

'Maybe 1919, just after Poland became Poland again. After the war.'

'My father was born the next year. His parents were newly married, I suppose.'

I had no picture of my grandparents, let alone my great-grandparents, before. My great-grandfather is muscular with a moustache, like a middle-aged Omar Sharif. My great-grandmother Jula wears a headscarf and looks determined, strong, and confident. Seeing her gives me strength and makes me cry, in a good way, sitting next to Renia. We both have tears in our eyes, our bodies are touching and it's comfortable, as we look at our ancestors.

Amba is tucked up on a day bed, and we have drunk Tokay. Ula is doing her best to translate. Ula is the daughter of the baby on the animal skin in the photograph. I remember her, she came to live with us in York, as an au pair, in the year before the worst year. When I was twelve. Now she has snow-white puffy hair, and I am a foot taller than her. Between them these lady relatives have managed to usher us into too many churches to count. As they say in Poland, 'You could open a tin of fish and the Pope will be inside.' Naturally the Polish pope.

Ula in particular is trying to save my soul. Under her influence I kiss the bones of St Faustina, the nun who painted Jesus with his heart shining out in a spectrum of colours. St Faustina apparently followed his direct guidance, the other nuns disapproved and were jealous of her. Queuing to kiss bones reminds me of the fervour of faith in India. Ula nudges me towards a piece of the cross embedded in the wall of the porch of the huge modern steel glass church, like an American church, with the giant Polish pope on high in brass over our heads. She whispers, 'Touch it. This means that now Jesus will be there when you die. To meet you, you see. Jesus will be there to meet you.'

I say nothing when she gets me to touch it again on the way out. It would be churlish.

We drive to the forest and hope to get lost there. But I should have known it, we are near a monastery, and they steer us there. Women are not allowed in, but the monk 'on the door' sells us postcards and charms. But Ula would frown if we said 'charms'. In the future I will notice that Amba leaves home with hers. The monks here venerate the skulls of past monks. I make the sign of the cross with holy water many times on many thresholds in Poland.

Renia shows us a photo of her father, towards the end of the war, twenty-five years after the family group photograph when he was so handsome, even suave, hopeful and young. In 1944 he wears the stripy overalls like pyjamas, he's emaciated, his features look as if someone has tried to rub them out.

'They broke him. He was in the prison here in Kraków. He was in the Polish Underground. The prison we passed on the way to the forest, do you remember?'

Yes, I remember. And the street she gestured at in passing, saying over her shoulder, 'They shot so many people there, the Gestapo. So many.'

Amba and I compare notes, we both have time slippage here. And have heard feet running over cobbles, gunshots, trams squealing, the judder-judder of wheels on cobbles, breath held in courtyards. Seen the flags unfurled on the central square, heard the curt echo of boots on the castle staircases, the muffled drunken giggles of women. I have met the eyes of an old woman wheeling a shopping trolley below the castle down by the river, just after looking through peepholes at photographs of hangings that happened in the same place, on the same street. Our eyes locked with the shared knowledge of the stain.

Renia, a bit tipsy, smoking on her kitchen balcony like an errant teenager, tells me about my grandfather.

'He was an alcoholic, you know. You are old enough to know. It started in the trenches in Italy, they gave them brandy every day for breakfast. For courage. He died of grief and alcohol. Vodka. After your grandmother died he couldn't go on. In less than a year he had gone.'

We have been to the family grave in the baroque graveyard. That day it was full of the Turkish community of Kraków burying two young people killed in a car crash. We carried flowers, candles in glasses, a dustpan and brush, and some gardening gloves, walking in the opposite direction to the huge procession of Polish Turks in black. We have looked up at the apartment window my grandmother looked out of in the old town, while standing on the steps of the convent opposite.

Amba has recorded, has seen, our trip through the lens of her camera. Photo after photo in the mountains, eating cheesecake, in the Planty, will be lost with the camera. Renia gives me the photographs glued onto faded orange card that belonged to my grandmother. And there I am in shorts at the seaside in Filey, the fifth of her six grandchildren. The orange card is dog-eared. I think of my grandmother saying our names out loud, in a Polish room in a Polish street. Popping up to Rynek Kleparski market, preparing pierogi, she would have been hoping. In the lush blue and gold interior of the Mariachi church that Picasso said was the eighth wonder of the world, she would have been praying. Doing penance, lapping her rosary with Hail Marys, she would have been imagining us together. Touching our hair, sitting us on her knee, teaching us Polish. Laughing.

My grandmother never met my mother or any of her grandchildren, she never saw my father again either. After the war, my father 'settled' in Oxford. They would not issue him with a visa when he heard she was dying in 1963. She had glued the photographs he sent her onto orange card. Of him with the family as it grew, in gardens in Oxford, lanky in swimming trunks on the promenade at Filey, with me sitting in the fringed pram, the others clustered around eating ice creams, carrying buckets and spades. He'd sent a postcard to Kraków of Filey Beach, with an X marking the spot where we used to make our base. He'd sent a postcard to Kraków from the camp at Miranda de Ebro in Spain in 1942. A black-and-white picture of the Puerto de la Paz (the Port of Peace), in Barcelona. Hitler invaded Poland on 1st September 1939. Britain declared war on Germany on 3rd September, my father's nineteenth birthday was on 20th September. My father was a law student, and joined the Polish army.

I was brought up in this loss, like invisible snow falling all around me. Nothing was ever explained. 'Surviving, surviving,' I can hear him say. I think I'm still focused on 'Surviving, surviving', even now. Grief and loss were dedicated to God, and dwarfed by the suffering of Jesus nailed to his crucifix. I realise my father had PTSD long before it was coined, after those years in the camps, in Hungary, Spain, and France, and inherited from his father, and his . . . and his . . . and so on . . . The whole atmosphere of my father in photographs tell me this. Pre-war he looks wary but hopeful, fresh and gawky with big ears. Post-war he is haunted and gaunt, a black-and-white refugee in Oxford tweed, sallow, with pinched cheekbones. I have inherited the chasm of separation. And a reservoir of the emotions that he 'controlled' with his coping mechanisms of foul temper, common sense and electrifying silence.

There is another photograph I have of my father, sipping vodka from a small glass and wearing a string vest. Now I realise it's taken at Renia's, one morning in the 1980s. This is a man I don't recognise. I have never seen my father drink vodka.

'Really. You don't want to go there,' Renia says. 'Why do you want to go there? There is nothing there. My mother brought me up alone, you know. I had no father because of the war.'

She finds the photograph of the tall ghost of a man in the striped uniform.

'You see. Look. He was broken, he could not be a father, the Jesuits took him to Wisconsin after the war. I didn't know him. Why think about it now? You don't need to go, you know. What is the point? I will never go. Never. You feel headache? There is vodka for that. Water of life, it is . . . there is vodka for heartache, vodka for stomach, vodka for sadness, you know, vodka for everything.'

There is a cluster, a forest, a Manhattan, of different-shaped vodka bottles on her kitchen counter. Urek, her husband, in cologne and cravat, has Mongolian eyes. They meet mine filled with sadness and happiness at the same time.

Ula whispers, 'If you like, I will go with you. If you like, I will translate for you. I can go. Urek went, you know, with your father. And your sister.'

They never said, so I never knew. Pure Tata – he would never say, neither would my light blue sister, who lives in Spain now. I know Ula needs to go back home to Warsaw. I know she would translate beautifully, and I know I will miss her. But we need to do this ourselves, without her. We part as she gets on the tram to go and stay with her oldest friend, in Podgórze, south of the river, where the ghetto used to be.

WATER BOTTLE

'This sounds mad, but I've been wondering if it's OK to wear stripy pants.'

'Oh God, I was just thinking that. About my socks,' says Amba.

'I think it is OK. They wouldn't mind.'

'No. Today will change us, we will never be the same again.'

'That is true about every day, technically. Every moment in fact. But I know what you mean.'

Alone at home Amba has been studying European history, Germany is all over the syllabus. We are getting ready to go to Auschwitz, and each small decision finds itself under a magnifying glass. Yesterday I saw a train to Oświęcim, the Polish name, sitting empty and creaking on a shiny new platform. Also empty. The station is new now, you get to it through a mall, it could be anywhere. The old one sits empty and full of memories. Departures, arrivals. I can't face going by train, even a modern diesel with windows. We get a coach, it's the hottest June day they've had in Poland since records began. We clutch water bottles in sweaty palms. The water is never cold enough. We float past forests, but today every glade, every clearing, looks sinister.

The coach stops in the market town, a woman clutches empty bags and a shopping list, standing in the file of locals waiting to get off the bus, looking bored and impatient. She pushes a wisp of hair back behind her ears. When we arrive at the camp, the museum, the visitors' centre (whatever it is, names don't encompass it), the car park is heaving with coaches and cars. It's a popular destination. Security is airport tense. We are guided by a Polish woman in English: 'Stick together, stick together. We don't want to lose you.'

There are many groups and many languages. Here is the *Arbeit macht frei* gate and we have to walk through it, there's no other way in. The ground is uneven, the buildings look like old-style low-rise council flats. They're not. We are in a museum that's not a museum, being funnelled round in a troop. The processing of visitors is scrupulously efficient, to the letter, to the minute. I know there will be a room of hair, and a room of shoes, we all know. Here is the map of all the camps – concentration, prisoner of war, extermination – with

Auschwitz here at the heart centre. All the black lines lead to this destination: central, straddling east and west, convenient for transport. Technically it was in the Reich territory, which somehow, in some minds, made what happened here legal.

Here are the empty cans of Zyklon B, real yet ghostly in a vitrine. Here is the list of the numbers, of the many different peoples who were murdered here. Here is a room with a great heap of enamel kitchenware in an enormous bay, behind glass. Stencilled with flowers and geometric shapes, there are thousands and thousands of plates and bowls and mugs and kettles and coffee pots, piled high, piled willy-nilly. If you were told to pack one bag you would think about cooking when you got there, wherever it was. Tired from the journey, it would be the first thing you would want to do. Boil some water and put the coffee on. Eat together. And this great silent pile, this hill of hope, of everyday kitchen behaviour, is what undoes me.

The mountain of suitcases, with painted-on names, the huge heaps of shoes and boots in every stage of wear from smart and dainty to worn out with the soles hanging off. Piles and piles and piles of hair. In a glass case, a roll of cloth woven from hair, clinical, efficient, shameless. The wallpaper on the way down to the torture chamber cellar is peeling, is original, is a pattern of browns. Many hands have touched these walls. We troop in and out of clammy cells still thick with fear, with horror, imagining the minds of those experimenting on the people they called 'vermin', and 'pieces', after they'd been murdered. The aftertaste of torturers has a sadists' metal smell. This is cold vile hell, and I wonder why it still needs to be here, in a building. Schoolchildren trail in lines, bored, chewing gum, missing their smartphones. Time is rationed. Outside, in the air at last, is the wall where they shot people. There is no time on this breakneck tour to stop, to feel, to honour. No time to go beyond the visible. There is the knowledge of what happened here in words, and then the next block to visit. We are running out of water. It's so hot. We cluster obediently, I stand beside a bulky African American in a baseball cap with his grown-up children, we exchange winded glances, hollowed out with history.

After two hours we are told to meet up again in exactly ten minutes to get the bus together to go to Birkenau. We have seen the first prototype gas chamber/shower now, the holes in the roof where they poured the Zyklon B in, we have stood and looked at each other standing there in our casual summer clothes. We have seen the ovens, industrial, brick and metal, heavy duty. We have seen the suburban house where the commandant, Rudolf Höss, lived with his wife and five children, and the scaffolding where he was hanged after Nuremberg.

In the Ladies' we try to be quick. We get more water and then go to the edge of the heaving car park to reconvene with our group and our guide. But they're not there. Except for one man in the busy throng of anonymous people, it's so crowded. He recognises us. 'Where are all the others?'

'I don't know, I haven't seen the guide anywhere either. We haven't been long, had to get some more water.'

'Yes. Me too.' He brandishes a fresh bottle. 'It's so hot.'

'It's so full on.'

He is a thin Indian guy from Glasgow, he has come especially to Poland to visit the camp.

'I had to. I have been reading and thinking, and I just had to come. Then I will go straight home. And you?'

'My father was Polish, Catholic, from this area. My mother's grandfather was Jewish. Relatives died in the camps on both sides of my family. I think.'

My family history has been challenging to uncover. Friedrich and Leon died in Dachau as part of the 'extermination of intellectuals'. Sophie died in Theresienstadt. My mother's grandfather, Gustav Maximillian Schloss, was a Jew from near Nuremberg. He ran a hardware shop for a time in Demerara in the 1880s. I know that if my father had known that Gustav was German and Jewish, he would not have married my mother. I have discovered that Gustav and my great-grandmother, an Irish Cockney and a Catholic, didn't marry until after all six of their children were born. They had both been married before. They lived at various addresses separately and together in North London, where they are buried. I have a German family tree. The names toll: Gabriel, Sarah, Moses, Lazarus, Esther, Ludwig, Sophie, Max, Frieda, Siegfried and Gustav.

My siblings are settled all over the world now. Our children have Polish, French, German, Irish, Roma, English, West Indian, Ghanaian, Croatian, Serbian, Hungarian, Dutch and Danish roots. And these are the ones we know about. Roots go on spreading.

'We are all related. We are all the same,' says the Glaswegian Indian.

'Yes. We are. We must be.' I look at him with relief, with recognition.

Amba is looking briskly around, but our group has managed to vanish into thin air. So we get on the coach shuttle to Birkenau, a couple of kilometres down the road. The coach doors open and close with a sealed swish, effective, the air conditioning is slightly chilling. I clutch my water bottle like my life depends on it, wishing the water was colder, while realising that this thought is completely out of proportion and out of place.

We stand at the gate of Birkenau, the railway line goes through it. There is absolutely no sign of anyone else in our group. The Glaswegian agrees, 'I'd know them anywhere. Strange, after only two hours together, but I would. I don't understand it. I can't believe we've lost them, we did everything we were told to do.'

'Well, they've lost us,' Amba says, tapping her foot.

'But where can they all be?' I feel abandoned and confused, thirty people have disappeared.

Amba is impatient to get on with touring Birkenau. With a zealous look in her eye, she wants to make the most of this experience, especially after all the years holed up at home with me, being bored and ill. She knows she may well crash later, but now she is thirsty for knowledge. There is a bookshop, and the gate. The man on the gate is the rudest man in Poland. At my faltering enquiry, he stares at the three of us, obviously not a group, and spits on the ground, growls something incomprehensible and waves his hands dismissively at us. He doesn't care. There is nothing to say. The group has gone. We will wait for another guide in English to appear and tag along.

Amba can tell from the outside that I am collapsing inside. My voice has gone wobbly. I am becoming incoherent and, particularly to her, embarrassing. The rudest man in Poland has pierced something in me. The Glaswegian is still somewhat startled, but pragmatic. We stand by the gateway and wait. I am thinking about the people we have lost, completely vanished, did we dream them?

'Mum, you need to calm down. We can just go with another group. It doesn't matter.'

'That's it. It will be fine,' the man from Glasgow says softly.

'But . . . I can't . . .' Words fail, and I realise I can't control myself.

'Well, we're here, and we have to go on with the tour.' Amba is fully engaged with the process.

Now I am crouching in the gateway by the railway track. The rudest man in Eastern Europe glares at me and makes arm gestures as though I am a goose or stray dog.

'You can't sit here. You can't, Mum. Don't you want to go round?'

I don't know what I want, I have crumpled. I need to sit down and collect myself. I traipse into the bookshop, there is nowhere to sit down. But on the way out, in a grubby lobby, there is an enormous drinks machine and a small iron bench. I sit down on it. Amba goes off to scout for a tour in English. I want to disappear. I am shivering, although it's the hottest day on record. I need to do this. I am letting Amba down. She reappears and explains, 'We've found a group now, they're Irish.'

'Irish? Who's "we"?'

'Imran.'

'Who's Imran? Is he Irish?'

'The Scotsman. For God's sake, Mum. The guide is fine with it. He's Polish and quite hot actually.' She grins.

'What?'

'Come on. We have to go. Now.' She is slightly gritting her teeth and fully raising her eyebrows.

'I don't think I can.' But I follow her out weakly.

'I can see that.'

'No. But, well, I don't want to let you down.'

'I can go without you. If you're like this. I'd rather go on my own.' She is hissing, we're in public.

I am deflated and defeated suddenly, like a balloon. And she knows me well enough to recognise this. And it is the worst moment to be like this, it is inappropriate, disproportionate, self-indulgent. I feel ashamed. But I can't reinflate myself, summon myself miraculously to order at this very moment.

'But you . . .'

'Christ, I'm nearly an adult. Just let me bloody do this. What the hell do you think can happen to me?'

'How will we find each other again?'

There is a manic pulsing in my chest, a churn in my stomach, and my head pounds. Amba is bordering on angry now.

'I really think it's best if you stay here. But I really want to go on the tour properly, it's important I do this. And I can do it without you.'

I sigh. I am squeezing the life out of my water bottle. Amba watches me, looking at my clenched fist and my white knuckles on the plastic bottle. She backs away. There is a perfectly friendly group of young Irish women smiling at Amba, and I am overflowing with grief, with tears. I don't want us to be separated, the nice Scot smiles to reassure me.

'Don't worry. It is an emotional place. She will be quite safe.'

At the gateway to Birkenau where we have been standing wrangling, people were separated forever. To work and most likely to be eventually murdered, or to be immediately herded into the trick showers, and murdered. With a curt nod, a gesture, a bark. Right or left.

We look out at the scope of Birkenau, rows and lines and fences and watchtowers and hut chimneys, all forlorn in the fields. We all know that the industrial-scale gas chambers lie at the far end, the railway line right here leads over there. They troop off, listening to the young Polish guide, he seems to be making jokes. The bookshop is full of grey books on grey tables. I blunder through it, dragging myself back to the metal bench. The bench and the outsize Nestlé machine seem to mock me. I take off my shoes and look at my blisters, one has spread right over the top half of the sole of my right foot.

Ash Pond

I have an ethical discussion with myself and decide it is OK to have a latte from the coffee machine even though it is a Nestlé coffee machine. I need to calm down. Despite the rudest man in Poland on the gate of Birkenau, despite . . . despite everything here. I wish there was no I, not here, but I need a warm drink. I want to lie down. I need to feel what I am feeling, and accept that I feel it. I tend to my foot, the blister is full of watery pus, is bright pink. Although this ground, this land, is holding human hell, I have to believe in healing. I have to or I can't go on. And to go on I have to belief in myself.

In the blocks at Auschwitz, in the stench of gross barbarity, in the precise and frightening efficiency, is an experimental prototype, a clinical laboratory of what we are capable of. At Birkenau this has been scaled up big time, it feels endless, a pitiless wasteland. A city of cruelty. I am alone now, on the hottest day on record, clutching my water bottle. I hobble along guideless, finding my way by listening to myself, stopping when I need to. I do not hurry, I cannot rush. I have no fellow travellers, there is no commentary.

Slowly I come to one of the huts that is still complete, full of the wooden slatted three-tiered shelf beds. It is dark and empty, but it is not empty. The space echoes, it is cool after outside, eerie. It is both all too easy to imagine people crammed in here, fearful, hungry, lonely, ill, desperate, devastated, dying, wily, people robbed of their innocence. And it is impossible too, to grasp how all this could be here in the middle of the Polish countryside, close to a small market town. How this factory of the desecration of humanity could happen. I sense lost souls hiding in the woodwork in lonely agony. I stroke the wood and hear myself say out loud, 'It's safe now. You are free to go. There is freedom. It is OK to leave. There is light and freedom, your light and freedom.'

And it feels utterly inadequate and pathetic. But I have nothing else to give and nothing to lose, and this feels like my only authentic wish right now. I think I know why I am here. What are we all doing here? What can anyone do here? Could this ever be a place of peace? Wouldn't a green park, an arboretum, be better than these buildings and half-buildings, these watchtowers and fences, and the old railway line heading to the bleakest vanishing point?

I go on, and it is impossible not to notice the long grasses waving under the bluest of blue skies. There are wildflowers even in the ditches between the huts. There are poplar trees, their leaves weave in the wind in the distance, ahead. At the back, where I know the gas chambers must be. And it draws me on, the sense that I am meant to be here like this alone. I note the little columns of tour groups and keep my distance. So I approach the end slowly. I don't want to look, but it is also inevitable that I will look. They phrase 'they must have known' is on repeat in my head. I say it out loud. I climb up a watchtower to try to encompass the scope of it all. I climb down.

I am rationing my water, some to sip, some for the back of my neck. I am walking along with my shirt draped over my head against the beating sun. It is noon. I stumble past the ash pond. So there is water here, and all this time later, although the grass grows, there is a sense of no life in the water. The ash pond is where the ashes were dumped from the ovens, the incinerators. So all this grassy land is really bones and ashes, a graveyard with no graves, no headstones. There is no church, temple, or mosque, nowhere to sit, kneel, meditate or pray. Except the ground. The poplar trees are playing the breeze up there. The ash water is yellowy green, it looks ill, terminally ill. The soil is clayey, sticky. I can see the bombed-out just-as-they-were-left giant gas chambers now, like a war zone, rubbled and roofless.

There is a circle of young Frenchmen. A very old thin woman, dressed in navy with long white hair, stands still just outside the circle, a witness. The young men have their arms around each other's shoulders and they are singing, to the accompaniment of a tiny tinny tape player on the ground. The circle sways at the top of the steps to the cellar that was a gas chamber. They sing well, they sing with youth and soul. I sit on the grass under the poplar trees at a distance, a satellite. Now, here, I cry, properly, safely. I cry into the grass, into the earth, into the mass grave all around me, under me, in me. I cry for everyone and everything. I cry for my family, my children, my ancestors, for the earth, for people, for the waste, for the suffering. I sit in the grass on the hottest day letting the tears fall.

The Soviet-era monument is brutalist. I stumble away and walk back towards the gateway on the railway line, hop hobbling from sleeper to sleeper. Eking out drops of my water supply between my dry gullet and the top of my pounding head. I count the railway sleepers as I go, trying to make sense of the numbers. Trying to imagine the faces, the lives. Deaths. And everything that has come since.

Back at the bench, Amba is waiting for me, cross and thirsty.

'Where on earth were you? I've been waiting ages.'

Apparently, the guide was knowledgeable about prostitution in Auschwitz, about survival and music, death and degradation.

We are staying by the river back in Kraków. A pop-up cinema below the castle is showing *The Wall*, the Pink Floyd film, there are pink deckchairs everywhere. We sit on the grass looking at the river eating ice creams. Afterwards Amba decides to go off on her own towards the crowd by the river. Dusk is on its way. I sit on a pink deckchair and watch *The Wall* with Polish subtitles, waiting for the familiar lyrics to ring out over the river. And worrying about Amba's whereabouts. She is a teenager. It is difficult for both of us. I worry about worrying, and still worry.

When we find each other again she is angry with me, upset and humiliated by a creep propositioning, and then insulting her. The river is lit up with light reflections. We talk into the night, and now Amba needs to cry. Tears for the camps, for our heritage, for the way men are, for the way I am, for the way she is.

THAMES

The rendezvous point is by Gallions Reach, this is east East London. I have driven past an international arms fair, with a group of protestors waving placards and a lot of police presence. Now it's no man's land, wasteland, yet to be developed land bordering the Thames. I can see Frank, skinny, standing on a rise waiting for me. There is always that moment when you haven't seen your child for some time when you see them as a stranger. Then he becomes familiar. We mirror this effect. It is not so much 'It's good to see you' as 'Wow, it really is you'. I am not sure where the river is from here and he shows me, I stand on a wall to see it. Then he says, 'You can walk to it from here, but it's tricky now they've put this new fence up. It would be best to drive to the roundabout.'

He gets in the car and we drive to a roundabout three minutes away. There is nothing there, just road, fencing, scrubland, broken glass, litter frittering in the wind.

'Just park here.'

There is a plastic-bags-broken-glass-litter-strewn layby, but it is a nominal layby. We climb, me with my backpack, through a gap in the fence and over a hump. There is more litter I don't look at too closely, I just follow him. He's a faster walker than me, and I have to remind him to slow down. The airport is too close across the river basin. The noise is shattering. I have to brace my body each time there is a take-off or landing. We are walking through grassland, stubbly scraggy wildflowers and prickly shrubs. There is a path, there is a way, but I would lose myself alone. There are blue pipes coming out of the ground in places, intermittently there are concrete staircases that lead nowhere, there is graffiti. I follow.

'Here's the lake I told you about.'

There are bulrushes, swans, and a colony of ducks, there are dragonflies. The expanse of water is a sanctuary in the wilderness. I stumble past on the subtle path that is furthest away from the swans, who have stretched their necks and made it clear whose territory this is.

'There is always wildlife,' I think Frank says. I'm not sure, I'm puffing a little bit behind him. This is all in single file. Is he making an existential comment, or an ecological observation? Or both? We haven't seen each other for ages and I'm tuning into what he is like again, and how he's changed. There is something beautiful about this place, a limbo breathing out between roads and building blocks and the airport, with the river like an arm embracing the land.

'I had no idea it was so far.'

'I've had a tent in a couple of places, I'll show you. The main thing is to feel safe.'

The land is waiting for decisions to be made about tunnels or bridges to the south of the Thames. The nearest way across now is the Woolwich Ferry. Frank has been living outside in his last year at the university next to the airport. (Whoever thought that was a good idea?) There have been halls of residence experiences, bed bug experiences, multi-occupancy experiences. Under the staircases that lead nowhere is dry space, there are suitcases, pans, a cooker and gas bottle, and junk. The sun is shining, and there is a robin keeping tabs on us. We pass through thicket, then crackling branches of dry wood clipped back to make a tunnel.

'I did all this with secateurs. Here, this is my wood pile, keeps reasonably dry. I like to have a good blazing fire.'

We walk over a manhole cover and hear the echo.

'That's the underground chamber I told you about. Fantastic acoustics down there, it's a bowl really.'

'Shall we have some tea now?'

There is a tent in the middle of a clearing of young trees, there is the robin on a branch, up close. Frank gets a plank and lays it on the grass. You can see all the river sitting out here, we are on the edge of the bank. The water is grey brown and churning, stretching across to Plumstead Marshes, so there is a great sense of expanse, of air and openness. Like we're not in London after all. We sit on the plank, I get the flask and cups out and we drink tea and eat the sandwiches.

'Good bread. Home-made?'

'Yep.'

I think neither of us can believe we are here. It is like we are both alone, but together, as we sit in his hermitage with the robin eyeing the crumbs as we drop them. We look out at the line of cormorants on the girders and brickwork of the old piers. The river flows to its mouth. The piers are all askew, falling apart, sinking into silt. There are gulls yelling, and river craft, way out midstream. We are invisible here. I feel very relaxed sitting on the plank with my son by the Lower Thames. We fall into silence after the questions and answers, and the silence is such a relief after the questions and answers. The silence of acceptance. I am honoured he has brought me here.

I refuse to climb down the iron ladder into the underground chamber, it is a completely dark sphere, and I am not up for it. He says he's recorded some great music down there. Taking another route back to the roundabout and the car, hugging the river, we come across two birdwatchers in camouflage fatigues, wearing jaunty hats and smiling. It is a beautiful balmy sunny day. They have climbed in here too. We exchange greetings and small talk, it feels utterly normal.

'They're OK, those guys. They know I'm living here. They don't mind me. They come here for the birds,' Frank explains.

We drive to eat in a pub next to the developments on the marina. We wait for the woman Frank might marry. This is the first time I have felt scrutinised as a prospective mother-in-law, in an East End pub by a marina. The riverbank here is all built, nothing is left to itself. Hutch flats, transparent, with tiny balconies. A man on a laptop scratches his back as if he is alone as we walk past to the riverside. There is water everywhere, and the sound of it slopping around, contained in concrete. There are lines of parked white fibreglass cruisers with whimsical names. There's a chill coming off the water. This is not the Thames of willows draped over lazy rowing boats, here it is worn out, used up, dirty and dogged.

Between the pub and the main road is another bit of shrubby hinterland. Frank has another tent pitched here, closer to the university and the bus stop. There are old shoes lying about, old tarps. Frank made an art installation here, on top of a concrete bunker he unearthed. The tutor visited, and gave him good marks.

MARITIME

It feels far-fetched that the Woolwich Ferry still exists, but we drive onto it anyway. Ferrymen, girders, clanking, hydraulics, there's metal everywhere. The river narrows here. Every ferry is a crossing to another world. We are off to the south side, to see my poker brother in Clapham. The red-in-the-face footballing anarchist, my guitar-on-the-roof-in-the-middle-of-the-night brother. Frank has decided to come and guide me through the trawl of South London traffic. I have an *A–Z*, limited energy and limited good temper. We take a detour in Greenwich to the park.

Frank is watching me as if I am a novel creature. We are at point zero degrees longitude. There are schoolchildren en route to the observatory and Chinese tourists perched on walls for selfies and groupies, turning their smiles on and off automatically. I am pleased by the trees. From here the Maritime Museum is visible, and the Dome, which looks like a boil bursting on the loop of the river, which snakes relentlessly, despite all the buildings and cranes and noise, the river owns London. We find a knoll to sit under the trees on, a lookout place. And we look out to Woolwich and over to Beckton. The airport is toy-town small, the planes dinky. I light a charcoal disc, put it on a stone and sprinkle some frankincense into the bowl of the disc as it begins to smoke and throw out little sparks. We are bathed in the smoke of frankincense, it drifts into our hair and clothes.

After some time, I ask, 'What are you still doing here? You've finished your degree.'

And he tells me about an accident in the Thames in 1878. Over seven hundred people died. Day trippers, women and children mostly, on a trip from London Bridge to Gravesend and back. The *Princess Alice*, a paddle steamer, collided with *Bywell Castle*, a collier. The *Princess Alice* was sliced in half. From pleasure to panic, to terror, to loss. Over seven hundred bodies were laid out on the banks all around, by Beckton Gasworks, at Woolwich Dockyards.

'It happened there, near my riverside camp, where the cormorants were today. Gallions Reach. Before all this building and the Dome and, you know, before modern corporate London. When the East End was the East End, not full of hipsters.'

His arms sweep to include the whole cityscape, with the river always the focus, like a charm, a chimera. Like the whole of this built-up, Greenwich-eyed view of London is an illusion. And from here, with us cross-legged under the trees with our small incense offering, it could be. The nature of reality hangs in the air, the possibility of quantum consciousness, the meaning of our connection, the state of the planet, all of it, is something we are not powerless to contribute to. Even though I am ill and limited, and he is ostensibly homeless, sleeping rough. These words do not encompass the experiences we are having, of being here, now.

'Is this some kind of prayer, or ceremony?'

'I don't know. Does it matter? And if it is, it is very freestyle and non-denominational indeed.'

On Frank's side was the inventor of the Spinning Jenny, which opened the floodgates of the industrial revolution. His grandfather was briefly a communist, his grandmother a child invalid in a house where they gardened at night by candlelight to avoid the neighbours. On my side, I am still trying to fit the scraps and pieces together. I am still discovering I am not who I thought I was. I am Polish and French and Irish and German. I am Catholic and fractionally Jewish and practise neither. I am all of these and none of them. I was born in York, educated in London, lost in India, hidden in Wales. I am the daughter of a refugee and two Oxford graduates. I am the fifth child. I am a stepdaughter, twice. A mother of four. I am a woman, but much of the woman template out there in my lifetime has felt irrelevant.

Driving along the M4 to get to London with the knowledge of this other family tree under my belt, passing a swaying lorry in the fast lane, I put my foot on the accelerator and said out loud, 'I can do this, I'm German.' As though I was driving a BMW suddenly. And I laughed out loud as I felt a new strength course in my veins.

We laugh, we have to laugh. And Frank asks me, 'What do you do, when you can feel, well, I suppose people would call them ghosts. What do you do?'

'Well. Talk to them, tell them it's OK to leave now.'

'Like they're stuck. Kind of amateur exorcism, then. Hmm. I can't leave until I've finished there. That's the answer to your question.'

'You don't just mean recording music in the chamber?'

'No. I suppose I'll know when I've finished. My dreams have been pretty full on there, where we were.'

'By the river, with the robin.'

'Yeah, those piers, that stretch of water. Look, you can see it from here.'

We talk about Poland. About the green Sondico goalkeeper gloves my father bought him years ago.

'I suppose nowadays your dad's personality traits would be on some spectrum. I've had some weird hallucinations, you know, without drugs or anything. Scary. Like waking nightmares.'

'Like you've been in a war.'

'And you never let me have even a plastic gun.'

'Well, I think you had a water pistol. Plastic and guns, that's the measure of humans.'

'Cars . . .' We have to pause because a plane's coming into City Airport.

'Would having a toy gun have helped you navigate your life . . . my mistakes . . . your mistakes? Helped you to be a man?'

'What do you reckon? The modern world isn't designed for people, really. Men or women.'

'Nothing goes away until it has been accepted, processed, composted, and transformed. Yet collectively we are still pretending we live in a disposable culture.'

Pause. 'We'll never be normal, will we? I have tried.'

'I know you have. Same here.'

'Really?'

'Yeah, really.' We both laugh. 'I just wish I understood what I was carrying, knew what had happened before. The silence has been deafening.'

'Perhaps that's more normal than we think. The whole world's drowning in trauma.'

We breathe the tree air before tackling the road west. Before a night of vodka with my poker brother.

FIREWATER

We have dry cardboard and newspapers, we have a stick lighter, we have men's tea, women's tea, green tea, tea tea, yogi tea, mint from the garden tea, we have peanut butter and tahini and oatcakes and pumpernickel, we have chocolate. We feel royal. We have everything. And the fire is smoking and flaring and crashing and embering and glowing. It spits and crackles, it hisses, it makes poetry out of wood.

Being in a Welsh field again, with pragmatic optimism I put up a washing line between two tents. It sags, it will not do. I attach the rope to an ash tree in the hedge, and a branch snaps, it is still not right, it is not happy. So, mark three of the washing line is a shared project: two fresh poles staved and staked into the ground, with guy rope tethers. The washing line sings, is long and strong, could carry wet blankets and anybody's washing. I feel relieved. As my father would say, 'It will all come out in the wash.'

I am happy if there is water and a washing line and a fire. No matter what, all will be well, we can get our washing and ourselves dry.

The kitchen awning sags, catching a pool of rainwater. We poke it from underneath to run into a big bowl and collect it. It's nearer than going to the tap. We fill up demijohns and bottles with rainwater. It is delightful, and exhilarating to collect fresh clean rainwater, drink it and piss in the bushes. These things are connected.

We dig a round hole an ell and a half deep. I lie over it with my head looking down into the earth, into the dark. A thick blanket covering me means I can't see anything. I lie with my head in the earth smelling the damp black, breathing it in. Leaving what I know and what I think I know. When I come up again, everything, the trees, the sky, the tents, the grass, the birds, the smoke, water, fire, flowers, people, the world, seem miraculous, etched with wonder. I feel I have never been awake before.

And always, all through, we keep the fire alight, feeding it, tending it, poking it, watching it, our thoughts disappear in it. We think of it, forget and then remember it, running over in the rain, in the dark in the dawn in the early and the late hours, covering for each other, like it's a new baby. At night the fire burns slow and we sit close, lit by flames and embers. In silence and not in silence. The beech tree flutters and seems to move a little closer. In the corner of a field is synchronicity. Today we have witnessed clouds that look like dragons laying eggs, clouds that could speak. We look up into the night and are kissed by shooting stars. The stars are sending out messages. How can it be that this is where I feel most at home, most myself, in a field by a fire?

Over there somewhere are gong baths and samba, gospel and capoeira, Taizé and drumming, dancing and football, willow weaving and table tennis, saxophones and guitars, songs. One evening I go over and sweat in the sauna. Afterwards, by the outside fire, lounging on straw bales, are fleshy men looking like beached walruses. As I get dressed I feel their eyes on me. Their regard is musty and fusty, there is the whiff of power gone wrong over lifetimes. Men of my generation, they shift uncertainly in their skins. Their conversation brims with codes and trapdoors. Even though I am not their prey, I head back quickly. I do not linger.

And fire night comes around. The rave has happened, the marketplace, the processions, the demonstrations, the exhibitions, inhibitions are long shed. A fire in the centre of the field is lit at dusk. Football and Frisbee die down. Someone is walking along behind the hedge carrying giraffe cut-outs, so it looks like our antics are being scrutinised by passing giraffes. Drummers gather around the fire and almost naked people painted silver and gold caper and dance and sweat, teasing each other and the fire. People going wild.

Later down by the beech tree, a red imp appears, desolate. She weeps. Red body paint is imprinting the grass, making the green red. The fire heats and eats everything. We fetch flannels and towels and water from the kettle, and we wash her in the firelight dark. The shrieking drumming dancing and cavorting continues across the field a world away. We are washing the red away – three attendants, two women, one man, performing an ancient service. The red spreads. The ground is drinking. We are waiting on suffering. We are all desolate and all washing, trying to shed it. The cry of women in this world.

The next day at twilight a tall woman appears prepared with written slips of paper. She hesitates, picks up the axe and attacks the words on paper before throwing them onto the flames. As they burn, she holds the slab of rose quartz to her stomach.

When I find my log it's fat and heavy, and up to the task. The didge plays whale songs. Frankincense seeps in a trail up into the tree as I plant the log in the fire and watch it catch. It takes a long time to burn. Hours. As it burns it creates a perfect hollow circle within itself. A red sun of nothing. I watch the burning, turning to charcoal, frittering to ash. Until now there has been nowhere else to put the anger safely, the loss, the regrets, the fear, the waste.

I walk barefoot in the rain-soft grass. I shut my eyes and I can see the waterfall. I can hear it. I can see our feet mixed up together under the surface of the pool. I can sense the shadows of the trees playing over our heads. Hear the songs of the birds and flowers. I open my eyes and it's still there even if I can't see it. The waterfall, then and now, and tomorrow. The earth and the air and the water and the fire are mine, are me.

In the morning the sky is like red crumpled velvet. And the darkness of the coming rain is backing up behind it, slate grey. There are embers in the ashes. The fire is mostly ashes. We are travelling in different directions. The dew is perfect today. Afterwards there will be trails left in the dew. Dew prints of circles and loops, dew prints of moving sideways. It is enough to be reminded like this now and then, of how to live, in this life. With these glimpses of sonatas by the waterfall.

KAYAK

I have a kayak for two, it's blue. Each voyage is a full episode, an adventure. Upriver past the awful eddying under the old bridge, to where you can go no further beyond the bird echo gorge, through the steep untouched sides of forest. Over the rapids, where car noise does not reach, so our voices, the pouring of tea from the flask, bird calls and wing flaps are centre stage. Fish plop up, leaving circles that prove that that happened, otters and herons compete. If we stop paddling to drift it's utterly restful, a full massage. Time disappears on the water, where does it go? I can never guess how long has passed, the river is a world of its own.

Downstream past the lime kilns, the pubs and houses, we go across to the other side, to Lady Hamilton's house. It's out of place here, a stonking yellow edifice on its own with a ghost to match. Up close it's a disappointment: empty, freshly painted, a garden of slate shards, blue ceramic orbs, and sad ornamental trees that look like they belong on an old-style Christmas cake. Sterile. Frank and I get trapped behind the sand bar as the tide comes in, the wind whips up and the geese look on haughtily. Amidst currents, undercurrents, the channel, buoys, the cruisers and fishing boats, the kayak is more like a neat insect than a boat.

'It would be good to go to the sea.'

'Mmm. Maybe.'

We have worked up very gradually to using two paddles in rhythm, in some kind of unison. Worked out how the dry compartment opens and shuts. Got wet, got muddy, forgot to let the skeg out, forgot to bring the skeg in, used the wheels, not used the wheels. Found the best bag, snacks, shorts to wear. I sit in the front, legs crossed, paddling, navigating. Every time I get out of the kayak onto dry land, I feel more me, proud, messy, adventurous, fit even. In fact it's easy to go to sea, we just do. Paddle down the estuary and, keeping left along the beach, we just arrive. Leave the kayak in the dunes, plan for next time. Stow the paddles in the car. It feels almost too easy.

Torn in the heat of summer between swimming and kayaking, I get to do both some days. And we venture out to sea. The first time we time it with the high tide and the sunset.

So we get to investigate the outside of the cave for the first time, peer in, save it for another day. Exclaim at the trailing jellyfish, decide to just stop and sit as the sun goes down pink, orange, red. And the water is touched with leaves of rosy purples, and yellows, and so many blues, reds and oranges, always moving. There is a small swell, just an undulation to remind us we are being held up by all this water. I know that technically parts of our seas are actually plastic water now, but I am still bewitched. There's no sound but us, and right here, right now. We are far enough away from the beach we can barely see it. The cliffs undulate and fold onto themselves, bowls and pyramids and majesty in rock.

'It's so beautiful, perfect.'

'Incredible.'

'Amazing, it's like a video . . . a virtual reality game.'

'I didn't know you'd ever played a game, Mum.'

'I haven't. Weird, what has happened to me that I can't inhabit this moment without that thought? It's ridiculous. Is my brain really so malleable, so soupy?'

'Soupy? It is a ridiculous thought, but I know what you mean.'

'Mmm.'

The colours moving the water all around us are sensations, are voluptuous. The sun falls down to the horizon very slowly and we go very quiet. And beside us, we become aware of dolphins. They breach the water and show themselves, then dip under, and up, and keep taking good looks at us. And there's an electricity between water and air and them and us, here now, together in this fading lightshow.

When we return to the shore with the light path behind us, and reluctantly emerge because it's chilly now the sun's down, a woman in long shorts just says, 'Dolphins. We watched them from here.'

'Yes.'

On another voyage we paddle through a thick stew of moon jellyfish, each one has four pink Os. There are hundreds, thousands, swaying and sashaying. It feels like a mistake, or that I didn't realise it but we're on an odyssey, a quest with hazards and temptations. We are in a swarm, a sea cloud of pink jellyfish, endless. It's hard to avoid them with the paddles. And it feels like we have gone way beyond.

In the future, in Oxford Circus, I will join a woman with long dark hair covered in a long robe of feathers singing in all directions to Mother Earth. She will be standing on top of a bright pink boat marooned on tarmac in the middle of London, miles from the river, or any sea. The boat will be the same colour as the jellyfish. Beneath it will lie several human 'barnacles', locked on in protest.

I will think, *So it has come to this*, and feel both grief and relief. I will feel less alone.

In the future I will contribute my own teardrop of protest. And find myself communing with sea creatures and beings from the invisible world, after doing yoga on a thin blue plastic mattress in a police cell. There will be a turquoise blanket. I will not be able to tell where the nearest watercourse is, except inside me. I will sing a song to Oshun, the Yoruba water goddess, to keep my spirits up before I am released. Acoustically the tiled room will be excellent, like a giant shower room. We have reached the high watermark, the apogee, now.

We have. And we know we have. There is the child kneeling on cracked drought-beaten earth, leaning over, trying to drink from a disappearing dirty puddle. While at the same time in the floods people are drowning.

We went to the very back of the cave, jade sea sloshing in a semi-sinister way, Frank looking around to see if there was a convenient shelf to put a recorder on to record the sound of the slopping, and the change from cathedral to church, as the tide makes the water level rise and fall again, and the acoustics change. I just wanted to get out of there because that particular sea cave feels like a place that's not for people. And we went right out and round the end of the headland and stopped for peanut butter sandwiches on a pebble beach unreachable any other way. Seals were pupping and guarding and popping up everywhere like marshals. Their pups wailing from crevasses and cracks and invisible-to-us beaches. And we turned back round the headland, but the wind whipped up, so we were going backwards if we stopped paddling, and I was in front so I took all the splash and the waves were rising and the peaks and the troughs were immense, and on top of all this activity in that high wind there were additional Gusts that paused and then came at us fast like we were being mugged. And the Gusts came at intervals you couldn't predict, like contractions in labour, and hellish. And waves were crashing on the rocks so we couldn't hug the land. And the tide was coming out towards us. And a cruiser full of tourists looked over at us as if we were wildlife and curious. There was no slacking possible, this was a definite two-person full-on effort, dredging to the very bottom of stamina, endurance, strength, teamwork and then some, no breaks. And even while we were out there I thought, *This is just like our lives. Same fucking principles required.*

My body covered in goosepimples, my brain addled and charged with adrenalin and endorphins and sheer shock and fear and that will to survive whatever the cost, I exit the kayak in the frilling shallows. On the beach people play and lounge with nonchalance, as if the whole episode, all the edges of danger out there do not exist. Maybe they would look at refugees reaching land from life-or-death leaking boats with the same expression of mild interest, then keep on trying to light the barbecue, adjust the windbreak and eat the last chocolate biscuit, wishing it hadn't melted so much in the sun.

I realise I have come right out of my cocoon, my sleeping bag, my pod, my nautilus shell, out of the pile of old leaves I've been living in, hibernating, like the laptop and tortoises. Waiting to live again. I always remembered what it felt like, even if only in dreams. I stride up the beach valiantly.

There is no romantic happy ending here, unless I can count the relationship with myself. There are no neat threads tied up once and for all. My helicopter brother can no longer fly, and my poker brother can no longer play football. In the future there will be watering and waiting, shrinking, wilting, and growth. Lily will buy the very best wetsuit. Amba will feast on watermelons on an island with a lover. The kayak will be stolen.

Water eventually meets itself in one form or another. It all joins up. Inside each of us there's more water than anything else. On the surface of the planet too, and the ice is melting. In the future I will die, I hope with some awareness of dying, and living.

In the meantime, I swim while I can.

LENKA JANIUREK was born in York. After winning a competition at the age of seventeen, she had three plays on at the Royal Court Theatre, a platform play at the National Theatre, and one at the Other Place with the RSC in Stratford-upon-Avon. She has facilitated workshops in writing, drama, art and well-being, in schools, colleges, at camps, and in a women's prison. And worked as a baker, fundraiser, caretaker, green builder and researcher. She now lives close to the sea in Wales.

BRISTOL LIBRARIES
WITHDRAWN
SOLD AS SEEN